STRAIGHT MALE MODERN

STRAIGHT MALE MODERN

A CULTURAL CRITIQUE OF PSYCHOANALYSIS

JOHN BRENKMAN

ROUTLEDGE NEW YORK & LONDON

Published in 1993 by

Routledge
29 West 35 Street
New York, NY 10001

Published in Great Britain in 1993 by

Routledge
11 New Fetter Lane
London EC4P 4EE

Printed in the United States of America

Library of Congress Cataloging-in-Publication Data

Brenkman, John.
Straight male modern : a cultural critique of psychoanalysis / by John Brenkman.
p. cm.
Includes bibliographical references.
ISBN 0-415-90217-7. — ISBN 0-415-90218-5
1. Oedipus complex—Social aspects. 2. Heterosexual men—Psychology. 3. Psychoanalysis and culture. I. Title.
BF175.5.O33B74 1993
150.19'52—dc20 93-14035
CIP

British Library Cataloguing-in-Publication Data also available.

For SAM and BEN

and

To the memory of my mother,
DORIS EPLEY BRENKMAN
1926–1992

Contents

Acknowledgments

I am deeply grateful to the many friends and colleagues who at various stages of this work have responded with their encouragements and criticisms, especially, Jonathan Arac, Nancy Fraser, Gerald Graff, Fredric Jameson, Leonard Kaplan, Colin MacCabe, Nancy K. Miller, Michael Warner and Joseph Wittreich.

I also want to thank Ralph Cohen and Jacqueline Rose whose invitation to participate in a seminar on "Sexuality and History: Authors and Institutions" at the Commonwealth Center for Literary and Cultural Change encouraged a new direction in the project. A version of Chapter 6 and part of Chapter 7 appeared in *New Literary History* 23:4 (Autumn 1992).

For all her insight and the talk, I most of all thank Carla Kaplan.

Introduction

SIGMUND FREUD made many startling statements in his 1931 essay "Female Sexuality." Among them was his admission that the theory of the Oedipus complex he had refined and amplified for more than thirty years didn't really describe what he had always claimed.

It wasn't an account of human beings' most universal feelings toward parents, self and sexuality after all. It was merely a story about boys:

> We have an impression here that what we have said about the Oedipus complex applies with complete strictness to the male child only. . . . It is only in the male child that we find the fateful combination of love for the one parent and simultaneous hatred for the other as a rival.[1]

Freud was drawing heavily on recent work by Jeanne Lampl-de Groot and others who were increasingly demarcating how the vicissitudes of little girls' relationships with their mothers and fathers—and their sense of self—differed from the classical Oedipal model. A revision was in order. And Freud's own intervention has all the markings of an effort to contain the revision within the larger parameters of his own views.

Freud's own cases had yielded a pattern among women who had unusually close attachments to their fathers: this intense attachment had originally been directed at their mothers, often up until the latency period. "This being so," writes Freud, "the pre-Oedipus phase in women gains an importance which we have not hitherto attributed to it."[2]

These remarks have become a crux for various revisionists, feminist and non-feminist. They mark the belated opening onto the question of women's sexuality and moral development. The belatedness of Freud's insight meant that the whole of his work began to be reread with an eye to the difference or differences that would define the situation of women or femininity or Woman. Gender had decisively entered the psychoanalytic problematic.

Yet Freud's account of the masculine Oedipus complex itself has been relatively immune from critique. In Juliet Mitchell or Nancy Chodorow, for example, it serves as a benchmark against which to define questions of women's sexuality, identity or development. Even the radical critique of Gilles Deleuze and Félix Guattari's *Anti-Oedipus* ultimately preserved the Freudian paradigm, which they saw meshed with the whole machinery of capitalism and patriarchy. With Heinz Kohut or Christopher Lasch, the Oedipus complex is deemed obsolete; the family life and social values to which it belonged have been cast aside they believe by new trends that make Lasch at least downright nostalgic for the Oedipal drama of possessive love, fierce threats and internalized authority.

I am far less convinced of the demise of the Oedipus complex, and much more skeptical about Freud's account of it in the first place. If the Oedipus complex applies only to men, then it is not *about* what Freud thought it was about. It is not about the inevitable fate of libido, but about the shaping of masculinity. It is also, very specifically, about the shaping of male heterosexuality.

Freud foregrounds heterosexuality in taking stock of the "great difference" between male and female development:

> In the case of the male, his mother becomes his first love-object as a result of her feeding him and looking after him, and she remains so until she is replaced by someone who resembles her or is derived from her. A female's first object, too, must be her mother: the primary conditions for a choice of object are, of course, the same for all children. But at the end of her development, her father—a man—should have become her new love-object.[3]

Freud frequently admits that the picture of such unremitting, uninterrupted heterosexuality on the boy's part is a fiction. The "simple positive Oedipus complex," in which intense love for the mother and antagonism toward the father define the little boy's whole emotional world and then blossom into unambiguous adult heterosexuality, is so rare as to be virtually non-existent.

But if masculinity and male heterosexuality do not then take shape as the spontaneous outgrowth of the mother-son relation, what does mold the boy's masculinity and heterosexuality? Conversely, if the Oedipus complex is not the quasi-natural form in which masculinity and heterosexuality originate and develop, what is it? Where does *it* originate and how does *it* develop?

These sorts of questions go against the grain of Freud's most basic assumptions and whole style of thinking and theorizing by putting gender and the history of sexuality at the center of psychoanalysis. For Freud, and many who follow him, "gender" is an admissible category on very narrow grounds only. It can refer to the mental representations of masculinity and femininity as these come into play in the desires and identities of biological males and females. Some Freudians will give these representations a narrowly physio-psychological origin, others will give them the full scope of cultural images and symbols. Some will minimize, some maximize the kinds of conflicts and incongruities that are possible between biological gender and gender representations.

What is missing across this range of approaches, however, is an account of gender in terms of the social relations between men and women. The practices and institutions that distribute wealth, work, capacities, knowledge and power unequally and unevenly between men and women are not granted a crucial place in the theoretical or therapeutic preoccupations of psychoanalysis.

This limitation is particularly telling when Freud confronts the problem of norm and pathology in the Oedipus complex. On the one hand, he holds that the psychologically and socially normal resolution of the Oedipus complex is rare; seldom has a man passed through the "simple positive Oedipus complex" and attained an untroubled masculinity and heterosexuality. On the other hand, Freud continues to treat just this trajectory as normal. But if the normal Oedipus complex is so rarely achieved, what are the forces that interrupt its formation or compromise its outcome? And, conversely, what are the forces pressing to *form* the Oedipus complex and direct its outcome?

Freud knew that this question could not be answered with recourse to psychological categories alone. Yet he gave himself no other categories for actually describing the inner forming and resolving of the Oedipus complex. Instead, he attributed the pathological distortions of emotional and sexual life to the high demands of civilization. There is a confusion here too, however. For is the modern form of heterosexuality the norm that gets distorted? Or, on the contrary, is this modern form of heterosexuality a part of the distorting civilizing process itself?

While Freud can entertain the possibility that civilization *as such* is a pathological process, he eschews the alternative possibility of specifying *which* processes, institutions and practices are pathological. Such evaluations would bring psychoanalysis too close to politics, for it would require distinguishing among the institutions of our civilization, validating some, contesting others. To use Max Weber's terms, Freud devoted himself to "science as vocation" as an alternative to "politics as vocation"; he never contemplated challenging or blurring the separation of science and politics in his theorizing or in his therapeutic practice.

But it seems to me that a political interpretation is exactly what is called for as soon as the clear-cut distinction between norm and pathology breaks down. Jacques Lacan, for example, will conclude that the Oedipus complex is as pathogenic as it is normalizing. The norms of male heterosexuality are themselves traversed with pathologies. There is, in short, a *cultural pathology* of the Oedipus complex. The interpretive strategies required to understand it, however, cannot be derived directly from the main developments within psychoanalysis.

Among recent theorists perhaps no one has done more than Michel Foucault to create a new space of political criticism regarding psychoanalysis and the history of sexuality. He first of all definitively overturned what he dubbed the "repressive hypothesis." The repressive hypothesis supposes that society sets barriers to instinctual gratification. Sexual repression in the moral and political sense rests upon instinctual repression in the psychological sense. Consistent with Freud's own view of libidinal economy and of the conflict of instinct and civilization, the repressive hypothesis has been the mainstay of left Freudianism, from Reich to Marcuse and even Deleuze and Guattari. Left Freudians have interpreted the ideological and institutional norms of the bourgeois family and reproductive, marital sexuality as a constraint on sexuality, a barrier to instinctual gratification, designed to ensure the orderly reproduction of labor power.

"We must," writes Foucault, "abandon the hypothesis that modern industrial societies ushered in an age of increased sexual repression."[4] It is not that sexuality is repressed, but that sexualities are socially constructed and controlled. The social control of sexuality does not simply bar unwanted sexual practices or desires; it produces "normal" and "aberrant" sexualities alike.

Foucault, therefore, challenges the prevailing image of the bourgeois household evoked by social critics as well as psychoanalysts:

> Was the nineteenth-century family really a monogamic and conjugal cell? Perhaps to a certain extent. But it was also a network of pleasures and powers linked together at multiple points and according to transformable relationships. The separation of grown-ups and children, the polarity established between the parents' bedroom and that of the children (it became routine in the course of the century when working-class housing construction was undertaken), the relative segregation of boys and girls, the strict instructions as to the care of nursing infants (maternal breast-feeding, hygiene), the attention focused on infantile sexuality, the supposed dangers of masturbation, the importance attached to puberty, the methods of surveillance suggested to parents, the exhortations, secrets, and fears, the presence—both valued and feared—of servants: all this made the family, even when brought down to its smallest dimensions, a complicated network, saturated with multiple, fragmentary, and mobile sexualities.

This marvelous Foucauldian list quite nicely details the many practices and relationships that keep cropping up in Freud's writings. Every patient's family and history are rife with these complexities of power and desire, but Freud turns all these "sexualities" back to the triad husband—wife—child. As Foucault says, "to reduce" the bourgeois household's "multiple, fragmentary, and mobile sexualities"

> to the conjugal relationship, and then to project the latter, in the form of forbidden desire, onto the children, cannot account for this apparatus which, in relation to these sexualities, was less a principle of inhibition than an inciting and multiplying mechanism.[5]

Oedipal theory achieves just this reduction. The triangular relation of I—mother—father imbues the earliest relationships of the male child with the very form of heterosexuality and masculinity that supposedly defines the adult sexuality to which the "simple positive Oedipus" is then destined. All other sexuality looks like mere aberration, extravagance, irrelevance or substitution.

The heterosexual couple becomes not only the socially validated norm of sexuality but also the theoretical vantage-point on sexuality. By way of a paradox Foucault sees running through the whole discourse on sexuality in the 18th and 19th centuries, "heterosexual monogamy" could become the benchmark for the pseudo-scientific, medical, psychiatric, legal and penal descriptions and classifications of aberrant sexualities so long as this monogamous heterosexuality itself remained unclassified, undescribed, unexamined:

> Of course, the array of practices and pleasures continued to be referred to [heterosexual monogamy] as their internal standard; but it was spoken of less and less, or in any case with a growing moderation. Efforts to find its secrets were abandoned; nothing further was demanded of it than to define itself from day to day. The legitimate couple, with its regular sexuality, had a right to more discretion.[6]

The will to knowledge was directed at the sexuality of "children, mad men and women, and criminals" and at "the sensuality of those who did not like the opposite sex" and at "reveries, obsessions, petty manias, or great transports of rage." Heterosexuality enjoyed the privilege of a kind of protection *from* knowledge.

The resulting complicity between this intellectual enterprise and the legal persecution of gays and lesbians continues down to this day. Jonathan Goldberg has developed a chilling analysis of recent U.S. court rulings regarding sodomy which deny gay men the rights and protections enjoyed by heterosexuals because the heterosexual couple's sexual behavior is deemed immune from the state's intrusion. It is not to be looked into. Gay sexual behavior, on the other hand, can be subjected to just such intrusions. Who you *are* according to the psychiatric or juridical classifications determines the legality of what you *do*.[7]

Despite Freud's reputation for lifting the veil of Victorian propriety, psychoanalysis did not really break with this pattern it inherited from 19th century sexual science. Various behaviors and feelings were examined through the lens of heterosexual monogamy, while the heterosexual couple remained remarkably unexamined. Despite Freud's own considerable capacity for self-reflection, as in his self-analysis and in his theoretical work, he does not look at the conjugal couple except in their fantasmal presence on the primal scene and their ideal presence as the norm toward which the individual is drawn. Heterosexuality is therefore at once the lens and the blind-spot of psychoanalytic thinking.

"Heterosexuality" and "heterosexual monogamy" are in fact misleading terms. For the institution in question is, more precisely, *male-dominated heterosexuality*. Gender is a crucial axis in the organization of power and sexuality. It is not, however, clear whether Foucault really grants gender a place in this problematic at all. For one thing, the very idea that the social relations between men and women may be a structuring force in the distribution of power does not square with Foucault's own notion of the "capillary" nature of power. Second, in his various accounts of the body and power in modern society, Foucault "treats the body," as Sandra Lee Bartky has argued, "as if it were one, as if the bodily experiences of men and women did not differ and as if men and women bore the same relationship to the characteristic institutions of modern life."[8]

Male-dominated heterosexuality is, as Adrienne Rich has so compellingly argued, *compulsory heterosexuality*. Her argument complements Foucault's to the extent that it looks at the social construction of sexuality, asserting "that heterosexuality, like motherhood, needs to be recognized and studied as a *political institution*."[9] Rich's argument also, however, differs from Foucault's. She sees in compulsory heterosexuality an institution that organizes and facilitates exploitation of women by men. "The extent and elaboration of the measures designed to keep women within a male sexual purlieu" point up, she argues, "the enforcement of heterosexuality for women as a means of assuring male right of physical, economical, and emotional access."[10]

Freud was well aware that there was no innate disposition to heterosexuality fueling our society's heterosexual disposition. But he did not comprehend the consequences of this fact. The repressive hypothesis, whether in its Freudian or Reichian variants, cannot explain what makes heterosexuality compulsory because it does not grasp that compulsory heterosexuality is a male-dominated institution. Though psychoanalysis gives itself the theoretical task of explaining how sensibility, identity and sexuality are shaped by "civilization," it fails to make the connection to specific institutions. First and foremost, it does not connect the Oedipus complex to compulsory heterosexuality.

A cultural critique of the Oedipus complex needs to work out those missing connections. This critique shares many of the intellectual tasks that Rich assigns to the feminist investigation of compulsory heterosexuality:

> Historians need to ask at every point how heterosexuality as institution has been organized and maintained through the female wage scale, the enforcement of middle-class women's "leisure," the glamorization of so-called sexual liberation, the withholding of education from women, the imagery of "high art" and popular culture, the mystification of the "personal" sphere, and much else. We need an economics that comprehends

> the institution of heterosexuality, with its double workload for women and its sexual divisions of labor, as the most idealized of relations.[11]

How does the Oedipus complex connect the individual male's identifications and desires to the institutions and representations that secure male dominance in modern society? How is the Oedipus complex itself shaped by the imperatives of those institutions and the meanings of those representations?

While Freud realized in 1931 that his Oedipal theory was androcentric, he did not realize how it was androcentric. Freud began theorizing the Oedipus complex at a point in the 1890s when most of his patients were women. His first decade of therapeutic practice had accumulated several cases in which women recalled being sexually abused by male relatives, usually their fathers. When Freud began to doubt the reliability of these memories, he advanced the hypothesis that the women had harbored erotic wishes toward their fathers as little girls, and that these wishes were later reversed and preserved in the form of the "seduction" memories.

However, this shift from the adult's misdeed to the child's fantasy did not become a coherent feature of the psychoanalytic theory of neurosis until Freud also reworked the whole hypothesis from the standpoint of little boys rather than little girls. The origins of neurosis were then unambiguously attributed to the child's repressed sexual longing for one parent and rivalry with the other. This first consolidation of Oedipal theory was complete by around 1910 in the wake of the case of the Rat Man. Having grounded the neuroses in the Oedipus complex, Freud would go on to make it the cornerstone of the socialization process as a whole. It became the key to normalcy in the writings of the next two decades, including all the crucial work on the castration complex, sexual difference and so on.

This whole trajectory—rejection of the "seduction" theory, the Oedipal origins of neurosis, the Oedipal framework of maturation, theory of sexual difference—followed from theorizing males in the guise of theorizing the human psyche. As a consequence, the eventual recognition that Oedipal theory applied only to male children should have challenged not only psychoanalytic ideas about femininity and female sexuality but also about masculinity and male sexuality. It should have called into question the Oedipus complex itself.

The Oedipus complex is the pattern of emotions and relationships that typically leads boys in our society into the roles, habits and practices of compulsory heterosexuality, into socially validated forms of masculine identity and heterosexual desire. The "simple positive Oedipus complex" would represent, therefore, a kind of perfect mediation between a boy's particular identifications and desires and the institutions of compulsory heterosexuality. However, since this perfect mediation is a fiction, it cannot be granted the status of a mental structure or psychological agency somehow "in place" in the human psyche. The forming of the Oedipus complex has to be grasped as a more complex, more ragged, more open-ended process. How do the male child's conscious and unconscious representations of his earliest relationships, especially to his parents, come to mesh or clash with the demands of compulsory heterosexuality?

The cultural critique of the Oedipus complex is, therefore, a two-sided task. It has to develop a revisionist reading of Oedipal theory, and it has to work out the links between the Oedipus complex and compulsory heterosexuality. I believe that an *immanent critique* of psychoanalysis is still essential because the psychoanalytic resources for a critical understanding of male-dominated heterosexuality are far from depleted.

Foucault cannot ultimately, therefore, provide the blueprint for this project. He considers psychoanalysis too complicit in the power-knowledge regime he analyzes in the 18th- and 19th-century discourse on sexuality. This position in my view underestimates how psychoanalysis taps alternative sources of knowledge about sexuality in our everyday and our expert culture. A political criticism of compulsory heterosexuality, male dominance and the patriarchal cultural inheritance that legitimates these institutions needs those sources of learning to fashion a language of critique.

An *immanent* critique will also, however, be a *critique* of psychoanalysis because Freudian theory has steadfastly refused to make the connection between the forms of experience it theorizes and the specific institutions of modern male-dominated society. Just as importantly, this critique does need to draw on another aspect of Foucault's archeology of knowledge and theory of power, namely, the notion that forms of knowledge are entwined with specific modes of social practice. The material and institutional dimensions of psychoanalysis are several and cannot be dissociated from its specific intellectual assumptions and procedures: the clinical practice built on a medical model, the interventions into family life, the pressures of professional associations, the making of a vocation within a particular social and political context and so on.

This book is divided into three parts. In Part One, "Theorizing Males," I work out an immanent critique of the psychoanalytic theory of the Oedipus complex as it was established by Freud and then significantly elaborated and refined by Paul Ricoeur and Jacques Lacan.

Ricoeur saw in fatherhood a complex cultural symbol whose layers link up infantile Oedipal experience with the social spaces of the household and the market as well as with religious and secular patriarchy. Lacan's concept of the individual myth points beyond Freud's triangular Oedipus complex, in which I—mother—father can look like fixed roles simply played out in stereotypical wishes and conflicts. In theorizing males, these revisionists of Freud help bridge the theoretical gap he leaves between psyche and society, even as they remain caught up in an affirmative interpretation of patriarchy.

In Part Two, "The Freudian Structure of Feeling," I turn to the various cultural, social and political contexts in which Freud actually formulated his Oedipal theory: Habsburg Vienna; Austrian Jewry under the pressures of anti-Semitism and assimilation; the bourgeois household whose sexual and family dramas shaped Freud's patients' lives; the economic and intellectual imperatives of Freud's profession; the crisis of Austro-Hungarian liberalism.

From this angle, the Oedipus complex is a kind of distillation of the biographical patterns which Freud encountered in his self-analysis and in his patients' histories, and which preoccupied other intellectuals and writers as well. I use Freud's self-analysis, the case history of the Rat Man and Kafka's autobiographical writings to identify the kinds of crises in vocation, marriage and citizenship that Freud rewrote as the Oedipal drama of childhood. It becomes possible in turn to reread the Oedipal drama as an ordeal of socialization and individuation within a particular set of social spaces—the household, the market, the community, the polis.

In Part Three, "Oedipus: Individual Myth and Cultural Pathology," I complete what I am calling a cultural critique of the Oedipus complex. The Oedipal triangle I—mother—father is transformed into a five-term structure. I draw out the consequences of Lacan's notion that the father appears twice in the individual myth, as the symbolic father invested with authority and as the real-life father with whom the son identifies. The real-life father is, in Lacan's phrase, the *4th term* whose presence complicates the Oedipal triangle because of its discord with the symbolic father, the traditional *3rd term*.

I then argue that the mother, too, is a bifurcated figure. The mother as Oedipal theory always represents her—revered, tabooed, degraded—is in fact a symbolic figure fabricated in the discourse of male fantasy and patriarchal culture. She is the *2nd term* of the I—mother—father triangle. Hidden behind this cultural representation is the real-life mother, the *5th term,* a theoretical blank space in Freud and Lacan, the woman who actually raises the child.

Part One

Theorizing Males

I

Freud

FREUD'S THOUGHT relied more and more on the Oedipus complex to explain sexuality, maturation and the origins of neurosis. When he set out to consolidate psychoanalytic doctrine in the writings of 1923–25, he confidently asserted how "to an ever-increasing extent the Oedipus complex reveals its importance as the central phenomenon of the sexual period of early childhood."[1] He also settled on his most concise account of what he now called the "simple positive Oedipus complex":

> In its simplified form the case of a male child may be described as follows. At a very early age the little boy develops an object-cathexis for his mother, which originally related to the mother's breast and is the prototype of an object-choice on the anaclitic model; the boy deals with his father by identifying himself with him. For a time these two relationships proceed side by side, until the boy's sexual wishes in regard to his mother become more intense and his father is perceived as an obstacle to them; from this the Oedipus complex originates.[2]

The Oedipus complex is "positive" when heterosexual; the child harbors sexual wishes for his mother and a strong identification with his father shading into rivalry and hostility. The Oedipus complex is "simple" when unalloyed with the complications of the "negative" variant. In the negative Oedipus complex, the little boy's sexual longings are aimed at his father and his jealous hostility at his mother.

Even as Freud was shoring up his view of the Oedipus complex, he raised new issues that were overtly and covertly undermining it. Overtly, he took on the task of explaining how the Oedipus complex dissolves, since all his previous theoretical discussions had considered only how it forms. But he was also therefore immediately led to stress how thoroughly bisexuality complicates the outcome. Freud's definition of bisexuality remained equivocal. Sometimes it meant having both active and passive sexual aims, sometimes having both male and female love-objects. Children are bisexual in both senses. Freud never successfully distinguished the two senses of bisexuality, and he never even entertained the need to justify the axiomatic equation of activity with masculinity and passivity with femininity.

A paradox haunts Freud's reflections. The simple positive Oedipus complex marks out the path of normal maturation, and yet is so rare as to be a theoretical fiction. Freud usually finessed his puzzlement with a remark on the civilizing process and its discontents, emphasizing the son's difficulty in "detaching his libidinal wishes from his mother . . . and reconciling himself with his father": "it is remarkable how seldom [these tasks] are dealt with in an ideal manner—that is, one which is correct both psychologically and socially."[3] But the paradox is more insidious. For the closer Freud gets to pinpointing the precise form and role of the Oedipus complex in normalizing psychosexual and moral development, the more vexed his theory as a whole becomes.

Consider that in 1923 Freud was on the verge of recognizing that the Oedipal scenario he had so meticulously worked out for over thirty years did not really apply to little girls. The inevitable references to "the case of a male child," as in the passage from *The Ego and the Id* quoted above, were never merely for the sake of illustration or argument, but amounted to a severe theoretical limitation. Freud came to realize that the male model of the Oedipus complex could not be projected onto female sexuality and maturation. He then embarked on his several controversial, unsatisfying accounts of female sexuality.[4] In this flurry of theoretical revision, however, it never occurred to Freud to rethink the Oedipus complex itself.

If the Oedipus complex could not be generalized to girls, if it were not therefore the normal pattern of the processes of psychological development as such, should it still be viewed solely in psychological terms? What justified favoring concepts of mental life over those of social life? What justified notions of libido, object, aim, wish and repression over and above notions of socialization, gender and power? If the civilizing mission of the Oedipus complex promotes masculine identity and heterosexual desire but seldom truly succeeds, shouldn't this masculinity and heterosexuality be approached as uncertain cultural and social norms rather than clear-cut psychological signposts?

Freud spared himself any such extensive revisionist reflection by flashing the slogan "Anatomy is Destiny." The consolidation of the doctrine in the 1920s was partly illusory. Freud's sharp, self-assured theoretical focus was in fact rimmed with an aureole of uncertainty. It is from the irregularities in Freud's most mature theoretical writings that we can take our bearings on the new, unsolved questions. First, the Oedipus complex does not apply to girls, only to boys. Second, its "simple" and "positive" form seldom exists, if ever. This simple positive Oedipus complex appears to be the optimal route to achieving a normal outcome of psychosexual development and socialization. But, third, the socially normal outcome—unwavering masculinity, unambiguous heterosexuality—is atypical. And, fourth, the psychologically ideal outcome—a complete destruction rather than mere repression of the Oedipus complex—is nearly unheard of.

There is a new problematic to be recovered through a rereading of Freud's discovery of the Oedipus complex. Masculinity and heterosexuality are not beacons of maturity toward which the psyche inevitably plies its way. Nor are they a blueprint laid down for the erotic drives or for the discovery of self. The new problematic will have to orient itself toward questions of socialization, specifically, the modern male's socialization into masculinity, heterosexuality and forms of power inscribed in the social relations of men and women.

From this perspective, it is worth going back to Freud's first published use of the term *Oedipus complex,* for it came from a 1910 essay that was devoted, not to a general theory of sexuality, but to the pathologies of male heterosexuality. Entitled "A Special Type of Choice of Object Made by Men," it later became the first of the three *Contributions to the Psychology of Love.* Freud was trying to figure out what a man needed to fall in love, or be in love, with a woman. His clinical work had led him to postulate that the "necessary conditions for loving" arranged themselves according to various types. The 1910 essay concerned one such "special type."

Some men, Freud had found, could love a woman only when a particular cluster of preconditions were met. These preconditions could occur in various combinations of four motifs, but the first was always present and key to the other three:

(i) That there be an *injured third party.*
(ii) That the woman be in some way or another of *bad repute.*

(iii) That she be held in *high esteem.*
(iv) That she be in need of *rescue.*

Freud then connects this adult series of conditions for loving to an infantile series. He considers the connection to be causal and derives the adult series from the infantile one. Moreover, while the adult series amounts to an unusual, "special type," the infantile series is the normal, well-nigh universal Oedipus complex:

> It seems scarcely possible that the different features of the picture presented here should all derive from a single source. Yet psycho-analytic exploration of the life-histories of men of this type has no difficulty in showing that there is a single source. The object-choice so strangely conditioned, and this very singular way of behaving in love, have the same psychical origins as we find in the loves of normal people. They are derived from the infantile fixation of tender feelings on the mother, and represent one of the consequences of that fixation.[5]

The man who cannot love unless he sees himself rescuing an exalted yet fallen woman while harming a male rival was once upon a time simply a little boy who deeply loved his mother. Freud is convinced these two stories are intimately related. But he falters in trying to make the normal little boy's story the single source of the abnormal man's story.

In fact, he only succeeds in deriving two of the four motifs of the "special type" from the infantile series—the *injured third party* and the woman's *high esteem.* The presence of the injured rival Freud attributes to "the fact of the mother belonging to the father [which] becomes an inseparable part of the mother's essence."[6] As for the woman's high esteem, "the trait of overvaluing the loved one, and regarding her as unique and irreplaceable, can be seen to fall just as naturally into the context of the child's experience, for no one possesses more than one mother, and the relation to her is based on an event that is not open to question and cannot be repeated."[7] Let us accept for the moment the plausibility of these two interpretations, from within Freud's perspective at least, despite the fact that they beg the two questions of the specific social relations between men and women that make the mother *belong to* the father and the specific social practices that make the mother's childrearing role unique.

By contrast, Freud contradicts his own perspective when he interprets the other two motifs. To explain *bad repute* and *rescue* he covertly introduces elements that do not belong to infancy at all, but are part of latency and adolescence. From the moment he begins to discuss the motif of rescue, he openly contradicts the thesis of a single source. "In actual fact," he admits, "the rescue-motif has a meaning and history of its own."[8] It comes from the sense of being indebted to one's parents for one's existence. Freud conjectures that the child acquires this feeling of indebtedness when he "hears that he *owes his life* to his parents, or that his mother *gave him life.*"[9] Feelings of affection as well as wishes for independence are awakened by the awareness of indebtedness. The child wants to repay the debt and assert his own power and autonomy:

> The mother gave the child life, and it is not easy to find a substitute of equal value. With a slight change of meaning, such as is easily effected in the unconscious and is comparable to the way in which in consciousness concepts shade into one another, rescuing his mother takes on the significance of giving her a child or making a child for her—needless to say, one like himself. . . . All [the child's] instincts, those of tenderness, gratitude, lustfulness, defiance and independence, find satisfaction in the single wish *to be his own father.*[10]

Let us grant for the moment that a boy typically has an urge to repay his mother for giving birth to him. And let's grant that he pictures the repayment heroically as a rescue. And let's even grant that he then re-pictures his heroism sexually as making a child for her, perhaps because the phrase "owing your life" can mean both "being born" or "getting rescued." Even so, does it really make sense to assume that this urge and these pictures—and all the surmises and knowledges that nourish them—are complete during the supposed period of the infantile Oedipal drama? And how does the leap get made from wanting no debts to becoming one's own father?

Freud's own work frequently shows that sexual knowledge and even the basic meaning, let alone all the connotations, of *owing one's life, giving him life, giving her a child, making a child for her* and so on, undergo innumerable variations and revisions as the child grows. When Freud here makes the link between the special type of heterosexuality in men and the typical forms of affection little boys have for their mothers, he turns to representations that are in fact laden with the sorts of cognitions and fantasies that arise during latency and adolescence. The representations linking the infantile and the adult series do not unambiguously belong to childhood. They fall somewhere *between* the two series.

The motif of *bad repute* illustrates even more strikingly that the adult series does not simply derive from an infantile series. The motif does not appear within the boy's fantasies until two distinct developments, separated in time, become linked with one another and in turn permit the contrary connotations of *bad repute* and *highest esteem* to be represented in the same woman. The first development belongs to the intricate intimacies between mother and child. A bifurcation gradually emerges in the child's experience between the gratifications the mother provides and those she withholds. On the basis of this bifurcation a distinction is established between permitted and forbidden satisfactions, the former tending to develop as affection and care while the latter are increasingly differentiated as erotic satisfactions. The second development Freud attributes to the boy's encounter, especially in adolescence, with the opposites "mother" and "whore." Femininity is divided along a symbolic axis: women are mothers or they are whores. The polarization derives from class structure, since it is patently clear in all Freud's comments that it is the respectable bourgeois mother who is inevitably contrasted to working-class prostitutes or naughty peasant maids and servants. Freud suggests that the representation of this dichotomy plays into the adolescent's earlier disavowals of his parents' sexuality. After a long struggle against recognizing that his mother is a sexual being (she doesn't do what whores do), he joins the undeniable evidence to the dichotomous representation of women as mothers and whores, "telling himself that the difference between his mother and a whore is not so very great, since basically they do the same thing."[11]

According to Freud's own account, then, it is via this cultural representation that the properly Oedipal wish actually forms, that is, the wish to receive gratifications from the mother that are forbidden and distinctly sexual. Such a conclusion, however, runs counter to Freud's stated theoretical intention of showing that the infantile series is the single source of the adult series. In fact, the infantile series remains incomplete during the supposed Oedipal phase of early childhood. It cannot really become Oedipal until the culture impresses its stereotypes of femininity on the adolescent. And since the same stereotypes furnish the adult series with its ability to unite the motifs of *bad repute* and *highest esteem,* it makes little sense to claim that the infantile series causes the adult series.

A different kind of causality must be at work, one in which the retrospective relation to the mother and the prospective relation to some still unknown woman-to-love are forged simultaneously. Freud's interpretive and clinical work, as opposed to his theoretical arguments, show that the four elements of the infantile series cannot be connected to the corresponding elements of the adult series except by means of intermediary constructs in the form of experiences, cognitions and representations acquired during latency and adolescence. These intermediary constructs have proved to be more than mere bridges, since they determine the primary meaning of both the infantile and the adult series. They may fall *between* the two series, but neither series attains its structure or meaning except as an effect of the bridging itself.

I propose that the elements of the infantile Oedipal series are themselves determined, retroactively, by the intermediary constructs. Only by means of this retrodetermination does the Oedipus complex become Oedipal. Retrodetermination translates the Freudian concept of *Nachträglichkeit* by taking it in the strong sense of the capacity of later experiences to determine unconsciously remembered events *after the fact,* rather than in the weaker sense of "delayed effect" or "reactivation."[12] The infantile series does not cause the adult series, nor for that matter does the adult series cause the infantile. What counts are the intermediary constructs linking the mother-son relationship of childhood and the "object choices" of male heterosexuality in adult life. The infantile series is indeed reactivated in adult life according to Freud's account, but only by means of the retrodetermination of infantile experience in latency, adolescence and early adulthood.

Scrutinized anew, even the elements of the infantile series that Freud claimed were simple givens of infantile experience—the mother's *uniqueness* and her *belonging to the father*—only acquire their Oedipal meaning after the fact. When Freud defines the mother's uniqueness in her son's eyes, he conflates two aspects of the mother-son relation. There is the fact that the mother gave birth to the child, and there is the exclusivity of their relationship. The latter reflects the social practices that assign the mother primary responsibility for infant care, and it should have been obvious to Freud that those practices vary historically and cross-culturally as well as according to social classes. Indeed, his self-analysis had revealed that his Czech nanny not his mother had been the source of the most important infantile experiences in his own psychosexual development. The mother's "uniqueness" is not a constant of emotional life but a variable whose precise meaning is shaped by a complex of institutional and symbolic processes. None of these has so far found its way into the Freudian problematic.

Even the fact of giving birth is not an unmediated, natural datum. The question, "Where do I come from?" inevitably gets answered *from this woman,* but the answer never exhausts the question. One's genesis is multiple not unitary. The various markers of self-identity arise from different times and contexts, and they always have to be synthesized into the perception of oneself as a selfsame individual. Freud took account of this notion in *Group Psychology and the Analysis of the Ego,* suggesting that the genesis and recognition of one's "self" come from multiple networks of intersubjectivity: "Each individual is a component of numerous groups, he is bound by ties of identification in many directions, and he has built up his ego ideal upon the most various models."[13]

The biological fact of birth does not coincide with the social genesis of subjectivity and identity. Birth does of course acquire complex social meanings, in part because it serves as a metaphor for just this multiple social genesis of identity. One's own birth is at once fact and metaphor, singular event and cluster of meanings. It is therefore not, as Freud first suggests, "an event that is not open to any doubt and cannot be repeated." Lacan will show that the narrative of one's own birth and its circumstances functions as a kind of individual myth. And Freud himself frequently shows how the fantasies and cognitions of birth are constructed anew in the diverse moments of the child's intersubjective, libidinal life, beginning with children's "sexual researches" into sex and reproduction. Children "produce typical *sexual theories* which, being circumscribed by the incompleteness of their authors' own physical development, are a mixture of truth and error and fail to solve the problems of sexual life (the riddle of the Sphinx—that is, the question of where babies come from)."[14] Birth is not so easily fixed in one's own history. No matter how eager the researcher "there are . . . two elements that remain undiscovered by the sexual researches of children: the fertilizing role of semen and the existence of the female sexual orifice."[15] Freud also shows the unmistakable social content of the "family romances" through which children imagine for themselves different parents "who as a rule are of higher social standing."[16]

The mother's *uniqueness,* too, then, is subject to the effects of retrodetermination and continual revision. The revisions of the question *where do I come from?* can easily contradict one another or take shape around completely different desires or anxieties. Moreover, the evidence supplied by Freud suggests that they are increasingly connected to children's social understandings and aspirations. With this motif as with the others the meaning of the infantile relation to the mother proves susceptible to continual revision. And it is only by means of these revisions that it becomes reactivated in the erotic life of the adolescent or adult.

The remaining element of the infantile series—*the mother belonging to the father*—is, contrary to Freud's assertions, hardly an infantile perception at all. Here too a sequence of intermediary constructions has to intervene before this motif can reach its Oedipal significance, especially since it depends on both the "mother/whore" dichotomy and the motif of the *injured third party*. How does *belonging to the father* become, as Freud put it, "an inseparable part of the mother's essence"? And how does *belonging to* acquire a meaning that implies rivalry between son and father? The Oedipal crisis comes from the boy's perception that his father's relation to the mother has its own uniqueness, one from which he is himself excluded. Freud's own clinical work clearly implies that this crisis and this perception do not emerge all at once or with a single meaning. As the little boy experiences the division between the satisfactions his mother provides and those she withholds, he discovers a first solution to this challenge to the uniqueness or exclusivity of her relation to him. He disavows her sexuality. She simply does not indulge in the gratifications forbidden him. The cultural representation "mother/whore" confirms his disavowal by dividing women into two kinds that correspond to the two kinds of satisfaction. At this moment, the mother's *uniqueness* is secured by placing her at the one extreme of the symbolic opposition of mother and whore. But the son's eventual recognition that his mother is a sexual being disturbs this solution and provokes a new form of the earlier crisis. Now he must integrate in the person of his mother both poles of the "mother/whore" dichotomy.

Only at this point can the father assume the role of rival in the Oedipal sense. For only now can he be perceived as the one who has a claim on the sexual satisfactions forbidden to the son. The mother's *belonging to the father* finally acquires, or becomes fitted to, the social meaning of possession or exclusive right in accord with the practices of male-dominated monogamy. By the same token, the son's desire—the *wanting-to-have*[17]—becomes a *need-to-possess* only as he sees that the satisfactions forbidden him are the exclusive right of another. Only as the father's relation to the mother is grasped simultaneously as sexual and possessive can the son encounter his own sexual wishes in their Oedipal form. His desire is Oedipalized.

The boy's identification with his father *retrodetermines* his Oedipal attachment to his mother. This hypothesis answers to René Girard's critical commentary on Freud. Girard identifies an ambiguity in Freudian theory. Sometimes Freud gives primacy to the attachment to the mother, sometimes to the identification with the father. He can seem to make such identification the starting-point of the Oedipus complex, as in the following passage from *Group Psychology and the Analysis of the Ego:*

> Identification is known to psycho-analysis as the earliest expression of an emotional tie with another person. It plays a part in the early history of the Oedipus complex. A little boy will exhibit a special interest in his father; he would like to grow like him and be like him, and take his place everywhere. We may say simply that he takes his father as his ideal. This behaviour has nothing to do with a passive or feminine attitude towards his father (and towards males in general); it is on the contrary typically masculine. It fits in very well with the Oedipus complex, for which it helps prepare the way.
>
> At the same time as this identification with his father, or a little later, the boy has begun to develop a true object-cathexis towards his mother according to the attachment [anaclitic] type. He then exhibits, therefore, two psychologically distinct ties: a straightforward sexual object-cathexis towards his mother and an identification with his father which takes him as his model.[18]

The passage is striking because, as Girard suggests, it goes against the grain of Freud's usual sequencing of the Oedipus complex according to which the little boy's primal attachment to the mother develops into an object-love which then encounters the barrier and model of the father. The passage seems to acknowledge that Oedipal desire is a modeled desire; it does not simply unfold the little boy's attachment to his mother.

"There is a clear resemblance," writes Girard, "between identification with the father and mimetic desire; both involve the choice of a model. The choice is not really determined by parentage, for the child can select as model any man who happens to fill the role that our society normally assigns to the natural father. . . . the mimetic model directs the disciple's desire to a particular object by desiring it himself."[19] By the same token, however, nothing justifies concluding that the child's attachment and desire toward his mother do not exist except through instruction by the father. Yet Girard is driven to just such a position. Straining to make "the universal double bind of imitated desires"[20] explain all manner of human relations, he has to eradicate all reference to the interaction of mother and child and is led, absurdly, to picture the *origin* of the child's relation to the mother in his identification with the father. Girard therefore overreads Freud's inability to synthesize maternal attachment and paternal identification, extrapolating from it the ultimate theoretical incompatibility of the Oedipus complex and mimetic desire: "The mimetic process detaches desire from any predetermined object, whereas the Oedipus complex fixes desire on the maternal object."[21]

Girard would simply cast aside the Oedipus complex and attribute the little boy's relation to his mother solely to his identification with his father. Surely there is an alternative to this dogma of mimetic desire. Oedipal desire *is* modeled and does require the mediation of identification with the father and other male figures. But this modeled desire is precisely a remodeling of the mother-son relation as it has developed in the history of their interactions. The temporality of *Nachträglichkeit* provides a surer clue to the impact of the Oedipalizing identification with the father. The living record of the past can be repressed, but it can also, Freud suggested, be altered: "If we do not wish to go astray in our judgement of their historical reality, we must above all bear in mind that people's 'childhood memories' are only consolidated at a later period, usually at the age of puberty; and that this involves a complicated process of remodelling, analogous in every way to the process by which a nation constructs legends about its early history."[22] Had Freud applied this line of thought specifically to the Oedipus complex he could in fact have synthesized his accounts of maternal attachment and paternal identification. He could have linked Oedipal and mimetic desire.

The son's desire is Oedipalized not in infancy, during the so-called Oedipal phase or infantile series, but retroactively from experiences during latency and adolescence. During the course of the child's life, the differing qualities of desire are successively divided into pairs whose contents and boundaries shift: provided vs. withheld satisfactions; affectionate vs. erotic feelings; permitted vs. forbidden gratifications. The Oedipal relation to the mother can crystallize only when the last of these bifurcations, having been inflected with connotations of possession, subsumes the other two and projects its scenario back across the earlier moments of the mother-son relation. And the connotations of possession are acquired through the social instruction and cultural modeling the son receives from the father or, more precisely, from his identifications with him.

The revisionist interpretation I am proposing revises as well the status of what Freud called the "diphasic onset of sexual development." Infancy, latency and puberty remain sharply marked off stages as in Freud's account, but his supposition that the Oedipus complex is fully formed in infancy, then repressed during latency and finally revived at puberty ignores the complex temporality of sexual development:

> Towards the end of the fifth year this early period of sexual life normally comes to an end. It is succeeded by a period of more or less complete *latency,* during which ethical restraints are built up, to act as defences against desires of the Oedipus complex. In the subsequent period of *puberty,* the Oedipus complex is revivified in the unconscious and embarks upon further modifications. It is only at puberty that the sexual instincts develop to their full intensity; but the direction of that development, as well as all the predispositions for it, have already been determined by the early efflorescence of sexuality during childhood which preceded it.[23]

I have shown that the formation of the Oedipus complex requires that the interaction of mother, father and son acquire, for the son, specific meanings. Those meanings turn out to be social meanings and cultural valuations. They are not parts of an intrinsic psychological response but have to be acquired through a long, multilayered learning process.

Every element of the Oedipus complex according to Freud—a boy's threefold wish to possess his mother, destroy his father and become his own father—turns out to be the outcome as opposed to the source of the boy's psychological, social and sexual development. The cognitions and fantasies that are supposed to underlie the infantile Oedipus complex do not take effect until long after infancy. The Oedipal formation requires that *belonging to* come to mean *possessed by,* and that *wanting-to-have* come to mean *needing-to-possess.* These revaluations of desire involve social meanings that, in Freud's own interpretations, belong to a boy's adolescent experiences, particularly his acceptance of cultural representations and social values embodied in the symbolic dichotomy "mother/whore" and in the roles of "possessor" and "possession" assigned men and women within the institution of male-dominated monogamy.

So, too, the third aspect of the Oedipal wish, *to be one's own father*, is a socially and ideologically mediated, rather than direct, expression of the little boy's sense that he owes his life to his parents. On the one hand, the wish takes shape from the sexual researches, family romances and individual myths through which he attempts to comprehend the social as well as sexual meaning of birth. On the other hand, the wish to be his own father is more an effort to abolish or erase the debt of existence than to repay it. It aims at forgetting the debt, as in Hamlet's negative expression of the same wish:

> This time is out of joint. O cursèd spite
> That ever I was born to set it right![24]

When Freud tries to ground the wish to be one's own father in the "impulses which strive at power and independence," he fails to show *how*, or *why*, the male child's movement toward autonomy and the exercise of his own capacities should come to express themselves as a struggle with a rival for the exclusive possession of someone's love. This aspect too of the Oedipal revaluation of desire remains unexplained.

Each aspect of the Oedipal wish points up, in fact, the need to view the Oedipus complex more broadly than Freud does. The Oedipus complex is a process in which desire and self-recognition are being shaped by cultural as well as psychical representations, by ideological as well as libidinal forms, by an array of social relations that includes but is not restricted to the family. Must the psychoanalytic field, then, be abandoned in favor of a sociological or cultural-historical standpoint? I believe, on the contrary, that psychoanalysis has an integral place in the critical theory of society and culture. It is necessary, however, to continue the *immanent critique* of psychoanalysis by disclosing and pursuing the questions that are *determinately absent* in Freudian theory, that is, those questions that become compelling within Freud's theory but remain unprocessed by the theory itself.

The critical reconstruction I have developed thus far of Freud's account of the Oedipus complex provides a framework for pursuing the determinately absent questions. The Oedipal relation, including its capacity to connect infantile and adult sexuality, is constructed from fantasies, cognitions and representations that belong to a whole field of social practices and cultural symbolizations that shape the maturation of males. These intermediary constructs bear the stamp of a process of socialization-individuation in which immediate family relationships—son-mother-father—are just one component. The role played by these intermediary constructs has also suggested an alternative hypothesis to Freud's regarding the mode of causality in the Oedipal relation. I have applied another Freudian concept, the *Nachträglichkeit,* to suggest how the Oedipal meaning of the infantile relation to the parents is determined retroactively. Once restructured, the infantile relation in turn fuels the subject's adaptation to specific forms of heterosexuality, by anticipation (male fantasy) and in actuality ("object-choice"). The effort to comprehend this retrodetermination puts a whole new set of questions on the agenda, questions that are at once immanent to the psychoanalytic theory of the Oedipus complex and absent from it:

What are the specific forms of autonomy and independence the male subject acquires, or comes to anticipate, in the course of his socialization-individuation?

What values and norms are embodied in these forms of autonomy, and how do they relate to the society's prevalent modes of work, exchange, citizenship?

How do these norms and values affect the formation or the dissolution of the wishes characteristic of the Oedipal conflict?

What are the effects the modern restricted family has on those valuations and norms that form the Oedipal relation and the mature heterosexuality in which it supposedly dissolves?

How does the role of the father—as rival, threat, model, authority—become established?

To these questions will eventually be added others which are central but which psychoanalysis has generally failed to ask because of its deep-seated inability to comprehend the relevance of the historical forms of male dominance and women's oppression:

By means of what cultural forms and social institutions does a mother come to figure at once as the object of the incest taboo and the model love object in male heterosexuality?

How, on the other hand, do the childrearing practices the mother assumes in her social role foster or hinder, affirm or contradict, the actual and potential forms of her child's autonomy, role-identity and sexuality?

These questions underscore the bearing of social theory and cultural interpretation on the psychoanalytic problematic. With this perspective, however, comes a new order of problem and dispute. For now psychoanalysis, like social theory or cultural interpretation, faces the task of either legitimating or criticizing, affirming or negating, accepting or rejecting, specific norms and values embodied in the institutions and representations that play a part in the formation of the Oedipus complex.[25] The Oedipus complex is integral to a process of socialization-individuation whose goal is for young men to adapt to the symbolic-institutional configuration made up of male-dominated monogamy, the restricted family, capitalist social relations and patriarchal culture. To understand this configuration one cannot exempt oneself from assessing, however tacitly or explicitly, the legitimacy of specific social institutions and the validity of the prevailing cultural symbolizations that accompany them.

2

Ricoeur

THE OEDIPUS COMPLEX invites a clarification of psychoanalysis's intersection with cultural interpretation and social theory. Paul Ricoeur has set an important precedent, beginning with discussions in *Freud and Philosophy*[1] and culminating in an essay on "Fatherhood: From Phantasm to Symbol."[2] And he does not shy away from assessing the legitimacy of the social institutions he analyzes or the validity of the symbols he interprets. Ricoeur also mounts a very important methodological challenge to Freudian theory by searching out the institutional as well as the symbolic processes that are integral to the Oedipus complex's formation and outcome. He places the family scene back within culture and society. And the relevant social and cultural processes are ultimately shown to be integral not extraneous aspects of the Oedipus complex.

Ricoeur links the Oedipus complex and patriarchy by showing that fatherhood is a symbolic construct enmeshed in the Western cultural tradition, and he links the Oedipus complex and capitalism by showing that the form of personhood implicit in the Freudian account of the father-son relation is an economical-juridical construct derived from capitalist forms of property and contract.

However, his project has to be contested on political grounds even as it is built upon on theoretical grounds. For Ricoeur's rich exposition of fatherhood as symbol is also a defense of the patriarchal character of Western culture. His interpretive procedures aim for a preserving rather than a critical understanding of the cultural traditions of patriarchy. And, while he surpasses the limits of psychoanalysis by connecting the father-son relation to property and contract in capitalist society, he ends up in a contradictory defense of possessive individualism.

Ricoeur's own starting-point is dissatisfaction with Freud's understanding of culture. The weaknesses in Freudian cultural interpretation, he argues, also come back to haunt the more specialized concerns of psychoanalysis. Freud keeps trying to explain cultural works and symbols—in this instance, the symbolizations of fatherhood—by deriving them from the archaic or infantile organizations of the libido. The concept of sublimation remains ambiguous, even confused in Freud. It is a concept of libidinal economy insofar as it refers to the transformation of sexual investments into sublimated ones. Less obviously it is also a concept of value; sublimation requires, as Ricoeur puts it, an "innovation of meaning" insofar as the renunciation of an immediate satisfaction gives rise to a symbol whose own powers of satisfaction lie in its collective or communal value.

Ricoeur agrees with Freud that the higher level of cultural expression does indeed derive from the archaic level of individual or collective childhood. But he also stresses that the relation between the infantile and the adult, the archaic and the sublimated, is not a one-way path of determinations. An individual's sublimated activities and experiences may lead "back" to repressed infantile urges and wishes, but it is also true that the individual's desires have been educated "forward" to collectively validated symbols and actions. These two perspectives are in effect incommensurate and yet refer to the same process.

To solve the dilemma Ricoeur proposes that two methods or procedures of interpretation have to be worked up and coordinated. *Regressive interpretation*, as in Freud, can disclose the sequences of intermediary constructions that lead from sublimated figures back to the archaic figures originally invested with libido. *Progressive interpretation*, the possibility of which Freud uncovers but fails to develop, should then reconstruct the sequence of symbolizations moving from the archaic to the sublimated. Such sequences of symbolization are the movement of "self-symbolizing" that creates culture. From renunciation arises an innovation in meaning. The symbol at once refers back to the figure lost and establishes a new, more collectively binding figuration of desire. For Ricoeur, the incommensurate perspectives of libido and value are then resolved. The archaic can be seen to imply the higher level, the higher level to amplify the archaic.

Ricoeur tests out the regressive-progressive method in "Fatherhood: From Phantasm to Symbol" by tracing the movement of the father figure from the archaic Oedipal drama of childhood to the sublimated symbols in which fatherhood lays claim to the whole of culture. I am going to summarize in some detail the "self-symbolizing" of paternity. Ricoeur works out three interlocking developments each of which he associates with a distinct intellectual tradition and field of inquiry: the psychoanalytic, the Hegelian and the hermeneutical. The psychoanalytic field addresses the archaic drama of desire in childhood. The Hegelian field explains the socialization process that makes an individual a rights-bearing subject with regard to property and contract. And the hermeneutical field concerns itself with the most highly sublimated and religious symbols of the father. These three sequences in the symbolization all follow the same pattern. In each the father figure first forms at an archaic level, then dissolves and finally reappears in a higher, symbolic function.

First comes the psychoanalytic field: *the father figure in an economy of desire*. Ricoeur couches his careful redescription of the Freudian account in a terminology that emphasizes how the shadings of meaning in the Oedipal relation to the father change. Like Freud, Ricoeur models his account on the male child without remarking on the problems posed by drawing universalizing conclusions from gender-specific formulations. And he too begins by postulating infantile omnipotence.

According to this story, the infant initially demands that all his desires be fulfilled and refuses any renunciations. This omnipotence encounters a barrier when the little boy discovers that he does not possess all his mother's love since she loves the father. Puffed up with his supposed megalomania and omnipotence, the little boy projects "the phantasm of a father who would retain the privileges which the son must seize if he is to be himself."[3] With this fantasmal form of the antagonism of father and son there emerge the two primal symbolizations of the struggle's possible outcome. Either the son will kill the father, or the father will castrate the son. The son's literal identification with the father—desiring exactly what he has, wanting to replace him—confines the father-son relation to the paired symbolizations of parricide and castration.

The Oedipus complex "dissolves" only when this literal, murderous identification with the father gives way to a series of symbolic identifications based on the generational difference of father and son. The fantasmal wish to murder the father is replaced by the expectation of taking his place in the succeeding generation. The son now stops fantasizing a deadly struggle for omnipotence and, instead, recognizes that his father is mortal. The violence that permeates the primal fantasies is replaced by the representation or *symbol* of fatherhood.

This symbolization of fatherhood restructures the father-son relation on the basis of *mutual recognition* and *reciprocal designation:*

> It is in terms of the meaning of mortality that there will be articulated a representation of fatherhood distinct from physical begetting and less attached to the very person of the father. Begetting is a matter of nature, fatherhood of designation. It is necessary that the blood tie be loosened, be marked by death, in order that fatherhood be truly instituted; then the father is father because he is designated and called father.
>
> Mutual recognition, reciprocal designation: with this theme we touch on the frontier that is common to psychoanalysis and to a theory of culture. We enter psychoanalysis by the concept of instinct, at the boundary line between biology and psychology; we leave it by other limit-ideas, at the boundary line between psychology and the sociology of culture. Identification is such a concept, and Freud exerts himself to repeat that he has not resolved the problem that such a concept introduces. To resolve it will require a change of field.[4]

The change of field will be the shift to the Hegelian account of the individual's socialization. The concept of identification has to broaden out beyond the family drama in order to include the individual's participation in the whole of social life. Identification in this enlarged sense will have to include the individual's role-taking, self-consciousness and the experience of equality with others.

By the same token, Ricoeur does not believe this change of field simply abandons the Freudian problematic. It is a question, rather, of redefining the "permanence of the Oedipus complex." Ricoeur agrees with Freud that the Oedipus complex persists beyond childhood. Mutual recognition and symbolic designation dissolve the Oedipal fantasies formed in childhood, but the Oedipus complex survives transformed. Ricoeur disagrees, however, with Freud's tendency to associate this permanence of the Oedipus complex with the "object choices" made in the erotic life of men. The reappearance of maternal fixations in the heterosexual experience of grown men does not, Ricoeur argues, exhaust the Oedipus complex's continuing power. Freud errs by staying within the vicious circles of sexuality. He concerns himself only with the neurotic outcome of the Oedipus complex. The nonneurotic outcomes involve the permanence of the Oedipal relation in a very different sense, namely, the recurrence of the symbolic father through other figures of social and cultural life.

The second field of paternal interpretations is therefore the Hegelian field: *the father figure in a phenomenology of spirit.* Freud dates the dissolution of the Oedipus complex at around age five or six. What follows is mere latency, the years awaiting adolescence and the onset of the second phase of psychosexual development. As I argued in the first chapter, there are many flaws in Freud's supposition that the Oedipus complex is fully formed, let alone dissolved, by age five or six. Too many experiences and knowledges belonging to latency as well as adolescence contribute to the forming of the Oedipus complex. Ricoeur too sees a problem at this juncture. Though he does not doubt that the Oedipus complex forms in infancy, he rejects the notion that the maturation the son must undergo for the Oedipus complex to dissolve could be provided by the family drama or infantile psychosexual development.

Maturation takes place at the social-cultural level of mutual recognitions and symbolic designations. "The movement of recognition," according to Ricoeur, "originates in another sphere than fatherhood and sonship."[5] Self-consciousness, in Ricoeur's reading of Hegel, proceeds through culturally produced forms; "philosophy . . . attempts to order them in intelligible series which permit us to sketch out an itinerary of consciousness, a path on which an advance of self-consciousness occurs."[6] The son's self or self-consciousness has to form outside the family and sexuality. The son

> attains to subjectivity only by the long detour of the signs that subjectivity has produced from itself in works of culture. The history of culture is, even more than individual consciousness, the great matrix of these signs. . . . [Self-consciousness] unfolds henceforth in the great empty interval which stretches between the dissolution of the Oedipus complex and the final return of the repressed on the higher levels of culture. For the economy of desire, this great interval is the time of subterranean existence, the period of latency. For the *Phenomenology of the Spirit,* this time is filled in by all the other nonparental figures which build human culture.[7]

The cultural tradition furnishes the forms of recognition, including self-recognition and role-taking, from which individuals fashion the self. Hegel, Ricoeur is suggesting, captured the dynamic process of these symbolizations of selfhood. Even though the process is detached from family relations, it follows an analogous path. Desire is again transformed by means of new forms of recognition and designation.

The Hegelian field starts with an assumption that corresponds to the megalomania or omnipotence of infantile desire. It is the notion that desire—or the immediacy of life—is extravagant, unlimited. This extravagance originally expressed itself in the fantasy of murdering the father and was restrained by the fantasy of being castrated. But now extravagant desire is submitted to the dialectic of master and slave. Just as mastery must run the "risk of life" by conquering the immediacy of life or desire, so too the slave "is raised above formless, unshapen desire by the rude schooling of thingness."[8] Desire enters into a dialectical relation to labor. In Hegel's words, "Work . . . is desire held in check, fleetingness staved off; in other words, work forms and shapes the thing."[9]

Ricoeur then makes a decisive shift in his reading of Hegel. He turns to the *Philosophy of Right* rather than the *Phenomenology of Spirit* to establish "the fundamental nonparental relationship, starting from which fatherhood can be rethought."[10] Master-slave still echoes the father-son relation. The fundamental nonparental relationship resides, rather, in *property* and *contract.* They reground mutual recognition and the interplay of desires in a juridical relation that is "stripped of all concrete bonds." The faintest hint of the father-son relation is removed. Individuals who enter into contract encounter one another as persons rather than as fathers and sons or masters and slaves.

Once again it is a question of what shapes extravagant desire, forming and constraining the arbitrary will. The social practices that come into play are forms of negotiation:

> And what is noteworthy about the contract is that another will mediates between my will and the thing and that a thing mediates between two wills. Thus is born, from the negotiation between wills, a juridical relation to things: this is property; and a juridical relation between persons: this is the contract.[11]

Accordingly, property and contract institute the *person,* in the strongly normative sense of an individual with rights. The autonomy of one's person is also a mode of possessiveness. It is protected against the intrusions of others just like one's property. The body becomes one's *own body.* It is here that Ricoeur makes his most far-reaching revision of Freud. Only a rights-bearing, self-possessing person can participate in the dissolution of the Oedipus complex: "if the person is posterior to the contract and property, if even the relation to the body is posterior to these, then the same holds true for mutual recognition of father and son; it is as free wills that they can now confront each other."[12] The family drama of childhood and the transition from infantile sexuality to latency cannot, therefore, as Freud proposes, dissolve the Oedipus complex.[13] The son's identification of his desire with the father's and the conflicting wills of father and son cannot be resolved until the son encounters his father without fantasies of murder or castration. They have to meet not as father and son but as rights-bearing persons whose desires and wills are mediated by contract and property.

No sooner has Ricoeur's rewriting of Freud taken the modern Oedipus beyond the family scene than the Hegelian dialectic sends him right back to it. The itinerary followed by the evolving forms of selfhood and of sociality now has to undergo one more dialectical turn. Fully socialized and transformed into a contracting, possessing, rights-bearing person, the son must be transformed again. The son overcame the family to become a person and proprietor; he must return to the family to become a husband and a father. At that moment, the ethical life of the family community surmounts the rights-bearing person. Looked at from the standpoint of the family, the matured man has to become "a member of . . ." rather than a wholly independent person. Looked at from the individual man's standpoint, the ethical life of the family beckons him to become a husband and father. The father figure thus returns once again in a new guise. "The father can be recognized only as the spouse of the spouse."[14] The father is a father only by virtue of marriage.

A new parallelism can be seen at this point between the psychoanalytic and Hegelian fields. In the Oedipal economy of desire, the son had to recognize that the mother and the father "belong with" one another. At the corresponding moment in the Hegelian dialectic of socialization, the recognition of their sexuality attains a higher form:

> Thus, sexuality is recognized—the sexuality of the couple that has begotten me; but it is recognized as the carnal dimension of the institution. This reaffirmed unity of desire and spirit is what makes the recognition of the father possible. Or, rather, the recognition of fatherhood, for in this astonishing text on the family [*Philosophy of Right,* esp. para. 163–164] the father as such is never mentioned. What is mentioned are the Penates, that is, the representation of fatherhood in the absence of a father who is dead.[15]

Hegel's allusion to the protective gods of the Roman household interprets marriage as the act of union that makes the couple, ultimately the whole family, into a single entity. Hegel stresses how the family members surrender their individual personalities to this entity: "the family becomes one person and its members become accidents."[16]

Ricoeur stresses how this surrender of individuality depends upon the power of *representation*. The "one person" of the family does not exist except as a representation. Moreover, the personhood of the family is different from the personhood of individuals. It cannot in fact be embodied by any individual family member, not even the father. Earlier, property and contract obliterated the father figure altogether. Now the father figure returns, but as a representation effectively detached from the literal, begetting father. The Penates "are the dead father raised to a representation; it is when the father is dead, when he is absent, that he passes into the symbol of fatherhood."[17]

The family stands at both ends of the dialectic movement Ricoeur has described through his psychoanalytic and Hegelian interpretations. The family provides the first stage of Oedipal consciousness as the primal scene of natural begetting and fantasized murder and castration. And ultimately, after the innovation of new forms of selfhood and sociality, the family is the scene of ethical life. Between these two extremes fatherhood has followed the trajectory *from fantasy to symbol*, "from nonrecognized fatherhood, mortal and mortifying for desire, to recognized fatherhood, which has become the tie between love and life."[18]

Following the Freudian and Hegelian interpretations is the hermeneutical field: *the dialectic of divine fatherhood*. Western religious representations provide Ricoeur with a third field, that is, the third level of the symbolism of fatherhood and the third method of interpretation. The religious designations of fatherhood are for him the "highest" or most sublimated forms. Ricoeur uncritically rehearses one theme of the Christian theological tradition that has historically been a vehicle of religious anti-Semitism, namely, the notion that Judaism and the Old Testament are foreshadowings that Christianity and the New Testament completed and transcended. In every other respect, his account is a rigorous inquiry into the textual and existential manifestations of God the Father.

Ricoeur spurns searching the Bible for "theological abstractions" that might define God. Instead, he seeks to establish, interpretively, "how God occurs in the various discourses which structure the Bible."[19] In the Old and New Testaments alike, Ricoeur delineates how each specific designation of God occurs within a specific form of discourse. It is then a matter of establishing the relation to God achieved by the collectivity or individuals who participate in that discourse. The emphasis falls on the semiotics and pragmatics of religious representation.

The Old Testament contains two prevalent forms of discourse, historical narrative and covenant. In neither is God fundamentally a father. The historical narratives, or sagas, of the Old Testament apprehend "Yahweh as the sovereign hero of a singular history, punctuated with acts of salvation and deliverance, of which the people of Israel, as a whole, is the beneficiary and witness."[20] The only father is Israel itself. "Yahweh is 'god of our fathers' before being father."[21]

Nor does kinship or ancestry play a fundamental role in the second discursive form. The covenant, too, casts God's relation to Israel as that of a hero. God is designated or symbolized by means of a promise rather than a metaphor of generation. "The Priestly Document (Source P) articulates this theology of covenants around three themes: Israel will be constituted as a people; Israel will receive the gift of land; Israel will enter into a privileged relation with God."[22] Promise is anterior to paternity, expectation to ancestry: *I shall be your God.*

The Biblical texts in which theologians have been most prone to see God as progenitor or origin are all in fact modes of promise or prophecy. Ricoeur reads the Creation Myth as essentially the narrative of the founding of a historical people. It is the "preface to the history of acts of salvation."[23] Even the giving of the Law is less a paternal commandment than a gift founding the special relation between the historical collectivity and its hero. The symbolism of fatherhood is latent in the historical narratives and covenants, merely alluded to in God's role as hero or as god of our fathers. In fact, the father figure is held off when God speaks most directly. The revelation of God's name, Yahweh, in the pronouncement *I am that I am* does not call forth any *imago* of the father. This imageless naming of God "eschews any reference to fatherhood [and], moreover, in actively dispelling idols, amounts to a dissolution of all anthropomorphism, of all figures and figurations, including that of the father."[24]

Only the Christian discourse unambiguously designates God the Father. Jesus, Ricoeur argues, introduces a new form of prophecy through the promise of the kingdom to come. He replaces historical narrative and covenant with the *invocation.* This new discursive form is an act of speaking to God rather than speaking about him or being spoken to by him. It alters the relation to God. The Old Testament prophets performed invocation only reluctantly or indirectly. The Lord's Prayer by contrast makes the direct address, "*Abba,* which we could translate by 'dear father.' Here is completed the movement from designation to invocation. Jesus in all probability, was addressing himself to God in saying 'Abba.' This invocation is absolutely unprecedented and without parallel in all the literature of Jewish prayer. Jesus dares address himself as a child to his father."[25]

Historical narrative and covenant establish an external, collective relation to God the hero; the invocation of the Lord's Prayer establishes an inward, personal relation to God the Father. The Christian addresses God in the words of Jesus, a son speaking to his father. Through this discourse the relation to God is internalized. The becoming-intimate of the relation to God establishes the complex range of feelings the Christian experiences as spirituality.

Even this act of naming the Father gives prophecy or promise precedence over ancestry. The invocation

> does not look backward, toward a great ancestor, but forward in the direction of a new intimacy on the model of the knowledge of the son. In the exegesis of Paul, it is because the Spirit witnesses our sonship (Romans 8:16) that we can cry *Abba,* Father. Far, therefore, from the religion of the father being that of a distant and hostile transcendence, there is fatherhood because there is sonship, and there is sonship because there is community of spirit.[26]

Christian interiorization has, then, three aspects. It makes the relation to God intimate. It transforms the experience of collectivity and solidarity, by supplanting the Jewish experience of a collectivity's own history with the individual Christian's inner experience of the "community of spirit." And, finally, on this basis God is symbolized as the Father.

One more innovation of meaning is attributed to the shift from the Judaic to the Christian tradition. The orientation toward individual rather than collective salvation, and toward transcendent rather than historical deliverance, alters the meaning of fatherhood and death. Ricoeur argues that Christian religious symbolism so transfigures the death of the father that it effaces the connotations of murder. For Ricoeur, the death of Christ accomplishes this transfiguration on a higher level than the Oedipal recognition of the father's mortality or the representation of the dead father by the Penates. The crucifixion replaces *being killed by* with *dying for*.

The innovated meaning brings forward the element of compassion in the father's death. It absorbs the primal economy of desire and the secular power of representation into a new symbolization of desire and reconciliation:

> The Just One is killed, certainly, and thereby the aggressive impulse against the father is satisfied by means of the offspring of the archaic paternal image; but at the same time, and this is the essential point, the meaning of death is reversed: by becoming 'dead for another,' the death of the Just One achieves the metamorphosis of the paternal image in the direction of kindness and compassion. . . . [I]f Christ is here the Suffering Servant, does he not reveal, in taking the place of the father, a dimension of the father to which death by compassion belongs primordially? In this sense, we could speak truly of the death of God as the death of the father. And that death would be at the same time a murder on the level of the phantasm and of the return of the repressed, and a supreme abandonment, a supreme dispossession of the self, on the level of the most advanced symbol.[27]

Ricoeur gives a kind of dialectical completion to his interpretation of fatherhood by postulating that Christian symbolism is the highest achievement of Western culture's designations of fatherhood. The progressive interpretation of fatherhood claims to disclose a trajectory of symbolizations. In the beginning are the murderous impulses of a megalomaniacal infant toward a fantasized all-powerful father. And at the end, dialectically reversing this origin, are the saving compassion and self-abandonment of a son become father.

In constructing the dialectic of fatherhood, Ricoeur has established a path of symbolizations he claims create fatherhood in Western culture. Along one edge of this path the death of the father has progressed through a series of figures or symbols. With each new figuration, the father's death becomes less laden with conflict. The first death of the father was his fantasized murder at the hands of the son. That figuration was transformed by, and into, the son's acceptance of the father's mortality. The father figure next takes the form of the Penates, a representation that at once alludes to the father's death or absence and expresses the paternal spirit of the family community. And, finally, the Christian transformation of the Judaic God re-creates the union of absence and presence, fantasized murder and symbolic reconciliation, aggression and devotion. The Christian symbolism makes the death of the father coincide with the revelation of the father. All at once the symbolization of fatherhood satisfies the urge to kill the father and expiates all such urges, adduces an attitude of sonship and intimacy toward the father and gives the father-son's death the meaning of *dying for*.

Along the other edge of this same path has developed the education or cultivation of desire. Each renunciation of desire has given rise to a new figuration of desire. First came the infantile megalomania of omnipotent desire. It was constrained by fantasmal fears of castration before breaking forth anew in the individual's mature erotic life. This pattern is then repeated and transformed on the scale of institutions. Extravagant unformed desire stirs a will to possess but is checked in the experience of labor and reshaped through property and contract; desire then reappears in the form of the ethical bond of marriage and family, deprived of its caprice and integrated into the institutions of spirit. Finally, the Christian experience completely overcomes the megalomania of desire through the abandonment of desire. At this ultimate point in Ricoeur's dialectical construction, receiving the *promise of fulfillment* takes the form of the *abandonment of desire*. Desire fulfilled and desire renounced ultimately become one and the same, just as the father killed and the father revealed became one and the same. The cultivation of desire and the symbolizations of the death of the father are corresponding processes. The two edges of a single path, they have followed the same "ascending dialectic." For Ricoeur, of course, this single path is not merely the effect of the interpreter's ordering of the representations, it is the dialectical progression or evolution of Western culture.

This dialectical progression can be criticized by scrutinizing either its supposed end-point or its supposed turning-points. I will for the moment merely describe, without criticizing, the end-point of Ricoeur's construct. This ultimate horizon is Christian faith, understood as the individual's inner experience of the promise of personal redemption. The symbolization *God the Father* places the subject in relation to a limit beyond which lies whatever cannot be satisfied in one's own desire or accomplished through one's own effort. The symbolization of fatherhood here signifies a power to satisfy and reconcile, in Ricoeur's phrase, "beyond desire and effort." This power of the father lies beyond not only the individual's desire and effort but also beyond that of humanity as a whole: *Thy will be done*.

This beyond-will-and-effort embraces the two paradoxes overtly expressed in Christian faith. Namely, that the killing of the Son who represents the Father is at the same time the Father's compassionate act of dying for . . . ; and that to renounce one's own desire is at the same time to receive the promise of fulfillment. In sequencing the paternal symbols as he does, Ricoeur makes these paradoxes the meaning to which all the other symbolizations of fatherhood and refigurations of desire aspire; symbolized fatherhood and cultivated desire always contain, latently or incompletely, the limit beyond-will-and-effort at which renunciation is fulfillment.

I readily confess a suspicion—a lack of faith, really—toward the interpretive procedure that leads to this outcome. But I am going to focus my criticisms of Ricoeur's dialectic on its turning-points rather than its endpoint. For it is at the turning-points that he is most acutely aware of the social and historical situatedness of the Oedipus complex. My doubts can therefore be directed at material rather than spiritual realities, questions of social theory rather than theology.

Ricoeur isolates two experiences that transform the maturing male's conflictual, fantasy-ridden family relationships into his reconciling recognition of, and self-recognition in, family roles and norms. The first turning-point involves vocation and marks the point at which a young man becomes a rights-bearing person by participating in the practices of contract and property in a capitalist market society. The form of sociality and selfhood experienced in the marketplace dissolves the fantasmal, conflictual relation between father and son. The son becomes a person. At the next turning-point, marriage transforms the person into a husband and father, making him the member of a single entity that transcends his own individuality. Conflict has been replaced by reconciliation and fantasy by role-taking.

While vocation and marriage have been the typical watersheds for young men's maturation in the bourgeois lifeworld, Ricoeur's dialectical account is flawed. The flaw is in part empirical and in part normative. Ricoeur expunges from the two turning-points all the inequalities that can inhabit and disturb the social-symbolic relationships he describes. Indeed, he has to attribute intrinsic harmoniousness to these relationships in order to make the dialectic and its norms work at all.

Consider the second of the turning-points first. The cornerstone of Ricoeur's account of marriage is his vehement repudiation of Kant's notion that marriage itself is a kind of contract. In argument and tone he follows in Hegel's footsteps:

> After having declared that the two parties to a contract are "immediate self-subsistent persons," [Hegel] remarks: "to subsume marriage under the concept of contract is thus quite impossible; this subsumption—though shameful is the only word for it—is propounded in Kant." . . . And indeed, in the ascending dialectic, we must look for the family quite beyond abstract right.[28]

Marriage, however, plainly does have contractual elements in modern societies. Not only are marriages recognized and regulated by the state, but all manner of marital disputes regarding divorce, custody of children, property, child support, inheritance and so on, are subject to legal resolution in a manner that positions husband and wife as rights-bearing, contracting individuals.

The fact that there are massive inequalities in these relations, that women do not in fact enjoy the full protection of the law, should not keep us from seeing that the norms and rules of contract operate in the so-called domestic sphere. "Equality" does not *describe* the marital relation, but it does come into play as a *norm* rightfully *evoked* to denounce inequalities between husbands and wives. When Ricoeur, like Hegel, bars juridical and contractual relations from marriage, he in effect banishes women from the domain of rights and solidifies the androcentric standpoint of his whole project.

Rights, equalities and personhood are placed outside what Ricoeur likes to call the "spiritual-carnal institution" of marriage. On the one hand, then, marriage and family are viewed as *Sittlichkeit* (ethical substance) without a trace of the juridically mediated relation between "immediate self-subsistent persons." The two parties to marriage are in short not persons. On the other hand, a man becomes a mature member of the family through marriage by virtue of having already attained his personhood in the social practices of property and contract. Consequently, only the personhood of men figures in the realization of marriage as ethical substance, while the personhood of women is rendered irrelevant to the nature of family, marriage, childbearing and childrearing. Ricoeur pictures men acquiring and then overcoming abstract right, women simply lacking it.

In failing to account for the rights women claim with regard to their roles as wives and mothers, Ricoeur misses a crucial component of marital

conflict. The impact of such conflict on the child who witnesses it surely must be counted among the main ingredients of the Oedipal relation. How do the inequalities and injustices in the social relations between men and women manifest themselves in the couple whose life together furnishes children with the materials for their Oedipal representations? This question Ricoeur blocks, first by expelling the juridical-contractual dimension from marriage altogether and then by bifurcating the pathological and the normative effects of marriage. He attributes the pathological effects solely to the little boy's apprehension of his parents' marriage in its "natural" dimension as sexuality; he then links the normative resolution of the resulting conflicts to the boy's eventual discovery of the carnal-spiritual dimension of marriage. Had Ricoeur approached marriage in its fuller social and moral dimensions, he would have had to consider how the complex set of social relationships embodied in the heterosexual couple is a potential source of pathologies as well as norms.

Androcentrism also leads Ricoeur to postulate a false harmony in the matured male's autonomy and independence. The young man, he argues, achieves independence in the experience of property and contract: "as person, I possess my life and body, like other things, only insofar as it is my property." When women claim the right to their own bodies in the political form of sexual and reproductive rights, they not only complicate this androcentric idea of body and right but they also directly challenge the legitimacy of treating the carnal-spiritual institution of the family as a domain of male mastery superior to their own rights. The heterosexual couple has been shaped by, and contends with, conflicting forms of right and autonomy. Had Ricoeur approached heterosexuality on these terms, he would likewise have had to approach the family as the site of complexly constructed norms—abstract and concrete, contractual and customary, juridical and ethical—which do not neatly array themselves on a transcending arc from the sexual to the spiritual, from abstract right to ethical substance, from fantasmal jealousy to adaptive role-taking.

There is a one-sidedness, too, in Ricoeur's whole discussion of property and contract. Once again he expunges actual inequalities—and their potential effects—this time from the relations between individuals, groups or classes who meet one another in the market-mediated processes of labor and exchange. For while the capitalist market, including the cultural, psychological and legal norms that make it work, does bring individuals into a relation of equality at the moment of buying-and-selling, it is by no means devoid of power relations. Indeed, the market can create, reproduce or intensify the power of one individual or group over another, including the capacity to exploit. Property and contract complicate power relations, sometimes exacerbating, sometimes ameliorating them, but they do not transcend them or transform them wholly into relations of equality. Yet that is the task Ricoeur assigns them in the ascending dialectic that overcomes all the traces of power symbolized by the Hegelian master and slave.

The account of property and contract stems from Ricoeur's uncritical adaptation of what C. B. Macpherson identified as the crucial premise of possessive individualism. The concept of man as *infinite consumer* or *infinite appropriator*—which reappears in Ricoeur, through Hegel and Freud, as the megalomania, the extravagance, the omnipotence of desire—has historically been "needed to provide the incentives and justify the power relations of a capitalist market society."[29] But it also comes into conflict with democratic commitments to equality. Classical liberalism believed it could bring together a notion of freedom built up on the assumption of infinite appropriation and the notion of equality evolved in Western democratic traditions. Modern society has tended to belie that promise.

I think Ricoeur is at one level fully aware of this. He might well subscribe to Macpherson's argument that political thinking must sharply distinguish individuals' free self-development from their unlimited appropriation: "The justification of liberal democracy still rests, and must rest, on the ultimate value of the free self-developing individual. But insofar as freedom is still seen as possession, as freedom from any but market relations with others, it can scarcely serve as the ultimate value of modern democracy."[30]

Ricoeur obviously recognizes that possessive individualism cannot anchor a theory of socialization and moral development or provide an adequate rendering of the traditions and values that are actually sedimented in sexuality, family life and education. In his search for correctives to this possessive individualism, however, he draws on an uncritical view of *compulsory heterosexuality* and *male dominance,* construing them to be the institutional-symbolic matrix that overcomes yet preserves individual right.

In sum, Ricoeur's account of male socialization in the bourgeois lifeworld follows the pattern of overlooking the inequalities and injustices that disturb vocation and marriage. Moreover, after failing to identify the specific injustices that stem from male dominance or mastery, he imagines that injustice itself can be transcended through, precisely, a higher form of male mastery. This higher form supposedly belongs to religious experience, and it is at this point that Ricoeur's use of religious hermeneutics for the purposes of social theory invites closer scrutiny.

He argues, quite persuasively, that Christianity has contributed to Western culture a father symbol through which one is beckoned to seek reconciliation in the form of giving up desire and effort. Christ is the metamorphosis of the Father that completes "the conversion of death as murder into death as offering":[31] "He humbled himself, and became obedient unto death" (Phil. 2:8). As father symbol, Christ is "the likeness of the father in accordance with which the giving up of desire is no longer death but love."[32] This love, for the one who answers the call of the symbolization, is an experience of entry into the "community of spirit."

Ricoeur the social theorist takes his vivid and learned accounts of the lived symbolization that creates Christian faith a step further. He attributes to this symbolization the power to reconcile the human community *beyond* desire and effort—and *beyond* justice. His starting-point is in itself extremely insightful. The "consciousness of injustice" rooted in Judaic and Greek traditions creates meanings of guilt over and above fears of vengeance, including the Oedipal fears Freud identified as the castration complex: "The fear of being unjust, the remorse for having been unjust, are no longer taboo fear, taboo remorse. The breaking of the interpersonal bond, the wrong done to the person of another, are more important than the threat of castration."[33] Ricoeur also recognizes that the consciousness of injustice does not guarantee the capacity to overcome the injustice. It is limited and fallible.

At this point, though, he associates the consciousness of injustice with the "judging consciousness," or conscience, on the model of an individual whose condemnations of self or other arrive at the impasse of resentfulness, combining the powerlessness to set things right with the gratification of pronouncing judgment. The meaning of guilt then passes a second threshold, "that of the sin of the just man, of the evil of justice itself. In this presumption of the honest man the delicate conscience discovers radical evil."[34]

Radical evil finds its mythical representation in the story of the Fall and its philosophical reflection in Kant's *Religion within the Limits of Reason Alone*. Evil actions carry out evil maxims, but these maxims could not have "originated" anywhere other than in human freedom. In Kant's words, "In the search for the rational origin of evil actions, every such action must be regarded as though the individual had fallen into it directly from a state of innocence."[35] In Ricoeur's:

> Evil would cease to be evil if it ceased to be "a manner of being of freedom, which itself comes from freedom." . . . For the enigma of this foundation is that reflection discovers, as a fact, that freedom has already chosen in an evil way. The evil is *already there*. It is in this sense that it is radical, that it is anterior (in a nontemporal way) to every evil intention, to every evil action.[36]

Beyond justice lies the prophetic-paternal promise that reconciliation is a giving up of desire and effort.

The leap of faith should not be allowed to disguise a flaw in the theory. Ricoeur simply has not exhausted the secular and social meaning of the idea of radical evil. We are all born and socialized into relationships and practices in which we harm others, or are harmed by them, before we acquire the values and the means required to alter those practices and relationships. We are always already entangled in webs of injury and wrong. But it does not follow that we must or should therefore seek reconciliation beyond justice. The eschatological vision obscures whole arenas of effort, like the polis, and whole modes of significant social action that transform lifeworlds in order to rectify, even belatedly, specific wrongs by eliminating their source.

Moreover, it is just because patterns of harm are anterior to individuals' specific agency that we should not expect watershed experiences such as vocation or marriage to wholly resolve the conflicts they respond to. By forcing that role upon them, Ricoeur gives false solutions to the Oedipus complex and fails to illuminate the unfinished nature of Oedipal maturation. The space for a social critique of the Oedipus complex is acknowledged ever so obliquely in the very turn that then simply obscures it, namely, the move to place genuine reconciliation in "the figure of the prophet, the figure outside the family, outside politics, outside culture, the eschatological figure par excellence."[37] Had Ricoeur admitted the inequalities and injustices within the practices of contract and property and marriage, and had he simultaneously held off the eschatological question, his rich exploration of the Oedipus complex would have led to other questions.

Principally, how might we account for the formation of the Oedipus complex without presupposing a dissolution of the Oedipus complex? For there is no reason to expect the individual's socialization into various fields of social practice, various symbolic frameworks and various moral and ethical norms to be more peaceful or complete than are these practices, symbols and norms themselves. It is just because the social relations in which we participate are complex and conflictual that our paths to forming identities and shaping desires are perilous.

3

Lacan

WHEN SELECTING the contents of his *Ecrits,* Jacques Lacan omitted his most salient contribution to the theory of the Oedipus complex. It was not a simple oversight. "The Neurotic's Individual Myth, or, 'Truth and Poetry' in Neurosis" represents a path not taken. In this essay from the early 1950s Lacan initiated a dialogue between psychoanalysis and social theory that he never brought to fruition. A few of the themes resonate in his later work, but the essay's central questions were abandoned:

How do the practices and habits of the modern family shape the psychosocial development of children? How does the father-son relationship typically become a focal point for various social relationships and conflicts? How does the traditional socialization of middle-class males into market-mediated practices of work and exchange mesh with their acceptance of father symbols?

When the *Ecrits* was put together in 1966, Lacan viewed "The Neurotic's Individual Myth" solely from the standpoint of the structuralist turn taken by his later work. He considered it noteworthy because it contained his first use of Claude Lévi-Strauss's analysis of myth. It was a step on the way to his own "placing of the unconscious within language."[1] I would like, in contrast, to retrieve the essay for its relevance to the kind of dialogue with social theory that Lacan dropped.

The essay's oblique, fuzzy language presents something of an obstacle. I intend therefore to rewrite Lacan's insights in Ricoeur's vocabulary. The result will significantly complicate Ricoeur's project and offer an alternative to several of his conclusions. The synthesizing of a man's identity which Ricoeur sees achieved in vocation and marriage has a far more precarious fate in Lacan's eyes. He never makes the assumption that bends Ricoeur's dialectic to its various resolutions. He does not assume that the formation of the Oedipus complex is intrinsically connected to a dissolution of the Oedipus complex.

Lacan does consider vocation and marriage the decisive moments in male maturation. He also shares the view that maturational crises are a process of forming an identity through experiences of mutual recognition. Classical psychoanalytic doctrine saw in the outbreak of neurosis a revival of infantile relationships prompted in adolescence or early adult life by the demands of independence. For middle-class men those demands typically build up around getting a job and deciding to marry.

Lacan sets up the terms of the problem in the meander of the following passage:

> To schematize, let us say that when a male subject is involved, his moral and psychic equilibrium requires him to assume his own function—he must gain recognition as such in his virile function and in his work, he must gather their fruits without conflict, without having the feeling that someone else deserves it and that he has it only by fluke, without there being any internal division that makes the subject the alienated witness of the acts of his own self. That is the first requirement. The other is this: an enjoyment one might characterize as tranquil and univocal of the sexual object, once it is chosen, granted to the subject's life.[2]

Lacan's imprecise prose nearly inundates his categories of social description. A more cogent critical analysis has to be teased out of his assertions. Note first that whereas Ricoeur assumes that all economic exchanges and contracts guarantee a sense of equality and equity, Lacan makes room for the question Ricoeur's perspective obscures: How is moral development affected by the instabilities or inequalities that an individual can sense in society's distribution of efforts and rewards? But Lacan quickly displays the familiar class-bias of psychoanalytic theory by modeling his example on the individual who feels he doesn't really deserve all he receives as opposed, say, to those who feel their efforts are being exploited for someone else's gain. Moreover, the perspective is androcentric in conceiving the efforts rewarded materially and socially solely on the model of profits, salary or at the very least paid labor without reference to the unpaid work women have traditionally performed within and outside the male-headed household.

Lacan's obscurity in part simply masks the fact that he is constructing a thoroughly androcentric view of the bourgeois lifeworld and then treating that particular lifeworld as coextensive with social life as a whole. The bourgeois male's uneasy feelings that he is getting more than he has really earned are surely worth explaining. But they need to be explained by showing how forms of social inequality can disturb individuals' self-recognition and sense of identity. Lacan unfortunately reverses the procedure and makes the example of the bourgeois male into the paradigm of identity formation. It should nevertheless be possible to make the necessary critical adjustments when evaluating Lacan's specifically psychoanalytic formulations in light of these biases.

What, for example, is really at stake when he asserts that a young man's maturation requires him to *identify with himself* as he performs his role or roles in society? What is the ordeal he faces when he must "become identical to himself and feel secure about the merits of his self-manifestation in the given social complex"? Identity formation has to acquire a new quality of permanence or consistency at the threshold of adult life. In the characteristic narrative patterns of the classical bourgeois period, particularly the *Bildungsroman,* men's life-histories culminate in the learning of a craft or choosing of a vocation. The contemporary analogue would be individuals' adoption of success-oriented goals and their expectation of money and status as the reward for good performance.

By saying that the young man must *identify with* himself as he carries out his new role-taking, Lacan is evoking what remained a central theme of his work, namely, the notion that self-identity is always formed through *identifications with*—. Children have very special reactions even at an early age to recognizing their own image in a mirror; they model themselves on others; and they recurrently accept the image attributed to them by others through labels, stereotypes or fixed expectations. As adulthood approaches, the role one takes on in one's social practices and interactions is yet another image with which one must identify. It has to be reproduced in one's everyday actions and relations. In "The Neurotic's Individual Myth," Lacan focuses on the moment in the maturation process where a young man is challenged to integrate this performance-oriented identity into the series of identifications on which the self has been formed since childhood through various intersubjective experiences.

Ricoeur arrived at the same question in more precise terms. How does an identity that has been forming in childhood through substantive, concrete bonds with others get integrated into an identity henceforth grounded in abstract relations of property, contract and right? He responded by arguing that these two sites of socialization—the family and the marketplace, concrete family bonds and abstract juridical-economic relations—furnish males with two types of identification with the father. The first is rooted in fantasy and rivalry, the second in mutual recognition and equality. Ricoeur further argued that the second type of identification supplants the first. In a third dialectical moment the father figure then returns as symbol rather than fantasy, and the matured male returns to the family in the role of husband and father.

Unlike Ricoeur, Lacan does not believe that vocation resolves the young man's boyhood relation to his father or that marriage ushers him into the higher symbolism of fatherhood. Ricoeur hews closer to classical psychoanalytic doctrine, viewing the unsuccessful resolution of such crises purely as a neurotic outcome of the Oedipus complex. The neurotic outcome is associated with an overly valued erotic tie to the mother and the incomplete acceptance of father symbols. The nonneurotic outcome is guaranteed by possessive individualism and compulsory heterosexuality. While Lacan was hardly a critic of compulsory heterosexuality, and only obliquely a critic of possessive individualism, he did accomplish a decisive break with classical doctrine by claiming that the father-son relation is itself the *source* of the pathologies in question.

Lacan sees a clash develop between the father symbols and the real-life father who becomes a vehicle for those symbols. According to Lacan's hypothesis, the modern father assumes—in the whole of his actual existence and conduct—the role of representing or embodying the cultural-symbolic function of fatherhood. The real-life father represents the father symbols to those around him. A son would be able to perceive *both* his father's actual existence and the cultural-symbolic meaning of fatherhood, accepting them without ambiguity or conflict, only if, in Lacan's phrase, "the symbolic and the real would fully coincide" in the father's experience and conduct. The real-life father would have to be the perfect embodiment of the symbolic father.

The modern restricted family imposes this requirement on the maturation process but thwarts its realization:

> Now, it is clear that this coincidence of the symbolic and the real is totally elusive. At least in a social structure like ours, the father is always in one

> way or another in disharmony with regard to his function, a deficient father, a *humiliated* father, as Claudel would say. There is always an extremely obvious discrepancy between the symbolic function and what is perceived by the subject in the sphere of experience. In this divergence lies the source of the effects of the oedipus complex which are not at all normalizing, but rather most often pathogenic.[3]

The dissonance in the son's perception of the father apparently goes beyond the simple fact that any actual father deviates to one degree or another from the effective ideal of fatherhood. Lacan's remarks suggest that the relation modern Western society establishes between the actual existence of the father and the symbolizations of fatherhood is inherently dissonant. Lacan's perspective contrasts with Ricoeur's on two counts. Where Ricoeur distinguishes the fantasized father from the father symbols and postulates a dialectical movement from the one to the other, Lacan distinguishes the father symbols and the real-life father and postulates a recurrent discrepancy between them.

However, Lacan's notion of the symbolic father remains too undifferentiated. Various designations of fatherhood have evolved in the multilayered heritage of patriarchy, and each has particular effects on the discourse and interactions in which it occurs. To get at what the bourgeois father represents or embodies, it is therefore necessary to uncover the entire scale of symbolizations condensed in the cultural designation "Father." Simply drawing on the discussions found in Freud, Ricoeur and Lacan, I propose that such an inventory of father symbols should at least include the following: *begetter, castrator, name-giver, law-giver, provider, protector, redeemer.*

What is it that links these various symbolizations and permits them to be associated in a single designation? Ricoeur touched on it I think when he implied that father symbols place the subject to whom they appeal in relation to something that cannot be satisfied or accomplished through one's own desire and effort. The Father is this *beyond-desire-and-effort.* The form of this limit varies with each symbolization, as does the discourse which communicates the limit. For example, the symbolization *castrator* or *law-giver* is communicated through a command spoken by the father and makes the limit to desire and effort appear in the form of a taboo or prohibition. The symbolization *redeemer* is, by contrast, communicated through prayers addressed to the father and makes the limit of one's own effort appear in the form of a promise the Other will fulfill.

The symbolic cannot fully coincide with the real in the modern restricted family because—to rewrite Lacan one more time—the symbols *beyond-desire-and-effort* are not compatible with the bourgeois father's actual existence. A real-life father's history, his life situation, the elements of his character, his achievements and failings, his fears and anxieties, all result from his actions, will and desire as they manifest themselves in his specific social circumstance. A son recognizes and understands his father by witnessing his actions and the countereffects of society, his will and the limits to its realization, his desires and the circumstances that satisfy or thwart them. The real-life father exists through his desires and efforts, yet he embodies or represents symbols of a *beyond-desire-and-effort.* Recognition and designation in the father-son relation are not, as Ricoeur would have it, complementary. They are discrepant. The father has to be recognized through the manifestations of his social existence, but he is designated through the contrary symbols he represents. The designated Father stands beyond-desire-and-effort, the recognized father bears all the physiognomy of desire and effort.

The burden of Lacan's claims would be to show that this dissonance is not merely localized or temporary, something sons simply get over, but that it is the generative structure of the father-son relation itself. I want now to sketch out such an argument with reference to two sets of father symbols—first, *begetter* and *name-giver;* second, *castrator* and *law-giver*—as they come into conflict with the recognitions or cognitions accompanying them. In each case, the discrepancy between recognition and designation can be seen to radiate out into other features of the Oedipus complex as traditionally conceived.

Begetter and name-giver. Lacan is right not to distinguish an "archaic" or "natural" relation to the father based on begetting from a later relation uniquely based on designations and recognitions. One's earliest inklings of sexual reproduction are forged in the interplay of designation. The meaning of one's own birth is never exhausted in the fantasies or knowledges of procreation, any more than it can escape them. One's birth is placed in the field of naming and symbolic filiation from the beginning. Filiation is an effect of designation, both in the sense that a man is the acknowledged father of a child only by being so designated, and in the sense that in patrilinear societies at least the father's name is the mark of paternity and kinship. Lacan conveys this aspect of fatherhood by dubbing the symbolic Father the *nom-du-père* or "name-of-the-father."

Intermingled with the designations *begetter* and *name-giver* are all the things children find out about their own birth in their search for answers to the question *Where do I come from?* Children's "sexual researches" seek what Lacan, playing on the astrological meaning of the term, calls the "constellation" of circumstances and actions, wishes and passions, that led up to their coming into the world. In this constellation the father is designated *begetter* and *name-giver*, but he also appears altogether caught up in his real life. The child gathers a narrative concocted from family legends, anecdotes, tell-tale phrases, even jokes. It is the story of the circumstances of the parents' union and the child's conception, the place of the marriage in the father's erotic history, the vicissitudes of his ambitions, his pleasures and sufferings and so on. Lacan calls this narrative of one's own prehistory an "individual myth," a kind of personal mythology of origins and identity pieced together from the steady stream of family tales that children so eagerly collect and revise.

The father appears, so to speak, twice over in the individual myth. He is there in the father symbols—marking a limit beyond the son's desire and effort, in the form of an origin—and he is there as a real-life person entangled in his own desires and efforts and thus a figure in whom the son can recognize himself. As I will illustrate later with reference to Freud's case history of the Rat Man, the Lacanian individual myth has a four-term structure as opposed to the classical psychoanalytic paradigm of the Oedipal triangle. In keeping with the discrepancy between the designated and the recognized father, father symbol and real-life father, the individual myth's narrative forms tend to split the father into two figures.

The bourgeois father's claim to embody symbolic-cultural fatherhood is continually thrown in doubt. His everyday life and conduct frequently belie it. His legitimacy is volatile. Lacan dwells on the pathos of this situation to the point of merely sounding the chords of masculine self-pity. Nevertheless, he does avoid the anachronism Ricoeur lapsed into when using the Penates to explain a man's recovery of paternal mastery in the household. The modernization of everyday life has included the decline of the myths, communal rituals and religious practices through which earlier social formations gave father symbols—ancestors, elders, household spirits and so on—a regular, integral presence in social life. Those symbols maintained a distance from the actual person of the father in the household. The modern father is far more closely identified with paternal symbols but therefore more thoroughly discrepant with them as well. It is this discrepancy which is formative of the Oedipal relation of son and father. The more the father seems to conform to his symbolic designation the less understandable is his real life, and conversely the more he is recognized in his real life the more deficient he appears with respect to his symbolic function.

Castrator and law-giver. The legitimacy of the father's moral authority is also volatilized by a discrepancy between designation and recognition. The designation *castrator* or *law-giver* is communicated in the form of the father's commands or the references to his authority on the part of the child's mother, siblings and others. Authority is proffered in the *nom-du-père*—that is, according to the pun Lacan intends, "in the name-of-the-father" or through "the father's 'No.'" As voice and representative of a law, the father again occupies the limit of desire and effort. But over against this father symbol stands the real-life father in whom the son recognizes someone like himself, his *semblable,* his likeness or counterpart.

This *identification with* the father is incompatible with the other slope of the father-son relation where the father's voice establishes him as a *transcendent* authority. In identifying with the father, the son's acceptance of his authority is disturbed because he sees someone who, like himself, is animated *by* desires and efforts rather than standing beyond them. In revering the father's authority, the son's identification is interrupted because he encounters a father who cannot be like himself, and whom he therefore cannot be like.

This much can be inferred from Lacan's discussion. But some further implications can also be drawn from it. For this challenge to the father's moral authority happens at a far more elementary level than the validity or rightness of his specific commands and pronouncements. There is a rent in the moral relation of father and son long in advance of the son's development of a capacity to question a command or judgment on the basis of acknowledged or tacitly shared criteria. The moral disequilibrium in the child's life cannot therefore be wholly attributed to moral immaturity, whether conceived developmentally or as the so-called omnipotence of desire. The disequilibrium comes from the relationship with the father, the very relationship that is supposed to eventually temper omnipotent desire and guide moral development.

Nowhere are the effects of this moral disequilibrium more in evidence than in what psychoanalysis classically considers the heart of the Oedipus complex, namely, the incestuous wishes that bind son to mother. As I have already argued in my commentary on "A Special Type of Choice of Object Made By Men," Freud's own interpretive and clinical work contradicts his suggestion that the Oedipal wish is an unmediated desire for the mother. Nor is this wish present from the beginning as some kind of primeval omnipotence of desire. The Oedipal wish has to be acquired. It is learned in the course of various social and cultural experiences. It is this learning process which shapes—and, indeed, reshapes—the mother-son relationship into its Oedipal mold. Lacan provides, quite unintentionally I think, a first glimpse at just how this reshaping occurs.

The father's "No" makes the mother the object of a taboo, but it is also from the father that the son learns what it means to desire her. The father furnishes the voice of the taboo and the scenarios of transgression. Lacan and his followers have all too frequently used this apparent paradox to hypostatize the interdependence of law and transgression. The notion that a law calls for an inclination to transgress it has an obvious truth, as does the longstanding psychoanalytic insight that the incest taboo promotes incestuous wishes. But it is far more important to stress how law and transgression do not derive from the same source in the social-symbolic context of the male-dominated restricted family. What counts is another discrepancy between designation and recognition in the father-son relation. The male child encounters the law limiting his desire in the voice of the command and the symbols designating the father *castrator* and *law-giver*. But it is through the process of recognizing himself in the father that he learns masculinity and heterosexuality. His relation to his mother *becomes* Oedipal only as he is socialized into masculinity and heterosexuality.

A further refinement on the idea of the *Nachträglichkeit* of the Oedipus complex can now be hazarded. A boy's identifications with his father are a framework for his lessons in his own social and sexual roles. These identifications are likely to be all the more significant the more the practices and values of compulsory heterosexuality and of the male-headed restricted family hold sway. At the same time, this father-centered learning process is itself continually supplemented, or contravened, by relevant experiences, cognitions and representations acquired throughout latency and adolescence. At each juncture what is learned has to be routed back through the boy's attachments to his mother and the whole unconscious record of his interactions with her. It is my hypothesis, then, that the male's unconscious relation to his mother is continually remapped as he acquires ever more elaborated forms of heterosexuality. In this way the cultivation of desire—

of male heterosexual desire and the "necessary conditions for loving"—acquires the complex temporality suggested by Freud's interpretations. The process that determines the male's adaptation to specific forms of heterosexuality retrodetermines the so-called Oedipal fixation.

Freud's regressive method of interpretation led from adult forms of heterosexuality back to childhood attachments, but he lacked a corollary progressive method that could chart the transformations of the mother-son relation. Memory is renewed but also revamped as new meanings, codes and representations reinterpret what has initially been lived through by means of other meanings, codes and representations. Or, to choose a metaphor closer to Freud's, new scripts are written over earlier ones on the palimpsest of the unconscious. As the norms and values of compulsory heterosexuality increasingly influence the socialized male's relation to women, the unconscious relation to the mother gets rescripted.

This learning process and this cultivation of desire are shaped by social meanings and cultural codes learned throughout latency, adolescence and early adulthood. Ricoeur made this point in general but failed to apply it to the learned forms of heterosexuality themselves. He simply postulated a progression from maternal fixation to mature heterosexuality, and attributed the progress to the sequence of father symbols. Lacan's reflections have challenged Ricoeur by showing that the various appearances of the father—as rival, as equal, as symbol—do not follow a dialectical sequence at all. Lacan has the further insight that the heterosexual learning process and cultivation of desire are shaped by the son's discordant relation to the father. The fact that the various moments of fatherhood revive a discrepancy between designation and recognition suggests, contrary to Ricoeur, that the return of the father symbol is less a power to reconcile than an incessant refurbishing of Oedipal pathologies. Yet Lacan too fails to fully appreciate how the resulting moral disequilibrium affects the psychic reality of the mother-son relation.

A new horizon-question now appears, one which never quite gets asked by Freud or Lacan and which Ricoeur answers unsatisfactorily: What ultimately is the link between the symbolizations of fatherhood and the cultivation of desire, specifically of male heterosexual desire? The question falls in part within the purview of social theory and cultural interpretation, in part within that of psychoanalysis. First, it is a matter of describing the institutional-symbolic webbing that connects father symbols, compulsory heterosexuality, practices of male dominance, the socially organized forms of interdependence between men and women (including their legal, civic and economic status as well as the sexual division of labor), marriage patterns, household arrangements and childrearing practices.

Second, psychoanalysis should be called upon, by the same token, to address how this institutional-symbolic complex affects structures of feeling and patterns of interaction, how it shapes and misshapes the inner world of individuals and, specifically, how men's desires and identities develop in relation to the particular historical forms of masculinity, heterosexuality and individuality in question. That is the task I think a cultural critique of the Oedipus complex has to fulfill.

The concept of the individual myth helps coordinate these various elements of social theory, cultural interpretation and psychoanalysis. The individual myth is a representation children use to map their family relationships. In the process they discover benchmarks of their own identity and aims of their own desires. They piece this representation together from the fragmentary materials at hand in their everyday lifeworld. But through this personal mythology they also begin to encounter the social relations, practices and institutions that create that lifeworld and society at large.

The individual myth is itself the mediating link between one's personal circumstances and relationships and the institutional-symbolic complex. The individual myth is therefore neither a universal mental structure nor a purely idiosyncratic narrative. It is shaped by the larger social world in which the child and parents participate, and it shapes the child's enlarging participation in that social world. So conceived, the concept of the individual myth can begin to force Oedipal theory to come to terms with its own immersion in history, society and politics.

Part Two

The Freudian Structure of Feeling

4

Rat Man

PAUL LORENZ was suffering obsessions and compulsions when he sought treatment from Freud in October 1907. At 29, he was unable to decide what course he should take in his relationship with a woman he had loved for several years. "His lady" had rejected his marriage proposal seven years previously and again three years ago. They remained close over the years. Freud does not reveal that they were first cousins. "It was true," Freud writes, "that he loved her very much, but he never felt really sensual wishes toward her."[1] In the throes of this idealized passion, he constantly vacillated between an intense admiration and just as intense an antagonism toward "his lady."

A similar vacillation marked his feelings toward his father, who had died eight years before the therapy with Freud. The father's death had stymied Paul's efforts to decide upon career as well as marriage. He postponed the completion of his legal studies and examinations for the next five years. Moreover, his father haunted his symptoms. The father could give him commands beyond the grave. And the patient's thoughts could likewise make the dead father suffer. Paul's illness took a new turn when, some four years before the treatment began, his mother suggested that he marry a relative's daughter instead of "his lady" and enter the family's business. This phase of obsessions and compulsions had culminated in August 1907 when the patient, while on military maneuvers in Galicia, fell prey to a frenzy of obsessive thoughts and compulsive actions designed to ward off a grotesque punishment he felt was going to befall his lady and his long dead father.

Freud's presentation of the case follows out several interrelated strands. The first strand includes all those elements of the father's life-story that were charged with significance for the patient. That strand is then made the basis for interpreting three others: first, the "precipitating cause" of the current phase of Paul's disorder; second, the obsessions and rituals that brought him into therapy; and, third, the transference relation established during the analysis. The significant elements of the father's history make up the core of what Lacan means by the individual myth: the narrative of those events and relationships which the patient views as leading to his own birth.

All four strands of Freud's interpretation are in fact narratives. Lacan suggested that the various narratives relate to one another as permutations of a single narrative structure. He drew his inspiration from Claude Lévi-Strauss's "The Structural Study of Myth." Lévi-Strauss analyzed several versions of the Oedipus myth. The basic elements of the myth could recombine through several permutations and still be shown to enact a relatively constant set of relations among any particular grouping of elements. That set of relations, or structure, rather than a supposed "original" version is, Lévi-Strauss argued, the key to the myth's meaning.[2]

The idea of narrative permutations is freely adapted by Lacan to the various "stories" that Freud's patient has lived, fantasized, remembered or simply been told. Accordingly, Lacan distills a narrative structure that is relatively fixed in the sense that each variant replicates a particular set of intersubjective positions, roles much like stock characters: Rich Woman, Poor Woman, Father, Friend, and a particular set of actions: borrowing, loaning, protecting, marrying, betraying. By the same token, the narrative structure is relatively fluid in the sense that each new combination only becomes meaningful in relation to a particular context of experience.

In summarizing the four narratives around which Freud organized his interpretations, I will try to bring out the sense of recurrent structures that organized Lacan's reinterpretation of the Rat Man.

The core narrative. The core of the patient's individual myth included two distinct stories Paul had heard about his father. One goes back to the days of the father's military service, and the other concerns his decision to marry. While in military service, the father had gambled away regimental funds entrusted to him and was only saved from dishonor by a loan from a friend. "After he had left the army and become well-off, he had tried to find this friend in need so as to pay him back the money, but had not managed to trace him."[3]

According to the second story, the father chose to marry the patient's mother at the expense of a "pretty but penniless girl" he loved. With the marriage, he secured a position in the business owned by his wife's relatives. The Rubenskys, Freud explains, are indeed the same family the mother later wants her son to marry into. What Freud does not explain is that the patient's mother and father are themselves first cousins. Paul had often heard this second story in the guise of his mother's supposedly lighthearted teasing of his father.

The two themes—leaving a debt to a Friend unpaid and replacing the Poor Woman with the Rich Woman—leave the dead father bearing a twofold debt: the money owed the Friend and the love owed the Poor Woman. In turn, according to the individual myth, Paul owes his own existence to just these breaches of faith on his father's part. They take on the significance of the events that led to his own birth. He is indebted to his father's indebtedness. The patient's symptoms, in Lacan's interpretation, are a protest against the symbolic debt of his existence, echoing his refusal to take control of his inheritance after his father's death, instead leaving it to his mother to dole out a monthly allowance to him. At the same time, his symptoms were a vain effort to settle his father's debts to the helpful Friend and the Poor Woman.

The precipitating cause. Only in the course of the analysis did Freud pinpoint the precipitating cause of Paul's current obsessions and compulsions. The mother's marriage plan not only held out the prospect of a lucrative position for Paul if he married the "rich and well-connected" girl, it invited him to abandon his lady and, like his father, desert the Poor Woman for the Rich Woman.

The obsessional ritual. Paul's ultimate crisis, a breakdown in effect, was a delirious episode that unfolded near the end of his military tour on maneuvers outside Vienna. A captain he particularly despised told him of an Oriental torture in which a vase containing rats was held up to the victim's buttocks until they bore into his anus. Upon hearing the story he was tormented with the thought *this is happening to my father.* A few days later he lost his pince-nez and ordered a new pair sent C.O.D. from Vienna to the post office at Z——. This same captain told him Lieutenant A. had received the package, so he owed him 3.80 *kronen.* Paul felt a sanction weighed against the repayment: *if I do that, the rat punishment will happen to my father and my lady.* The sanction was countered by a vow: *you must pay back Lieutenant A.,* a vow he felt compelled to keep even after learning that it was in fact not Lieutenant A. but Lieutenant B. who had paid the charges on the package.

Caught in a dilemma, he devised a scheme for fulfilling the vow *and* the sanction on the morning he was to leave for Vienna. He recounted the repayment ritual to Freud without explaining why a young woman at the post office as well as the two lieutenants had to be involved. His plan was as follows:

Himself, Lieutenant A. and Lieutenant B. should meet at the post office.

Lieutenant A. (who had to be repaid though he was owed nothing) would give 3.80 *kronen* to the young woman.

She would hand the sum over to Lieutenant B., thus reimbursing him for having originally received the package.

Paul would then repay Lieutenant A. the 3.80 *kronen* he had just laid out to set this ritualistic action in motion.

The scenario was designed to fulfill the vow by simulating a loan and repayment involving Lieutenant A. in strict obedience to the captain's command: "You must pay back 3.80 *kronen* to Lieutenant A." The young woman's presence went unexplained until the patient eventually revealed that it was really she who was owed the money all along. Lieutenant B. had no more to do with the package than Lieutenant A. Moreover, Paul had actually known he owed the money to the young woman *before* the captain told him to pay Lieutenant A. He suppressed this knowledge at the time, just as he deleted it from the first several renditions of the episode to Freud. In short, had he actually carried out his plan Lieutenant A. would do no more than give the young woman money in order that he might be promptly paid back by the patient, while Lieutenant B. would end up receiving money he was not owed and the young woman would still be out the money she was in fact owed! The patient, however, was unaware of any of these complications as he first thought up the plan.

On the morning of his trip, Paul hesitated between returning by train to Vienna or finding Lieutenant A. in order to make the trip to the postal station at Z—— and carry out the ritual. He was torn. He felt cowardly asking Lieutenant A.'s help, since he was merely trying to relieve himself of the pain caused by his own obsessions. And he felt cowardly not asking, since he thereby merely sought to avoid looking foolish.

> When in the course of his deliberation, the patient added, he found arguments so evenly balanced as these, it was his custom to allow his actions

> to be decided by chance events as though by the hand of God. When, therefore, a porter at the station had addressed him with the words, "Ten o'clock train, sir?" he answered "Yes," and in fact had gone off by the ten o'clock train. In this way he felt he had produced a *fait accompli* and felt greatly relieved.[4]

All along the route to Vienna, though, he was haunted by the thought he should stop at the next station, return by train to P—— to find Lieutenant A. and go with him to the postal station at Z—— to carry out the plan. At each stop, he recalculated the time the plan required and assured himself it could all be done with time to spare for him to get to Vienna on a later train. He would then let some factor or another convince him to stay on the train until one more stop and so on, through each leg of the journey. Upon reaching Vienna, he put himself in the hands of a friend, while still frantically devising ways to resurrect the plan.

Another essential fact came to light in the course of the analysis. Much of Paul's motivation for wanting to return to Z—— was, apparently, independent of the young woman who paid for his package, even though he did know she had spoken of her interest in him to another officer. It concerned, instead, another young woman, the innkeeper's daughter, who "had been decidedly encouraging to the smart young officer."[5] Once again he found himself drawn into, or perhaps drawn to, a situation pitting two women against each other for his feelings, as in the scenarios of the Poor Woman and the Rich Woman.

The transference fantasy and dream. A difficult period in the treatment began as soon as Freud asserted that Paul's father had abandoned the "pretty but penniless girl" for the sake of financial security offered by an alliance with the Rubensky family. The patient resented the suggestion his father had married for money instead of love. Meanwhile, he had noticed a young girl on one of his visits and assumed she was Freud's daughter. "She had pleased him," Freud remarks, without revealing that she was twelve years old, "and he pictured to himself that the only reason I was so kind and incredibly patient with him was that I wanted to have him for a son-in-law. At the same time he raised the position and wealth of my family to a level which agreed with the model he had in mind."[6]

He responded to Freud's suggestion about his father with insults and accusations directed at Freud and his family. His dreams became retorts to Freud's interpretation. "He dreamt that *he saw my daughter in front of him; she had two patches of dung instead of eyes.* No one who understands the language of dreams will find much difficulty in translating this one: it declared that *he was marrying her not for her 'beaux yeux' but for her money.*"[7]

The polarity between the Rich Woman and the Poor Woman has thus appeared yet again, now because marrying Freud's daughter would cause the patient to abandon his lady. It is striking how his love and his misogyny worked in concert thanks to this division between the Rich Woman and the Poor Woman. First his wish to marry the daughter, fueled by his social aspirations, intensified whenever he felt antagonistic toward his lady. And then, about-face, he would defend his love for his lady by deriding the daughter and insulting her as well as Freud's wife.

In sum, Freud sifts out four narratives: the father's story, the precipitating cause, the obsessional ritual and the transference fantasy and dream. Contrasting the interpretations that Freud and Lacan devise to understand these four narratives will help establish the salient categories of their respective conceptions of the Oedipus complex, or, what Freud in 1909 still called the "parental" or "father complex." Freud's approach will use these narratives to chart the patient's instincts and their vicissitudes, concentrating on the sexual urges of childhood and the barriers they encounter. Lacan will see, instead, a sequence of interpersonal or intersubjective combinations in which the patient has to map the benchmarks of his identity and desire.

Freud's interpretation can best be illustrated with reference to his account of the chains of association that connected the patient's first reaction to the rat story with the sanction and vow affecting the repayment of the 3.80 *kronen.* When Paul first heard the captain's story he had the thought *this is happening to my father.* Freud translates the thought as a wish: *may this happen to my father,* which might have expressed itself at the time as something like a silent curse addressed to the hated captain: *you ought to have the same thing done to you.* Such an identification or overlapping of the captain and the deceased father came from the patient's association of the captain's being "fond of cruelty" with the corporal punishment the father had meted out to the children throughout the patient's childhood.

Freud focused repeatedly during the treatment on his hypothesis that at some early age Paul had been "soundly castigated" by his father for "some sexual misdemeanour connected with masturbation," and that he consequently had not only repudiated the blameworthy activity but also harbored "an ineradicable grudge against his father . . . in his role as an interferer with [his] sexual enjoyment." Paul reported that his mother often recounted an episode he himself did not remember:

> When he was very small—it became possible to establish the date more exactly owing to its having coincided with the fatal illness of an elder sister—he had done something naughty, for which his father had given him a beating. The little boy had flown into a terrible rage and had hurled abuse at his father even while he was under his blows. But as he had no bad language, he had called him all the names of common objects that he could think of, and had screamed: "You lamp! You towel! You plate!" and so on. His father, shaken by such an outburst of elemental fury, had stopped beating him, and had declared: "The child will either be a great man or a great criminal!" The patient believed the scene had made a permanent impression upon himself as well as upon his father. His father, he said, never beat him again; and he also attributed to this experience a part of the change which came over his own character. From that time forward he was a coward—out of fear of the violence of his own rage. His whole life long, moreover, he was terribly afraid of blows, and used to creep away and hide, filled with terror and indignation, when one of his brothers or sisters was beaten.
>
> The patient subsequently questioned his mother again. She confirmed the story, adding that at the time he had been between three and four years old and that he had been given the punishment because he had *bitten* someone.[8]

From this incident Freud gleans the basic elements for the origins of an obsessional neurosis. The episode belongs to the early years; it involves unusually strong erotic or auto-erotic impulses, in this case oral and sadistic, which come to a catastrophic end; and intense love and intense hatred are so intermingled and inextricable as to have ramifications in every experience where the infantile repressed impulse reasserts itself. Looking to explain how this pattern of libidinal economy came into play years later while the patient was on military maneuvers, Freud shows how the rat story became the nodal point that gathered several of the patient's repressed impulses, memories and associations, including the childhood scene of punishment and rage. By the time Paul encountered the captain again and was told of the money he owed on the package this knot of associations was entangling virtually everything around him.

The sessions produced a host of rat associations. Among them were *money,* through the association with *feces* (*kronen*=shit) but also more specifically with the gambling debts of his father (a *gambler* is a *Spielratte,* literally, a "play-rat"); *penis* through associations Freud related to the patient's early, prematurely repressed anal-sadistic impulses; and *children,* through connections between the rats' gnawing and the patient's childhood biting episode, reinforced by a residue of the infantile tendency to consider the anus the birth canal and by the antagonistic feelings the patient held toward his lady because, it turned out, she was unable to have children. Many other related associations are scattered through the case history, and more yet in what remains of Freud's original record, but these should suffice to understand how Freud then translated and reconstructed the thoughts Paul had upon hearing the captain tell him to repay Lieutenant A. at a point, recall, when he himself knew he actually owed the money to the young woman at the postal station.

Freud's interpretive moves go as follows:

(a) Paul's account: When the captain told him to pay Lieutenant A., he felt a sanction weighed against that action: *If I do that, the rat punishment will happen to my father and my lady.*

(a') Freud's translation: *As sure as my father and the lady can have children, I'll pay him.* The translation construes the sanction as a derisive response addressed to the ill-informed, despicable captain and at the same time an insult aimed at his father and the lady.

(b) Paul: The sanction was immediately countermanded by the vow: *You must pay back A.*

(b') Freud's translation: The insults to his father and the lady had "called for punishment, and the penalty consisted of binding himself to a vow which was impossible to fulfill and which entailed literal obedience to his superior's ill-founded request,"[9] as though to atone for having insulted his lady while at the same time restoring a rigid respect for his dead father's authority: *Yes, you must pay back the money to A., as your father's surrogate has required. Your father cannot be mistaken.*

Freud's translations allow him to interpret the repayment ritual as a punishment designed to atone for the aggressiveness that expressed itself in the sanction against repaying Lieutenant A. The sanction is "really" an insult, the vow is "really" self-punishment and atonement. There results a kind of Oedipal version of slave-morality. Confronted with deep-seated memories of the father's punishing authority, the son, suffering from his rebelliousness, transforms his antagonism into a new configuration of atonement and self-punishment in the form of exaggerated obedience to the father's command. In keeping with the style of obsessional neurosis, the repressed aggressiveness toward the father and the lady is not simply unavailable to Paul's consciousness, but rather manifests itself in inexplicable forms. The repressed thought does become conscious but has the quality of an automatism that he then feels compelled to counter or undo.

Freud organizes his view of Paul's disorder in these terms and with reference to the father complex. "We may regard the repression of his infantile hatred of his father as the event which brought his whole subsequent career under the dominion of the neurosis."[10] Freud refines on this generalization by stressing that this hatred derives its force from aggressive infantile impulses of love, manifested in this case by the patient's infantile pleasure in biting:

> We may suppose, then, that in the cases of unconscious hatred with which we are concerned the sadistic components of love have, from constitutional causes, been exceptionally strongly developed, and have consequently undergone a premature and all too thorough suppression, and that the neurotic phenomena we have observed arise on the one hand from conscious feelings of affection which have become exaggerated as a reaction, and on the other hand from sadism persisting in the unconscious in the form of hatred.[11]

Accordingly, the patient's excessive devotion to his father is a reaction-formation designed to disguise and compensate for the grudge he holds against him, while the sadism that was suppressed in the same emotionally catastrophic moment that gave rise to the grudge still persists, now aimed at the interfering father.

The "partial paralysis of will" so pronounced in the case of Paul Lorenz reflects, Freud argues, the confusion that the melding of his love and hatred has caused. Freud cites the verses Hamlet sends to Ophelia—

> Doubt thou the stars are fire;
> Doubt that the sun doth move;
> Doubt truth to be a liar;
> But never doubt I love.[12]

—to illustrate, by inversion, the endless doubting characteristic of this patient and obsessional neurotics generally. "The doubt is in reality a doubt of his own love," Freud suggests. "A man who doubts his own love may, or rather *must,* doubt every lesser thing."[13] Doubt enters every pore of his experience, including the various protective measures that are themselves part of the individual's arsenal of obsessions. The compulsions that arise amount to

> an attempt at a compensation for the doubt and at a correction of the intolerable conditions of inhibition to which the doubt bears witness. If the patient, by the help of displacement, succeeds at last in bringing one of his inhibited intentions to a decision, then the intention *must* be carried out. It is true that this intention is not the original one, but the energy dammed up in the latter cannot let slip any opportunity of finding an outlet for its discharge in a substitutive act.[14]

When it comes to summarizing his theoretical overview of obsessional neurosis, Freud revives his longstanding assumption that psychical energy is a fixed quantity. It can be channeled to acts or to thought processes. Acts are "intended to bring about a discharge or to modify the external world"; thought processes require "smaller displacements of energy, probably at a higher level [of cathexis]."[15] Impulses inhibited from discharge in an act seek other channels, including symptom formation. What is striking about obsessional neurosis is that the symptoms take hold of thought processes, rather than the body as in conversion hysteria, intensifying and distorting intellectual activity in vows, obsessions, doubting, brooding and so on.

Freud's conclusions are couched in the vocabulary of libidinal economy:

> A thought-process is obsessive or compulsive when, in consequence of an inhibition (due to a conflict of opposing impulses) at the motor end of the psychical system, it is undertaken with an expenditure of energy which (as regards both quality and quantity) is normally reserved for actions alone; or, in other words, *an obsessive or compulsive thought is one whose function it is to represent an act regressively.*[16] (Freud's italics)

Freud's concepts undergo a characteristic shift in the course of his theoretical reflections on the Rat Man. It is as though Freud looks up close at the interpretations the analysis yielded, first with one eye, then with the other, creating two pictures from the same field of vision. Put another way, he uses two theoretical languages that do not translate one another. First comes a language of moral valuations and symbolizations used to explain the development of the patient's personality within his intricate family relationships. This Freudian genealogy of morals presents a Nietzschean drama played out in the theatre of the mind. The power of the father forces the weaker son into submission, but the son, in submitting, subjugates his own impulses and thus creates a new valuation, since his rage at the father is transformed into a loathing of his own weakness and a self-deceived feigning of filial affection and respect. New values of delicacy, self-examination, affection and respect are born on the ashes of the son's broken willfulness. Then, in the blink of an eye, this perspective disappears and is replaced by the economic perspective, a zero-sum game of psychical energy channeled to acts, organs or thoughts.

The two perspectives remain incommensurate in Freud, their mismatch signalling his unfinished theorization of Oedipal pathology. And it strengthens the more general suspicion that Freud is prone to convert intersubjective and moral-symbolic interactions into psychic economy. The moral-symbolic moment, which indicates an active relation between self and others, gets reduced to a barrier that blocks an impulse and forces its rechanneling. There is certainly no easy solution to the difference between libidinal economy and moral symbolization. Ricoeur's proved unsatisfactory, despite his suggestive notion that two interpretive processes need to be combined, the regressive tracking of the derivations of libidinal intensities and the progressive reconstruction of the building up of symbols. Ultimately he incorporates the moral-symbolic moment exclusively to account for the success of socialization, sublimation or transcendence, never for the pathological outcomes, which he, much like Freud, relegates to the clashes of impulse and barrier.

Lacan opens another line of theoretical reflection by suggesting that the Oedipus complex generates pathogenic as much as normalizing effects. And his conception of the individual myth is an attempt to foreground the symbolic and intersubjective dimensions of the Oedipus complex. When he turns to the Rat Man, he proceeds to reconstruct the various elements of Freud's interpretation as a sequence of intersubjective situations rather than an intrapsychic process of wishes and punishments. However, his commentary is so allusive and incomplete that his revisionist interpretation has to be extrapolated as much as explicated. I have chosen, therefore, in what follows to elaborate on what I consider the most relevant and valid directions in Lacan's commentary, and to furnish the missing arguments and justifications for this reworking of Freud's clinical materials.

Let us begin with the repayment ritual. There is an obvious flaw in Freud's interpretation of the vow to repay Lieutenant A. For the vow does not really impose an unrealizable action, since Lieutenant A. is effectively incorporated into the ritual. He will give 3.80 *kronen* to the young woman, and Paul will repay him strictly in keeping with the wording of the captain's instructions. What is it then that makes the whole action impossible? Why is the ritual not only a fiasco but also a trap? The ritual set out to solve a puzzle posed by the core narrative. The father's twofold debt—repaying the lost Friend and repairing the betrayal of the Poor Woman—had come to represent, for the patient, the symbolic debt of his existence. "The situation presents a kind of ambiguity, of diplopia—" Lacan suggests, "the element of the debt is placed on two levels at once, and it is precisely in the light of the impossibility of bringing these two levels together that the drama of the neurotic is played out. By trying to make one coincide with the other"—that is, to repay both the Friend and the Poor Woman—"he makes a perennially unsatisfying turning maneuver and never succeeds in closing the loop."[17]

When Paul incurs the debt at the post office, it stands for both of his father's debts. The obsessional ritual seeks to repay the Friend and the Poor Woman. But circumstances render this imaginary resolution impossible on the level of real action. The two threads cannot be tied together. The first involves the connection between the father's gambling debt and the captain's command to repay Lieutenant A. "The captain's words," Freud comments, "had sounded to his ears like an allusion to this unpaid debt of his father's."[18] Freud is wrong, however, to identify the patient's situation with his father's. The associations provoked by the captain's story a few days later made a rather different connection. By repaying Lieutenant A., Paul would save his father from the humiliation of the rat punishment, just as the long lost Friend had saved him from humiliation and punishment in the gambling episode. The son does not so much identify with the Father as he identifies, or finds himself identified, with the fourth figure in this individual myth, that is, the Friend.

As for the emotional debts owed the Poor Woman, Freud presents the relevant elements without completing the interpretation:

> But the information that the young lady at the post office at Z—— had herself paid the charges due upon the packet, with a complimentary

> remark about himself, had intensified his identification with his father in quite another direction. At this stage of the analysis he brought out some new information, to the effect that the landlord of the inn at the little place where the post office was had a pretty daughter. She had been decidedly encouraging to the smart young officer, so that he had thought of returning there after the manoeuvres were over and trying his luck with her. Now, however, she had a rival in the shape of the young lady at the post office. Like his father in the tale of his marriage, he could afford now to hesitate upon which of the two he should bestow his favours when he finished his military service.[19]

Paul's motivation for returning to Z—— centered, as Freud establishes, on the innkeeper's daughter. Lacan draws the further conclusion that she had come to represent the Poor Woman who was being eclipsed by the Rich Woman because Paul had to visit the young woman at the post office and pay her the 3.80 *kronen.* In this strand of the ritual, the son does indeed find himself identified with the father, but now in the sense that the ritual, in replacing the Poor Woman with the Rich Woman, would cause him to replicate his father's debt to the Poor Woman in the very act of paying the postal debt.

Turning now to the transference fantasy and dream, the elements of the father's life-story, as condensed in the core narrative, enter into a new combination that is quite distinct from the obsessional ritual. Recall that the fantasy and dream were Paul's response to Freud's suggestion that his father married for money. The fantasy that Freud wanted him for a son-in-law condenses and combines the two stories from the father's past: *a Friend* (Freud) *alleviates his financial worries by giving him his daughter to marry.* Lacan believes Freud is too quick to see himself as father and the patient as son in the transference. It should have been clear in this fantasy that Freud was cast in the role of the helpful Friend (*Freund*). This links him not only to the figure from the father's past but also to several analogous figures in the patient's own life.

Freud became identified, for example, with a man to whom Paul had often confided his anxieties and self-accusations. This friend always reassured him he was not evil or morbid. That friendship resonated in turn with an earlier relationship between the patient and a tutor his family employed for him. The tutor's attention made him very happy and gave him the feeling of being a genius. But he was disillusioned and suffered an acute sense of worthlessness, considering himself an idiot and a dupe, when he discovered that the young man was merely ingratiating himself in order to pursue an interest in the patient's sister.

It is that sort of vacillation that likewise characterized the patient's relation to his analyst. Freud did clearly serve to encourage and protect Paul, but he also forced him to recognize a host of forbidden wishes, resentments and hostilities. He was not always a reassuring voice. In fact, he introduced the patient to therapy by reaffirming rather than denying that he was torn between a moral and an evil self:

> Was there a possibility of his effecting a re-integration of his personality? If this could be done, he thought he would be able to make a success of his life, perhaps more of one than most people.—I replied that I was in complete agreement with this notion of a splitting of his personality. He had only to assimilate this new contrast, between a moral self and an evil one, with the contrast I had already mentioned, between the conscious and the unconscious. The moral self was the conscious, the evil self was the unconscious.—[20]

The scene was thus set for the transference fantasy. The patient's own history, already resonant with his father's history, yielded the mytheme: *my tutor befriends me only to get my sister,* which is then replicated in reverse form in the transference fantasy: *my tutor befriends me only to give me his daughter.* The reversibility signals, in Lacanian terms, the patient's mirroring or narcissistic identification with the figure of the Friend, an identification marked by ambivalences of envy and gratitude.

The transference fantasy prepares for the dream, which itself completes the permutations involved in this rendition of the individual myth. The daughter with the eyes of dung not only derisively makes Freud's daughter the Rich Woman of the individual myth, it also, Lacan suggests, shifts onto her the ambivalence contained in the patient's identification with the Friend. Like the Friend, she is alternately, in Lacan's phrase, "protective and maleficent"—*protective* in that she provides him with desired money and status: the eyes of dung signify money; and *maleficent* in that her presence forebodes harm to his lady: her blank eyes are the sign of a harmful power. This last conjecture seems a stab in the dark on Lacan's part, until this dream is juxtaposed with a related dream in which a woman, with the glazed look of someone in a hypnotic trance, has the power to harm the patient's beloved lady even into the next world:

> She got up as though she was hypnotized, came from behind my chair with a pale face and put her arms around me. It was as though I tried to shake off her embrace, as though each time she stroked my head some misfortune would occur to the lady—some misfortune in the next world too. It happened automatically, as though the misfortune occurred at the very moment of the stroking.[21]

The dream confirms Lacan's interpretation of the transference dream, but what is remarkable is that it is reported only in Freud's "Original Record of the Case," which was unavailable to Lacan at the time of his lecture. Luck does not always, as we will see, exempt Lacan from providing evidence and argumentation.

The transference, in sum, has produced a new permutation of the individual myth. The figure of the Friend (the tutor, Freud) has been fused into that of the Rich Woman (Freud's daughter), thus lodging the two episodes from the father's past into a single element. But this semblance of a synthesis immediately re-encounters the unsolved puzzle—how to repay both the Friend and the Poor Woman—because the ensuing dream once again has the Rich Woman (Freud's daughter) dislodge the Poor Woman (the lady). Compare this narrative permutation to the obsessional ritual. There the Poor Woman was fused into the Friend. The trip to the postal station at Z—— would give the Poor Woman her due and repay the Friend. That scenario's impasse arose from the necessity of including the young woman at the post office since she henceforward represented the Rich Woman usurping the love owed the Poor Woman.

In each permutation of the individual myth, then, the impasse of the twofold debt is reproduced whenever the narratives attempt to fuse the Friend into the Rich Woman or Poor Woman, or vice versa. What explains this tendency? Why should the patient's dreams, transferences, fantasies, symptoms and life situations tend to condense the father's two debts into a single act, whether of *identification* (with the Friend) or of *love* (for the Poor Woman/Rich Woman)? The core narrative might provide the answer, since its premise is that the father gained his ability to repay his military friend only by marrying into the Rubensky family. Based on this premise the later narratives would contain the structural impossibility of giving the Poor Woman her due and repaying the Friend at the same time.

This explanation, however, is not very satisfactory. It postulates a merely mechanical repetition of the father's story in his son's narratives, but the permutations just charted suggest that the narrative combinations of the individual myth are considerably more various. Indeed, variability is what distinguishes the individual myth from the classical Oedipal triangle. The classical conception views the Oedipus complex as an original set of fixed emotional attachments and rivalries which then replicate themselves in other arenas. The Lacanian individual myth, by contrast, is a map of relationships and roles which can be occupied by various combinations of people.[22]

Lacan seems to toy with two other explanations. The first focuses on the symbolic debt that makes the Rat Man indebted to his father's indebtedness. The second explanation looks, instead, to the connection between masculine identity and heterosexual love. In elaborating on these two explanations, I will once again supplement Lacan's sparse argumentation while trying to capture his approach as faithfully as possible.

(1) *The symbolic debt.* The designation of the father as *begetter* establishes within the father-son relation a symbolic debt of existence. For Freud's patient, the constellation of circumstances to which he owed his existence included his father's two debts. According to Lacan, his tendency or compulsion to repay both debts as though they were one was an effort to accomplish the impossible task of not owing his existence to his father, or more precisely, to his father's acts of betrayal. On the one hand, then, Paul tries to repair the paternal breach of faith and thus eliminate his own symbolic indebtedness. But, on the other hand, with every such attempt to free himself from his burdened paternal legacy he finds himself identified with his father or the father's substitute in the guise of the Friend. What animates the many scenarios and brings them to their impasse, therefore, is the son's identification with his father, that is, the real-life father, and his recognition of himself in his father's likeness. The son's identification with the real-life father is distinct from his relation to the symbolic father, that is, the "name-of-the-father" in Lacan's terminology, or, here, the designation of the father as *begetter*. This identification establishes the "fourth term" in the individual myth. The fourth term complicates the triangular structure of the Oedipal son-mother-father. The father appears twice, as symbol and as likeness, symbolic father and real-life father, designated father and recognized father. This fourth term frequently appears in the form of another man who stands in for the individual's father, a friend as in the case of the Rat Man, a stepfather, an uncle or as in the case of Hamlet stepfather and uncle in one.

To interpret the effects of the son's identification with the fourth term, Lacan drew on one of his most innovative revisions of Freudian theory. Lacan had revamped the theory of narcissism from the vantage-point of Hegel's account of the struggle for prestige, stressing how it connects the mutual recognition between two individuals and their awareness of death. He also suggests that the Freudian and Hegelian problematics can be combined around the themes of language, love and mortality. The theory of the symbolic, dead Father claims that language, love and mortality are at once the key to fatherhood and the essential, humanizing mediations in human relationships in general:

> Before Freudian theory stressed in the existence of the father a function which is at once a function of speech and a function of love, Hegel, in his metaphysics, did not hesitate to construct the whole phenomenology of human relationships around death as mediator, the third element essential to the progress by which man becomes humanized in his relationships with his fellow man [*son semblable:* his likeness, counterpart, etc.].[23]

The mirror-phase is to explain why death—an imagined death, the imagination of death—figures in the experience of mutual recognition in the first place. The mirror-phase experience, Lacan argues, originates in infancy, well before a child learns to talk. I perceive the fully formed image (*Gestalt*) of another like myself or of myself reflected in the mirror, but this image stands in sharp contrast to the discordant sensations of my uncoordinated body. My body is whole over there, turbulent over here. I therefore encounter this integral body in an image and as an image before I am able to experience bodily integrity in actual movements or actions. I first encounter my "self" as an imaginary other, a double, a counterpart, a likeness.

My identification with this image has contradictory effects. On the one hand, it helps orient me in time by anticipating growth, maturity and mastery. On the other hand, I am thrown "back onto the level of a profound insufficiency, . . . a rift, . . . a primal sundering."[24] Jubilant recognition oscillates with this first implicit experience of death. The awareness of death manifests itself in the self's vacillation between depressive and aggressive reactions to the other. In depressive fantasies my own uncoordinated body is represented as a wounded, torn or cut up body, while my aggressive fantasies lash out against the image—ambiguously myself and another—that provoked this experience and make it the target of my impulse to wound or tear or cut to pieces. In Lacan's view, the mirror-phase ordeal of identity and estrangement, unity and discord, exaltation, depression and aggression, is liable to revive whenever an individual's self-recognition hinges on an identification with another—which is to say, in any instance of mutual recognition.

It is this ordeal of self-recognition that Lacan discerns in the son's relation to the real-life father. With regard to the Rat Man, he turns his focus to the maturational crisis Paul faced as he approached the necessity of deciding his vocation and his marriage plans. These anticipated events were the thresholds of his independence. They oriented him toward his future self; they mirrored him back to himself as another. Paul could not cross this threshold because his self-recognitions remained frozen. He was trapped in a repeated drama where his own role was fixed by his identifications with his father, even as he tried vainly to achieve independence by cancelling his symbolic debt to this same father.

Paul's dilemma suggests to Lacan a pattern typical of the father-son relation. The son's identification with his real-life father is ever at odds with his resolution of the symbolic debt. He can neither fully accept nor successfully reject the designation of the father as *begetter*. The individual myth maps the bifurcation between the identification and the symbolization, for it not only designates the father as *begetter* but also includes him as the likeness in which the son recognizes himself in an alienated form. When the son encounters the paternal double, or finds himself doubling the father, his recognitions are transfixed by the "imagined or imaginary death" that flashes up alternately in his unacknowledged hostility toward the father or in the deadening of his own desire and action.

On this basis Lacan effectively rejects a central motif of the Freudian theory of the Oedipus complex, namely, the notion that the son's relation to death stems from sexual rivalry for the mother's affections and first manifests itself in the impulse to murder, in Ricoeur's phrase, "the phantasm of a father who would retain the privileges which the son himself must seize if he is to be himself." The violent alienations Freud's patient suffered—now turned outward in aggressive fantasies, now turned inward in depressive mortifications—replay, according to Lacan, the mirror-relation to the father and its insistent return as the "fourth term" of the Oedipal drama. As in the theoretical dialogue I established earlier between Ricoeur and Lacan, Lacan here again points out that it is the son's identifications with his real-life father not his rivalry with a fantasized father that are formative of the Oedipal relation, and further that this identification continually troubles symbolic fatherhood rather than being transcended by it.

(2) *Masculine identity and heterosexual love.* Lacan's second approach to explaining why the Rat Man recurrently, unconsciously seeks to resolve both debts in a single act of identification or of love builds on the first explanation. In choosing a vocation, Paul faces the task of identifying with himself in the taking of a social role. In deciding his marriage plans, he faces the task of choosing a partner in, as Lacan puts it, an "undisturbed," "univocal" heterosexual relationship.

Lacan further asserts that these tasks affect one another. They form two mutually affecting poles. Moreover, each pole is susceptible to the imaginary drama of narcissism or the mirror-phase. As regards the Rat Man's pathologies, Lacan proceeds—in an interpretation I will partly dispute—to view the patient's narcissism as the basis not only of his relation to his father but also to the lady. He emphasizes "the deadening symbols that tie the subject narcissistically to his dead father and his idealized lady," and offers a new explanation of the tendency for the Friend and the Rich Woman/Poor Woman to be fused. The images of the dead father and the idealized lady "support one another," Lacan argues, "in a symbolic equivalence typical of the obsessional, the one an image of the fantasmal aggressiveness which perpetuates it, the other an image of the mortifying cult which transforms it into an idol."[25]

The father, though dead, remained a presence in the patient's life, literally a ghost Paul expected to appear at midnight to witness his sexual acts of defiance. For example, he would stop studying and prepare to masturbate by "open[ing] the front door of the flat as though his father were standing outside; then, coming back into the hall, he would take out his penis and look at it in the looking-glass,"[26] defying a father who had always been annoyed by his son's "idleness at work." As regards the cult of the lady, his love for her was completely split off from his sexual experience except when he would imagine that she was affected, also like a shadow or ghost, by his sexual acts, as in the dream about the affectionate hypnotic or in one of his fantasies which pictured the lady hidden inside the body of a prostitute so that whoever had intercourse with the prostitute was also having it with the lady.

While I will rebut Lacan's claim that the aggressiveness against the paternal double and against the lady can be derived from one and the same structure of narcissism, I do think Lacan discerns a crucial pattern in Paul's life. According to his hypothesis, the patient was caught in a cycle in which his identity and his love—that is, his *masculine* identity and his *heterosexual* love, indeed, his masculinity and his heterosexuality—alternated as sites of crisis. When his relation to the self stabilized, the sphere of love was disturbed by a "doubling" of the woman. Conversely, when his love relation would cohere, his sense of identity and social recognition was disturbed by a "doubling" of the self. Lacan's description of this process, with reference to the Rat Man and more generally, is worth quoting at length, for it reweaves many of the themes I have examined and can serve to summarize the Lacanian reinterpretation of Freud's case history:

> Now, each time the subject succeeds, or approaches success in assuming his own role, each time he becomes, as it were, identical with himself and confident that his functioning in his specific social context is well-founded, the object, the sexual partner, is split—here in the form *rich woman or poor woman.* What is truly striking in the psychology of the neurotic—all we need do is enter, no longer into the fantasy, but into the subject's real life to put our finger on it—is the aura of abrogation which most commonly surrounds the sexual partner who is the most real to him, the nearest to him, whether in a love affair or in a marriage. On the other hand, a figure appears who is a double of the first and who is the object of a more or less idealized passion which is pursued in a more or less phantasmatic way, in a style analogous to that of romantic love, and which grows, moreover, into an identification of a fatal kind.
>
> Conversely, if the subject makes an effort in another aspect of his life to find the unity of his feeling again, then it is at the other end of the chain, in the assumption of his own social function and his own virility—since I have chosen [!] the case of a man—that he sees appearing beside him a figure with whom he also has a narcissistic relation insofar as it is a fatal relation. To the latter he delegates the responsibility of representing him in the world and of living in his place. It is not really himself: he feels excluded, outside his own experience, he cannot assume his particularities and contingencies, he feels discordant with his existence, and the impasse recurs.[27]

When the young man overcomes the doubling of the self by accepting his vocation, along with its responsibilities and rewards, he tends to experience a doubling of the love object in some variant of the "mother/whore" dichotomy. And, vice versa, when he stabilizes his heterosexual love relationship, he tends to undergo an alienating doubling of the self. Lacan attributes these phenomena to the same narcissistic structure, but this assertion seems to me patently false. Even if the doubling of the male self and the doubling of the female love object alternate as two poles in the young man's experience; and even if the doubling of the love object involves a narcissistic, deadening tie to one of the women—it nevertheless does not follow that the two phenomena have the same origin or the same meaning. There is reason prima facie to assume they have very different origins and meanings, since the doubling of the self is associated with identifying with the father and deciding upon a vocation, while the doubling of the female love object derives from the cultural representations of the "mother/whore" dichotomy.

Lacan might well have guided his inquiry further in the direction of the social problematic these formulations hint at. Instead, in a gesture that seems typical of psychoanalytic thinking, he was satisfied to explain the disturbances within masculine identity and heterosexual love alike in terms of a postulated infantile or archaic experience: the mirror-phase. At that point, he closes off the promising dialogue he had initiated between psychoanalysis and social theory. He even shortcircuits his own most original contribution, namely, the "fourth term" and the discrepancy between the "third term" or symbolic father and the real-life father. The crisis provoked by the "fourth term" is, on the one hand, typically intensified as the son anticipates entering into the field of property relations and social labor and, on the other hand, it is a crisis of mutual recognition on the model of the Hegelian master-slave dialectic. One would then expect a theoretical reflection that gave its due to the institutional-symbolic complex that links masculine identity, market-mediated forms of labor, property relations and the male-dominated restricted family.

The mediating role of death in the father-son relation, reinterpreted in terms of the mirror-phase's "imagined or imaginary death," is simply not adequate to explain why the son's identification with the father is at once *role-forming* and *rivalrous*. Yet this is the heart of the pathogenic moment Lacan uncovered in the father-son relation. The son's integration into socially normed behavior at the same time unleashes a disintegrating tendency toward self-alienation and aggression. Such a situation invites a social and cultural reflection. Freud would have read the social and cultural processes from the standpoint of an intrapsychic economy in which the demands of civilization—that is, the socially normed behaviors—are so heavy that the impulses they repress eventually erode the individual's personality altogether. Lacan opened the prospect of another reading when he transformed the intrapsychic into an intersubjective problematic.

The limit beyond which he could not take that problematic is now perhaps clearer. Following his parlance, the symbolic father is the *3rd term* of the Oedipus complex and the real-life father the *4th term.* The individual myth is a four-term structure which maps family relationships (I—mother—symbolic father—real father). But this structure also maps the points at which those family relationships are traversed by larger social relationships. The interaction of the *I* and the *real-life father* is inseparable from economic, juridical and moral processes; the discrepancy between the *symbolic father* and the *real-life father* is inseparable from patriarchal cultural traditions, family structure and compulsory heterosexuality. From this standpoint, beyond Lacan, the individual myth can be said to map the extrafamilial onto the intrafamilial field of intersubjectivity.

The need to account for an intersubjectivity not limited to family relations is even more telling when it comes to interpreting the *2nd term* of the Oedipus complex, that is, the mother as object of the son's incestuous wishes. The mirror-phase is starkly inadequate to explain the origin and meaning of the "mother/whore" dichotomy. Settled psychoanalytic doctrine makes nothing seem quite so self-evident as the *2nd term.* That the mother is at once and primarily incestuous object, forbidden object and model object for her male offspring is axiomatic in Freud, Ricoeur and Lacan.

But consider anew how the mother has actually figured in the formative texts of Oedipal theory, in particular, Freud's "A Special Type of Object Choice Made By Men" and Lacan's "The Neurotic's Individual Myth," texts still not altogether controlled by the doctrines they were giving rise to. Freud's Oedipal mother does not appear until produced through the social cognitions and cultural representations her son only fully acquires in his adolescence. The Oedipal mother is the "mother" generated by the "mother/whore" dichotomy. She is a symbolization produced within a masculine, masculinist discourse on love and sexuality. Indeed, if the "incestuous" attachment to the mother is a configuration of love and desire meaningfully comparable to the adult forms of male heterosexuality, then it is, as I have argued, an attachment which is constructed on the threshold of the "adult series" and retroactively produces the "infantile series," reinterpreting the whole history of the boy's interactions with his mother.

Lacan asserts that the Rat Man's idealizing, cultic, mortifying relation to the lady can be explained ultimately by reference to the mirror-phase ordeal. In fact, the material he is interpreting suggests something very different. As a *2nd term,* the mother figures in the Rat Man's individual myth only insofar as she is designated the Rich Woman as opposed to the Poor Woman in the structure of representations that narrates the *father's* desires and betrayals. Add to this the fact that Lacan, following quite unawares in Freud's footsteps, manages to develop a full-blown interpretation of the Rat Man's Oedipus complex without really referring to his mother at all. Neither the mother nor any meaningful pattern of her interactions with her child can be retrieved from this case history.

Is this lacuna simply proof of the incompleteness of Freud's analysis? Not exactly. It is indirect evidence, rather, that the Oedipal form of the mother-son relation does not inhere in the mother-son relation itself. The Oedipal mother is an element of the individual *myth* and is fabricated in the androcentric field of *male* intersubjectivity. The *2nd term* of the Oedipus complex, far from being the male's most primal or natural or originating relationship, is a *symbolic* construct. It is produced from the masculine discourse on love, including its stereotypes of the female object, and from the son's troubled identifications with his father. The Oedipal mother is a *symbolic mother,* as assuredly a complex creation of culture as is the symbolic father. Psychoanalytic theory has therefore occluded a *5th term* in the Oedipus complex: the *real-life* as opposed to *symbolic* mother, that is, the woman whose practices and activities rearing the child generate the actual fabric of mother-child interactions. There is obviously something about psychoanalytic therapy and psychoanalytic theory that has tended to let the symbolic, Oedipal mother eclipse the real-life mother.

Such a maneuver, therapeutically and theoretically, seems consistent with a trend in both Freud and Lacan. For the distinction, and possible dissonance, between the symbolic and the real mother raises yet more questions about the whole pattern of social relationships within which the socialization of children takes place: the sexual division of labor, compulsory heterosexuality, the social relationships between men and women, the institutions and the symbolic legitimations of male dominance. Freud and Lacan steered clear of this social problematic so long as they hid the practices of women behind the symbolizations of "woman." Each distilled a structure, intrapsychic in Freud's case, limitedly intersubjective in Lacan's, from multilayered, active relationships within society and the family. Those symbolizations and distillations will now have to be reinserted within the social process that they at once imitate and mask.

5

Hidden Faults

IN ORDER TO ELEVATE the Mother to the theoretical keystone of the Oedipus complex Freud had to abstract women from their relationships as spouses and from their actual activities as mothers. Oedipal theory glanced at the social relationships women participate in only to ultimately seal them off from the theoretical purview of psychoanalysis. The mother's actual childrearing activities were eclipsed by the symbolic mother spun from the loom of male fantasy. So, too, the mother's actual relationship with her husband dropped from sight even though the husband's power over his wife counts among a child's most formative perceptions of family relations. Freud himself wrote of marital conflict as early as 1905, "If there are quarrels between the parents or if their marriage is unhappy, the ground will be prepared in their children for the severest disposition to a disturbance of sexual development or to a neurotic illness."[1] Not until R. D. Laing, David Cooper and the anti-psychiatry movement was Freudian psychoanalysis confronted with its inattentiveness to the politics of the family, the whole tissue of power relations, strategies, deceptions and contradictory injunctions that emanate from the modern household and so often turn hearth into fire storm.

While psychoanalysis reached its achieved form by occluding women's actual experiences and practices, its origins lay in another act of disregard, namely, Freud's decision to discount the testimony of his women patients who told him they had suffered sexual abuse in adolescence or childhood at the hands of fathers, stepfathers, uncles and older brothers. The most significant challenge to Oedipal theory in the past decade has in fact come from the feminist and revisionist critics who have reinterrogated Freud's repudiation of his earlier "seduction theory" of hysteria. The criticisms have struck at a central tenet of psychoanalysis, since psychoanalysts have traditionally credited the disavowal of the seduction theory with making way for the Oedipus complex in Freud's thinking.

By concluding that his women patients had not after all been "seduced" by a male relative, but had rather fantasized such scenes of seduction based on their *own* repressed wishes, Freud attributed the basis of neurosis to children's incestuous wishes rather than adults' incestuous acts. He simultaneously accorded the "psychic reality" of fantasy the same import as the "material reality" of remembered events. The paradigm shift was not complete, however, until the emerging concept of the Oedipus complex could be modeled on the *male* child's fantasies rather than the little girl's experience whether real or imagined. From around 1909 on, the more androcentric the new theoretical model became the more convincing it seemed.

Freudians have generally been incapable of seeing that these various elements of Freud's shifted paradigm are not necessarily indissociable. Anna Freud's response to Jeffrey Moussaieff Masson exemplifies the dogmatic faith that psychoanalysis would not have existed had Freud not recanted his seduction theory: "Keeping up the seduction theory would mean to abandon the Oedipus complex, and with it the whole importance of phantasy life, conscious or unconscious phantasy. In fact, I think there would have been no psychoanalysis afterward."[2]

But, in fact, nothing logically prevented Freud from exploring the "psychic reality" of fantasy, that is, the fact that fantasies can have the same degree and kind of psychological power as memories, *and* simultaneously holding that there was a high correlation between sexual abuse and hysteria in his women patients. Nor does his view on either of these questions require him, logically, to model the psyche on the male perspective. But the formative forces of Freud's thinking were not of course only logical. They were also social, political and autobiographical. The most persuasive criticisms of Freud's rejection of the seduction theory have turned to biographical and ideological explanations. They lay the blame in very different, not altogether compatible ways. Together, however, they make a decisive critique of Freud's reasoning and bring sharply into relief many of the unanswered questions and unsolved problems of Oedipal theory.

Masson's *The Assault on Truth: Freud's Suppression of the Seduction Theory* is based on his archival work, especially a reexamination of Freud's entire correspondence with his friend Wilhelm Fliess, the Berlin physician, a nose and throat specialist, with whom Freud shared his deepest thoughts and feelings between 1887 and 1902. The editors of the original published version of the correspondence, Marie Bonaparte, Anna Freud and Ernst Kris, deleted many passages, including many that could have muddied Freud's later explanations for recanting the seduction theory.[3] Masson's own interpretations are by turns insightful and seriously flawed. He melodramatically casts himself as a hero of truth battling Freud the deceiver and a host of latter-day disciples, treating Freud's every misstep or faulty reasoning as a sure sign of illicit motives and undeniable evidence of intellectual or moral misconduct. He grants far too little room for the legitimate intellectual doubts and confusions that played a part in Freud's thinking. Nevertheless, so long as you keep setting aside the overstatements, Masson's work convincingly undermines Freud's rationale for abandoning the seduction theory.

Masson brings together persuasive evidence that Freud's patient Emma Eckstein nearly died on account of Fliess's malpractice in an operation on her nose, and that Freud's loyalty to his friend led him to interpret, with true Hippocratic zeal, Eckstein's massive hemorrhaging from the nose as hysterical bleeding induced by her own unconscious fantasies. Because this highly charged crisis occurred as Freud was reconsidering the validity of the seduction theory, Masson jumps to the conclusion that Freud abandoned the theory *in order to* protect Fliess and preserve their friendship. There is certainly plenty of reason to believe that this episode impinged on Freud's thinking, perhaps indeed confirming him in the idea that fantasy and innate sexual disposition rather than trauma might be the cause of neurosis. However, he might just as easily have used the Eckstein episode to reconfirm his seduction theory by simply assuming that the cause of her supposed symptom (bleeding) lay in a trauma yet to be uncovered in her analysis. The episode, in short, is actually inconclusive in its bearing on Freud's thinking. Its significance stems from the fact that it shows Freud, at this critical juncture, capable of shifting the blame for a woman's traumatic experience from the actions of the man who harmed her to the fantasies of the woman herself.

While Masson is convinced he can identify unambiguous motives for Freud's about-face, the important evidence he amasses actually tends to support a different interpretation of the pressures on Freud's thinking. After Freud advanced his seduction hypothesis in a paper before the

Society for Psychiatry and Neurology in Vienna in April 1896, he reported to Fliess he had "met with an icy reception from the asses, and from Krafft-Ebing the strange comment: It sounds like a scientific fairy-tale."[4] Richard von Krafft-Ebing was at the time head of the University of Vienna's Department of Psychiatry. Within two weeks Freud felt the impact of the Viennese psychiatric and medical establishment's disapproval. "I am as isolated as you could wish me to be," he wrote in a letter to Fliess first brought to light by Masson. "The word has been given out to abandon me, and a void is forming around me."[5] Five months later, in the famous letter of September 21, 1897, Freud revealed to Fliess "the great secret that has been slowly dawning on me in the last few months. I no longer believe in my *neurotica* [theory of the neuroses]."[6]

It is essential to take account of the professional pressures weighing against Freud's adherence to his seduction theory. Freud's self-analysis abundantly shows, and his biographers have repeatedly confirmed, how thoroughly his intellectual endeavors were intertwined with the sexual, emotional and political meaning his career had for him. But there is no reason to believe he let loose of his convictions about the seduction theory in a simple bid to gain professional approval. He did not openly reverse himself until 1905 when he published the *Three Essays on the Theory of Sexuality;* in the interim he had published the two most important works of his career to that point, *The Interpretation of Dreams* (1900) and *The Psychopathology of Everyday Life* (1901), without having attempted to rehabilitate himself in his colleagues' eyes.

The more salient point emphasized by Masson—and only partially acknowledged by the editors of the Standard Edition[7]—is that despite the definitive-sounding statements Freud made to Fliess in the September letter he continued to credit his patients' stories of rape and seduction long after. In fact, he obviously hesitated to make any definitive theoretical or therapeutic turn. The sense of a sudden, irreversible insight was merely transitory in 1897. It was then retrospectively exaggerated in Freud's 1925 *An Autobiographical Study,* where he placed the overcoming of his initial "error" and "credulity" neatly on the path of the discovery of Oedipus:

> When, however, I was obliged to recognize that these scenes of seduction had never taken place, and that they were only phantasies which my patients had made up or which I myself had perhaps forced on them, I was for some time completely at a loss. My confidence alike in my technique and in its results suffered a severe blow; it could not be disputed

> that I had arrived at these scenes by a technical method which I considered correct, and their subject-matter was unquestionably related to the symptoms from which my investigation had started. When I had pulled myself together, I was able to draw the right conclusions from my discovery: namely, that the neurotic symptoms were not related directly to actual events but to wishful phantasies, and that as far as the neurosis was concerned psychical reality was of more importance than material reality. I do not believe even now that I forced the seduction-phantasies on my patients, that I "suggested" them. I had in fact stumbled for the first time upon the *Oedipus complex,* which was later to assume such an overwhelming importance, but which I did not recognize yet in its disguise of phantasy.[8]

In this rendition of his intellectual autobiography, Freud attributes his period of doubt to the process of searching for a new explanation, not to any continuing uncertainty regarding the reality of seduction. Instead, he merely grants that "seduction during childhood retained a certain share, though a humbler one, in the aetiology of neuroses. But the seducers turned out as a rule to have been older children."[9]

So goes the official version of the birth of Oedipal theory and the death of the seduction theory. It is not a trustworthy guide to the actual shifts in Freud's thinking. It is not even reliable empirically. The claim that in the supposedly rare instances of childhood seduction the seducer is usually an older child does not square with the actual list of seducers that continued to crop up in Freud's own published and unpublished work: Freud's own nanny, Herr K. in Dora's case (with the complicity of her father), the Rat Man's nanny, the stepfather of the Rat Man's fiancée, the young woman's father who broke down in a tacit confession of his guilt during the daughter's first—and last—consultation with Freud. By 1931, Freud returned yet again to the notion that an experience of seduction lies at the root of neurosis—only to attribute such experiences to the erotically charged attention mothers lavish on infants. The seduction hypothesis never completely disappeared, yet whenever the fact of seduction had to be acknowledged Freud averted the scene every one of his 18 patients from the 1890s recollected: a child is molested by her father. Why this aversion? What led Freud to consider all these testimonials fabrications?

In his 1897 letter to Fliess, Freud spelled out four factors that had thrown the seduction theory into doubt: (1) No analysis had come to a therapeutically successful conclusion. (2) In every case, including his own self-analysis, the father was accused of perversity, and he now doubted that the frequency of abusive fathers could be so high. (3) The unconscious does not distinguish true from imagined events. (4) Even such traumas as his patients reported, traumatic secrets so dire, could not have overcome the "resistance of the conscious" as readily as happened in the 18 cases.

Masson is exactly right, I believe, to accuse Freud of succumbing to the very prejudices he had overcome when he advanced the seduction theory in the first place. By suddenly disavowing the word of his women patients, Freud fell back on the presumption of paternal innocence which he had in fact seen exposed several times. Going back to his days in Paris, he had been convinced by considerable psychiatric documentation and forensic evidence of the extent of the sexual abuse of children in his society.[10] His own practice had corroborated those findings by providing an in-depth examination of the childhoods of his 18 patients. Masson shows that the scholarly evidence Freud later drew upon to justify his reversal was so flimsy that it could not have seriously weighed against these sources.[11] When Freud suddenly considered siding with the fathers and disbelieving the daughters in 1897, he had not uncovered specific processes of fabrication in the cases themselves. As the reasons enumerated for Fliess suggest, Freud's scepticism took the form of a purely theoretical, essentially deductive problem. The theory, the technique and the stories were not adding up.

The fact that none of the analyses was really successful certainly has to be given its due. The sense of failure must have stung all the more because of his colleagues' disdain for his ideas. More to the point, however, is the fact that Freud was led to expect—going all the way back to his work with Charcot and then Breuer—that if the cause of a neurotic symptom were a forgotten trauma, then the symptom should be relieved as soon as the patient achieved a fullblown recollection and recognition of the trauma itself. This was not happening in the patients he was analyzing, since their symptoms persisted even after the revelations of paternal abuse. Why, though, was he ready in September 1897 to seek an explanation that contradicted his patients' testimony? The answer, I believe, lies in three factors that were shaping Freud's theoretical response to this whole professional and intellectual crisis: his unexamined sexism and patriarchal attitudes; a significant glitch in his self-analysis; and the limitations built into his intrapsychic theoretical assumptions.

Marie Balmary has made a significant connection between Freud's self-analysis and his theoretical assumptions in her important book

Psychoanalyzing Psychoanalysis: Freud and the Hidden Fault of the Father. Her view runs counter to Masson's as regards the motives for Freud's renunciation of the seduction theory, but complements and extends Masson's argument against the official psychoanalytic position. The barrier Balmary finds in Freud's theorizing is the same one I have been examining in several contexts, namely, his inability to establish the intersubjective context of the problems he was exploring.

Balmary argues that Freud got off track from the beginning by trying to understand the rapes and enticements his patients reported solely as the victim's trauma rather than the perpetrator's misdeed. Freud stuck to "a medical discourse, without moral coloration," according to Balmary. "Sometimes he makes an opening toward the interpersonal relation at the origin of neurosis, then he returns to the individual, immerses himself in the study of psychical phenomena, and returns to neurology."[12] It seems to me that this theoretical bias in turn kept Freud from evaluating his therapeutic failures as anything other than proof that his patients' stories were false; lacking a view of the damage done by a violation of trust, a rupture in the moral tie between self and other, Freud adhered to his expectation that symptoms caused by trauma would disappear with the revelation of the trauma.

The other line of argument Balmary develops proceeds by reversing the direction of Freud's self-analysis, the fragments of which lie predominantly in his letters and in many of the dreams and slips analyzed in *The Interpretation of Dreams* and *The Psychopathology of Everyday Life*. In the crucial months of 1896–97, Freud was also mourning the death of his elderly father, Jakob Freud. When Freud declared to Fliess in the letter of September 21, 1897, that he was questioning all the analyses on which he had based the seduction theory, he remarked that "in every case the father, not excluding my own, had to be blamed as a pervert."[13] By altering his theoretical hypothesis, Freud was exonerating his father from some unspecified charge of perversity.

At the same time, Freud was taking a decisive step toward Oedipal theory by transferring guilt from father to child. Balmary summarizes her view as follows:

> What Freud took to be reality, the rape of all hysterics by their father, would afterward be revealed as phantasy. Freud would then realize that it was a question of repressed desires of the patient alone. He would

> "discover," after having believed the father to be guilty, that, in fact, the repressed desires of the son toward his mother would force him to become the murderous rival of the father. It is not the real fault of the father, but the fantasized one of the child.[14]

I want to insist again on the double transformation Freud effects in turning the seduction theory into Oedipal theory, the passage not only from trauma to repressed wish but also from young women's to little boy's experience. The "father's fault" passes from father to child. In the case of his patients, the father's real misdeeds become the daughter's fantasmal misdeed, her repressed desires. Freud will try to wring confirmation of the new theory from Dora. As regards his self-analysis, blame transfers from his father to himself. The son exonerates the father by assuming his guilt.

It is this moment in Freud's self-analysis which lays the cornerstone of the androcentric conception of Oedipal desire. Henceforth, the theoretical center of psychoanalysis is modeled on the male child's desire. The self-analysis fashioned the model little boy's desire in the Oedipal mode. "My self-analysis is in fact the most essential thing I have at present," Freud wrote Fliess on October 15, 1897. "One single thought of general value has been revealed to me. I have found, in my own case too, falling in love with the mother and jealousy of the father, and I now regard it as the universal event of early childhood, even if not so early as in children who have been made hysterical."[15] Oedipal theory begins in this quick extrapolation of a *universal event* from one boy's experience.

Balmary shows that Freud was utterly caught up in the very process of symptom formation that he was trying, unsuccessfully, to unravel theoretically. His self-analysis, mixed with his mourning of his father's death, was producing rather than dissolving symptoms. In Balmary's formulation, a neurosis develops out of the victimized child's effort to hide the father's fault by making it his or her own. "Unable to express the fault of the dominating, the dominated subject finds himself at fault. . . . The symptom alone denounces the guilty one, while the patient does everything to hide the fault."[16]

What was Freud's father's fault? It is impossible to know really, though Balmary develops a wealth of interpretive speculations about Freud's own symptom-formation by playing the complex material from his self-analysis off against the fragments of information now known about Jakob Freud. Freud biographers have unearthed two crucial facts that undoubtedly played a role somewhere in Freud's own individual myth. For it turns out that, contrary to the official family story, Jakob had been married not just once but twice before marrying Freud's mother Amalie; between his first marriage, which produced Freud's two much older half-brothers, and the marriage to Amalie there was a second, childless marriage to another woman whose name was Rebecca and whose fate remains unknown. The register of the Jewish population of Frieberg listed Rebecca as Jakob's thirty-two year old wife in 1852, but her name does not reappear on the 1854 register—whether because of death or divorce or some other reason there is no way to know. Because of the dates involved, however, it is sure that Freud's mother as well as his half-brothers would have known of Rebecca. Freud himself must therefore have had some kind of knowledge of the family secret, some inkling of the skeleton in Jakob's closet. The second discovery taints the image of the father a bit more, for records unambiguously show that Freud was born on March 6, 1856, not on May 6, the date he had always celebrated as his birthday. The difference is not altogether trivial since Jakob, 40, married Amalie, 20, on July 29, 1855, a not so respectable seven months before Freud's actual birth date.

Obviously, for a good psychoanalyst this is more than enough to run with! And Balmary weaves a compelling, though occasionally unconvincing, interpretation from a skein of threads in Freud's dreams, slips, preoccupations, daily habits, travels, statue collection, reading in literature, myth and religion and so on, which keep leading back to Rebecca-figures, suicide, abandonment, illegitimacy. The theoretical value of Balmary's interpretations actually outweighs their psychobiographical accuracy. For no matter what flaws might mar her biographical speculations she has greatly enriched our understanding of the context in which Freud missed a crucial opportunity to grasp the interpersonal and moral origins of neurosis.

For, as Balmary suggests, whenever Freud "speaks of 'the motive force' for the formation of symptoms he abandons the field of intersubjective motives and limits himself to [the] intrapsychic mechanism."[17] The father's fault is hidden behind the child's guilt and desire. Once Freud came to doubt that the source of hysterical symptoms lay in trauma he gravitated immediately to another intrapsychic hypothesis, namely, that his patients must be harboring a repressed desire strong enough to force its way around the repression and express itself as a symptom. *That a symptom always refers back to a repressed wish* became a Freudian axiom, preempting a very different hypothesis: namely, *that the intersubjective dynamic of a family lie could induce repression and symptom formation.*

The second hypothesis was preempted by the intrapsychic orientation of Freud's theoretical vocabulary, though it was perfectly consistent with his therapeutic experience. The first hypothesis found easy expression in his theoretical vocabulary, though it seemed to contradict the original evidence of his therapeutic experience. But did it really contradict his patients' testimony? Freud could have left open the possibility that the impulses, affections and desires of his patients had *in some way* been stirred at the time of an assault or "seduction" by a male relative, *and* that the experience was fundamentally traumatic, a confusing, many-edged source of physical, emotional and moral pain, an experience that could not be assimilated. The two hypotheses are not intrinsically incompatible, as Freud and many of his proponents and critics have assumed.

Freud failed to find the theoretical means of holding the two ideas, desire and trauma, together. There is ample evidence, on the other hand, that for years after his supposed "discovery" and about-face he in fact held them together empirically, continuing to record in significant numbers his patients' recollections of sexual abuse. He let the two ideas coexist, without a genuine theoretical resolution, so long as his Oedipal theory was still in the making. He did not unequivocally withdraw the seduction theory in the period that runs from the Dora sessions (1900) through his publication of her case history and the *Three Essays on the Theory of Sexuality* (1905), in which he apparently repudiated but actually just revised the seduction theory.[18] Not until the theoretical focus had completely rotated over to theorizing males did Freud complete the basic paradigm of Oedipal theory; only at the time of the Rat Man (1907-1909) and the essay "A Special Type of Choice of Object Made by Men" (1910) is the seduction theory finally overthrown and the evidence of sexual abuse pushed definitively into the background.

To have found the theoretical means of placing trauma and desire in the same process of symptom formation Freud would have had to overcome the kinds of significant social prejudices and biographical barriers that Masson and Balmary identify. These pressures caused him, instead, to overlook the need for a concept of etiology that might embrace trauma and desire at the same time. He thus allowed himself to be satisfied with the drastic conclusion that since trauma alone could not explain his female patients' symptoms, those symptoms must have arisen from the patients' own repressed incestuous wishes to commit the very acts they claimed their fathers forced upon them. In adducing this strong form of what Foucault called the repressive hypothesis Freud succumbed to the popular, medical and legal prejudices of his time: respectable men wouldn't commit such acts; hysterical women are liars.

Freud's misogynistic, sexist, masculinist attitudes are not, however, sufficient to explain the ingredients of his initial about-face in 1897, let alone the solidification of the Oedipal theory in 1910. He had another reason for supposing that a desire was required to form symptoms. He was evolving a therapeutic technique in which the dialogue between patient and analyst was propelled by the patient's own repressed wishes. Free association did not give rise to merely random musings; it took its bearings on the wings of desire. What Lacan would later call the "direction of the cure" was oriented and propelled by the subject's desire. Therefore, according to this whole line of reasoning, in order for the symptom to be unraveled and resolved, the patient's desire ultimately had to be implicated in the original forming of the symptom.

How, though, is it conceivable to attribute both desire and trauma to childhood seduction? How can one and the same experience be a catastrophic explosion of wishes and an incomprehensible violation? The insight and wisdom that Freud lacked when faced with these questions are richly provided by Maya Angelou's recollection of childhood rape in her autobiography *I Know Why the Caged Bird Sings*. Angelou conveys both the pain the rape caused her and the love it implicated and shattered.

The rape took place shortly after Marguerite, as Angelou was then called, and her brother Bailey were reunited with their elegant, blues-singing mother in St. Louis. One morning her mother returned home after staying out all night only to leave again for the day. Marguerite was left alone with the mother's angry boyfriend. He called her over to him and displayed his erection. Threatening to kill her if she cried out and to kill Bailey if she breathed a word, Mr. Freeman took hold of her and pulled her pants down:

> And then.
>
> Then there was the pain. A breaking and entering when even the senses are torn apart. The act of rape of an eight-year old body is a matter of the needle giving because the camel can't. The child gives, because the body can, and the mind of the violator cannot.
>
> I thought I had died.[19]

The rape actually followed two earlier incidents in which Mr. Freeman had molested her. On the first occasion he had caressed her and made her touch his penis. Then he held her to his chest while he masturbated. She felt a moment of intense affection in being held so close, and she felt as though her years of yearning after something long lost were finally being gratified:

> Finally he was quiet, and then came the nice part. He held me so softly that I wished he wouldn't ever let me go. I felt at home. From the way he was holding me I knew he'd never let me go or let anything bad ever happen to me. This was probably my real father and we had found each other at last. But then he rolled over, leaving me in a wet place and stood up.[20]

He told her he would kill Bailey "'If you ever tell anybody what we did.'" The threat only threw her into a confusion about her part in what happened: "What had we done? We?" It was her first secret from Bailey, and afterwards she "began to feel lonely for Mr. Freeman and the encasement of his long arms." A few days later he put her in his lap and pressed his erection against her. "Then he pulled me to his chest. He smelled of coal dust and grease and he was so close I buried my face in his shirt and listened to his heart, it was beating just for me."[21] Mr. Freeman then went back to ignoring her, and her own anxious expectations of his affection and her fears of losing his attention gradually faded away until the day her mother's insouciance aggravated him. The brutal rape left Marguerite injured. Mr. Freeman was found out and arrested, convicted and freed and then murdered, perhaps by Marguerite's uncles.

The child was left burdened with a guilt she connected to the lie she told when asked at the trial if Mr. Freeman had ever touched her before the rape. She was paralyzed by moral confusion and afraid to expose her earlier feelings and the secrets she had kept:

> I couldn't say yes and tell them how he had loved me once for a few minutes and how he had held me close before he thought I had peed in my bed. My uncles would kill me and Grandmother Baxter would stop speaking, as she often did when she was angry. And all these people in the court would stone me as they had stoned the harlot in the Bible. And Mother, who thought I was such a good girl, would be so disappointed. But most important, there was Bailey. I had kept a secret from him.[22]

She later blamed herself for Mr. Freeman's death—"A man was dead because I had lied"[23]—since her lie had served in her own mind to preserve her innocence and heighten his guilt. Yet Mr. Freeman himself seemed to summon this lie at the trial, just as he had exacted her silence before:

> I looked at his heavy face trying to look as if he would have liked me to say No. I said No.
>
> The lie lumped in my throat and I couldn't get air. How I despised the man for making me lie.[24]

According to Christine Froula, who first showed the relevance of Angelou's book to the whole debate inaugurated by Masson, Marguerite is confused "because her memory of her own pleasure in being held by [Mr. Freeman] seems to implicate her in his crime." The social condemnation of women's pleasure contravenes her desire to tell the truth. Froula discerns in this episode a pattern typical in cases of sexual abuse and part of a larger "cultural script" in which women are silenced: "Taking [Mr. Freeman's] death as proof that her words have power to kill, she descends into a silence that lasts for a year. Like Helen's sacrificial speech, Maya's silence speaks the hysterical cultural script: it expresses guilt and anguish at her own aggression against the father and voluntarily sacrifices the cure of truthful words."[25]

The child's moral confusion is what Freud always failed to interpret, whether in his seduction theory or his Oedipal theory. The emotional authority and the menace Mr. Freeman's words carry when he commands Marguerite to silence in order to hide his own actions resound in her ears as a call to hide her own undesignated, still enigmatic deeds. The adult's fault is already being reinscribed as the child's guilt. Moreover, her yearning for her missing father and her needs for affection, recognition and security are incongruous with the adult's aims. He exploits these needs up until his most violent act, which shattered them by engulfing the child in genital sexuality and subjugation to another's will.

The one thing that Marguerite managed to salvage was the sense of security afforded by her ties to grandmother, mother and brother—a restoration of the protective environment that most victims of incest never achieve. Even that she got at the price of the guilt-ridden lie that caused her to be "constantly morose" for several months and to impose a silence on herself for fear her words might kill others.

Angelou's narrative recovers and preserves the same dynamic of the experience of abuse that Freud must have encountered again and again in his analytic sessions. But he just didn't get it. Desire and trauma are thoroughly interlaced in the web of solicitation, command, threat and lie that are part and parcel of the rapist's actions. Freud brushed aside the moral interactions, this entanglement of wish and violation, the broken trust, in a single-minded search for the victim's desire. Nowhere has his single-mindedness been so devastatingly exposed as in the remarkable essays Charles Bernheimer and Claire Kahane have collected in the volume *In Dora's Case: Freud—Hysteria—Feminism.*

Freud's high expectations for the Dora case were fueled by the need for a clinical success that would justify his therapeutic methods and confirm his emergent Oedipal theory. Dora would be the patient to prove that repressed desires ultimately traceable to love and jealousy for one's parents were at the root of neurosis. To all appearances there had indeed been a trauma, but Freud could count Dora's so-called "seduction" scene a "precipitating cause" occurring in adolescence and referring back to repressed childhood wishes. Dora's life-history presented Freud with the opportunity to demonstrate that desire precedes trauma in the making of a neurosis.

The "precipitating cause" of Dora's illness was threatening to become a family scandal when Dora's father brought her to Freud. Two years before, when she was 16, Herr K., family friend and husband of her father's mistress, had propositioned Dora, and it turned out that he had also grabbed hold of her and kissed her in an incident when she was only 14. Frau K. herself was on intimate terms with Dora, who had looked after her children. Herr K. adamantly denied Dora's accusation; enlisting the support of his wife, who revealed that Dora had read books on sexuality at their home, he suggested she probably "had been over-excited by such reading and has merely 'fancied' the whole scene she had described."[26] Dora's father declared the accusations false and begged Freud, "'Please try and bring her to reason.'" Faced with these two men's declarations that a girl's story of attempted seduction was mere fantasy, Freud never for a moment doubted Dora's version. He saw through the father's effort and considered it a cynical attempt to silence his daughter to buy peace with Herr K. and protect his own affair with Frau K.

That is about all that Freud saw through, however. His critics have shown that every other significant feature of the case either remained opaque to him or was distorted by his own prejudices and aims. Freud was presented with a case begging to be approached from the standpoint of the interpersonal and moral origins of neurosis. Dora's predicament in the four years since Herr K.'s sexual advances is well defined by Steven Marcus: "The three adults to whom she was closest, whom she loved most in the world, were apparently conspiring—separately, in tandem, or in concert—to deny her the reality of her experience. They were conspiring to deny Dora her reality and reality itself. The betrayal touched upon matters that might easily unhinge the mind of a young person; the three adults were not betraying Dora's love and trust alone, they were betraying the structure of the actual world."[27]

Many commentators have decried Freud's dogged insistence that Dora should have welcomed Herr K.'s aggressive advances, and that her flight from Herr K. and into illness was a recoil against her own desires rather than against his power. Alternative interpretations have stressed the social and moral predicament that Dora (whose real name was Ida Bauer) found herself in. Maria Ramas argues that Dora's illness was a distorted protest against compulsory heterosexuality. "Ida Bauer's hysteria was exactly what it appeared to be—a repudiation of the meaning of heterosexuality":

> Given her hysteria and the *refusal* that lay at its core, her choice of Herr K. was truly ingenious. It allowed her to comply with the demands her family and culture placed upon her while at the same time allowing her to revolt against those demands—and to do so in the name of social propriety and social justice. She could comply with her father's wishes and wear the cloak of femininity by receiving the romantic attentions of Herr K., while knowing full well this was a doomed affair.

Reworking Freud's own belated interpretation of Dora's "deep-rooted homosexual love for Frau K.," Ramas also sees Dora's behavior as an ill-fated attempt to square the social demands of compulsory heterosexuality and the emotional demands of socially condemned lesbianism: "Ida's flirtation with heterosexual romance plummeted her into an erotic triangle with Frau K., while at the same time masking the fact that Frau K. was her primary 'object' of desire."[28]

In a similar attempt to describe Dora's illness as at once strategy and symptom, protest and trap, Madelon Sprengnether stresses how the roles of invalid and nurse were charged with contradictory social and psychological meanings because bound up with gender and class relations, from Dora's initial role as her father's nurse to her irritation when Herr K. treated her in the exact way she knew him to have treated a servant he previously seduced and abandoned:

> Dora's option for the role of invalid might be seen in this light as a desperate bid for affection and a means of avoiding, temporarily at least, the nurse/governess role, associated in both households with betrayal. Complicating Dora's situation is her role as nursemaid of the K.'s children and her intimacy with Frau K. based on the exclusion of Herr K., until the time of her father's affair. Deprived of the role (involving for her maternal rather than sexual ministrations) on which she had counted for eliciting the affection and attentions of members of both families, Dora, now excluded by her father and Frau K., is offered only one position, that of Herr K.'s mistress, rendering her powerless and vulnerable to further rejection.[29]

Freud was, in Sprengnether's phrase, *enforcing Oedipus* in Dora's case. He missed the maternal, as opposed to heterosexual, gratifications that Dora derived from nursing her father in his illness and caring for the K.'s children. Moreover, he missed—even after identifying Dora's "deep-rooted homosexual love"—how the crushing impact of compulsory heterosexuality shaped Dora's responses. Instead, Freud tended to view her homosexuality as a regression and her attempts to contend with compulsory heterosexuality as a manifestation of repressed heterosexual desire itself.

Freud failed in this whole attempt, therapeutically and theoretically, to place Dora's trauma and flight into illness securely within an Oedipal narrative. Dora's life-history somehow stood athwart the crucial shift in Freud's thinking. The case that was supposed to have vindicated this shift did not in the end yield to it at all. Even as Freud pressed his new hypothesis that incestuous desire rather than trauma was at the root of hysteria, Dora never did confess a longing for Herr K., since her rejection of him was a repudiation of male-dominated heterosexuality altogether.

A second factor was at play as well. In the aftermath of his self-analysis, Freud was unwittingly in search of an Oedipal theory modeled on male socialization. He would not realize until 1931 that the premises of Oedipal theory never really fit women's lives at all. In 1905, having only just embarked on his major theoretical revision, he badgered Dora to make her story conform to the Oedipus complex and was then constrained to explain, or explain away, the incompleteness of her treatment and his "fragment" of a case history. Faced with the failure of Dora's treatment and the shortcomings of the written account, Freud made a definitive, though unacknowledged, turn to the male model to sort out the theoretical confusions that haunted Oedipal theory.

As luck would have it, the Rat Man arrived on his doorstep in October 1907. This case proved to be the needed test of the male-centered conception of the Oedipus complex. As we have seen, it confirmed and refined the new paradigm. Freud gained this theoretical success, however, at the cost of a renewed disregard for the potential significance of sexual violence and male power in the making of modern neurosis. However, it was now not a question of the patient as victim, but rather of the patient as perpetrator.

The clinical notes found after Freud's death are the underbelly of the Rat Man's case history. They tell a tale of moral confusion and sexual violence that Freud expurgated in preparing the case for public discussion. However much he may have been motivated by the need to disguise his patient's identity, or perhaps to minimize the harm that would be done if family members or close friends saw through the various disguises in the published account, Freud's misrepresentations *also* bear on fundamental theoretical and interpretive problems. I think it would be as wrong here as in the case of Emma Eckstein to accuse Freud of deliberate intellectual distortion. The omissions do, however, reveal how thoroughly the new Oedipal paradigm relegated sexual violence and male dominance to the status of merely tangential facts when they might have been put at the very center of an interpretation of the Rat Man's pathologies.

For starters, discrepancies between the case history and the clinical notes need to be reassessed. The published case history recounts, for example, an event that occurred the same year the Rat Man fell in love with his lady. (It is unfortunately impossible to determine whether before or after.) Freud uses the episode to illustrate the patient's experiences of the omnipotence of his feelings and wishes:

> The second experience related to an unmarried woman, no longer young, though with a great desire to be loved, who had once paid him a great deal of attention and had once asked him point-blank whether he could not love her. He had given her an evasive answer. A few days afterwards he heard she had thrown herself out of a window. He then began to reproach himself, and said to himself that it would have been in his power to save her life by giving her his love. In this way he became convinced of the omnipotence of his love and of his hatred.[30]

Thus told, the episode suggests nothing in the immediate situation that could have stimulated the patient's fantasy of omnipotence. It must have derived from some earlier experience. There is nothing he did in relation to the woman that could haunt him in the wake of her death, and Freud will build on this fact to show that the sources of his pathological fantasies lay in his primordial relation to his father. The "death-wishes which he had felt against his father" had originally erupted in the biting and name-calling episode at the time of his older sister's fatal illness.[31] Wish, rage and dying were, according to this view, melded into the fantasmal "omnipotence of his love and of his hatred" that revived yet again with the woman's suicide.

The "omnipotence" is purely fantasmal—and in need of primordial sources—so long as his real-life desiring and refusing are unmixed with assertions of actual power. But Freud misleads on just this count. The clinical notes, which he normally wrote down in the evening after a session with the patient, reveal that the Rat Man was not at all the passive participant pictured in the case study:

> When he was twenty years old, they employed a dressmaker, to whom he repeatedly made aggressive advances but whom he did not really care for, because she made demands and had an excessive desire to be loved. She complained that people did not like her; she asked him to assure her that he was fond of her and was in despair when he flatly refused. A week later she threw herself out of the window. He said she would not have done it if he had entered into the *liaison*. Thus one's omnipotence is manifested when one gives or withholds one's love, insofar as one possesses the power to make someone happy.[32]

The altered details are telling. It was he not she who sought a sexual liaison. She did not seek out a declaration of his love but had wanted to be assured of his affection before consenting to sex. He did not give her "an evasive answer" to an unsolicited request for love but flatly refused to embellish his demands for sex with shows of affection. The "unmarried woman, no longer young" was, more precisely, a working-class woman employed by the Rat Man's family. By omitting her occupation while supplying—perhaps even inventing—her age, Freud makes her expectations rather than his actions seem inappropriate.

It seems obvious that the Rat Man, who at the time had never had sexual intercourse, had thought to exploit the vulnerability of an emotionally unstable, insecure woman in his family's employ. Before fancying himself all-powerful he intended in fact to wield his actual power. He sought sexual advantage in the social power that class and gender put at his disposal.

Not only did he fail, but the dressmaker's suicide thrust him into a tragedy where he surely did not want to admit playing any part. The feeling of omnipotence he confessed to Freud—my love could have saved her—was braggadocio that still served, ten years later, to cover his actual involvement. His self-reproaches were actually self-aggrandizement. For they heroize his emotional and sexual powers in an episode where in fact he had merely flaunted his social power while proving emotionally impotent and sexually ineffectual.

The fantasmal omnipotence deflects the moral reflection his behavior might prompt. Freud becomes complicit in this stratagem because he has no way of connecting moral harm or sexual violence to symptom-formation, whether in the case of victim or victimizer, woman or man, hysteric or obsessive. Following the newly congealed Oedipal theory, Freud lets real actions be transformed into fantasy: so long as the Rat Man's actual power and real actions are devalued, the fantasmal omnipotence that made him believe his love could have rescued the dressmaker is left in need of an explanation with reference to something more archaic, something infantile, something yet more primordially fantasmal.

The Rat Man's propensity to sexual aggression and abuse did not end with the dressmaker's suicide. In the second week of his sessions with Freud, he related an event that for him illustrated how he always managed to ruin his finest moments:

> *Oct. 12.*—He . . . told me how he spent the day. His spirits rose and he went to the theatre. When he got home he chanced to meet his servant-girl, who is neither young nor pretty but has been showing him attention for some time past. He cannot think why, but he suddenly gave her a kiss and then attacked her. Though she no doubt [!] made only a show of resistance, he came to his senses and fled to his room. It was always the same with him: his fine or happy moments were always spoilt by something nasty.[33]

The spectacular fall from cultivated Viennese theatre-goer to would-be rapist belongs to a pattern of bifurcated sensibility that permeates the Rat Man's relations with women more generally. He often masturbated "when he experienced especially fine moments or when he read fine passages"—he cites Goethe's *Dichtung und Wahrheit*—but his periods of masturbation also frequently had less refined causes, as when his infatuation with a servant-girl in Salzburg led to such intense masturbation that it "spoilt a trip" he had looked forward to taking.[34]

Bourgeois spirit and proletarian body are joined in the Rat Man's erotic longings in the form of a coupling of male self and female other. But this same social-symbolic mapping of sexuality is also torn asunder in the gulf he maintains between his idealized lady, whom he courted for nine years, and the several women with whom he had sexual intercourse during those years. "He always sought a sharp distinction," according to Freud's record, "between relations which consisted only in copulation and everything that was called love."[35] The polarization of *esteem* and *ill-repute* that Freud located in the "special type of choice of object made by men" has its corollary here in the dichotomy between the Rat Man's chaste idealization of his lady and his erotic pursuit of other women.

The clinical notes leave no ambiguity regarding the fact that all the women with whom he was capable of sexual relations were working-class. In addition to the episodes with the dressmaker and the servant-girl in Vienna, he had had sexual relations with the Salzburg servant who had inspired his masturbation and later with a Munich waitress. Back in Vienna he began to visit another dressmaker during the course of his treatment: "He is cheerful, untrammelled and active, and is behaving aggressively to a girl, a dressmaker."[36]

The power of his social superiority is recurrently articulated with his capacity for sexual experience. Yet social power and sexuality are constantly disarticulated in Freud's interpretations. The double imperative of Oedipal theory—that neurotic symptoms derive from earliest childhood and, specifically, from overwrought impulses prematurely blocked by obstacles—deflects Freud from any attempt to sort out the formative role played by the moral disequilibrium and the social hierarchy within which the Rat Man's life unfolded. As a result, from the first therapy sessions right through to the published case history, Freud doggedly asserts his barely confirmed hypothesis that everything goes back to the father's threatening interference with the Rat Man's pleasures—that is, ultimately to castration.

Freud's glimpse at an alternative is all the more striking because it does not survive into the published account. At issue is the Rat Man's sexual aggression against his sisters. In deleting all reference to these episodes, Freud's Oedipal interpretation instead places the origins of the Rat Man's pathological scruples, obsessions and impulsiveness completely in the biting and spanking episode which the family, not the patient himself, remembers from his earliest years. The discarded material shows how quickly Freud's assumption of infantile origins leads him away from the sexual violence in the Rat Man's life:

> *Nov. 17.*—So far he has been in a period of rising spirits. He is cheerful, untrammelled and active, and is behaving aggressively to a girl, a dressmaker. A good idea of his that this moral inferiority really deserved to be punished by his illness. Confessions followed about his relations to his sisters. He made, so he said, repeated attacks on his next younger sister, Julie, after his father's death; and these—he had once actually assaulted her—must have been the explanation of his pathological changes.
>
> He once had a dream of copulating with Julie. He was overcome with remorse and fear at having broken his vow to keep away from her. He woke up and was delighted to find it was only a dream. He then went into her bedroom and smacked her bottom under the bedclothes. He could not understand it, and could only compare it with his masturbating when he read the passages from *Dichtung und Wahrheit.* From this we conclude that his being chastised by his father was related to assaulting his sisters. But how? Purely sadistically or already in a clearly sexual way? His elder or his younger sisters? Julie is three years his junior, and as the scenes we're in search of must have been when he was three or four, she can scarcely be the one. Katherine, his sister who died?[37]

The attacks on Julie occurred, therefore, in the year that followed the dressmaker's suicide and his falling in love with his lady. The patient was then 21, his sister 18. Freud apparently did not seek to learn the details of these attacks and assaults.

Nor do the existing clinical notes shed much more light than the case history on the relationship between Julie and the Rat Man. A few entries before the notes break off there is mention of a significant anecdote regarding the jealousy Julie's husband exhibited toward the patient:

> Yesterday there had been a scene with his sister in which [her husband] had said it straight out. Even the servants said that she loved him and kissed him [i.e., the patient] like a lover, not like a brother. He himself, after having been in the next room with his sister for a while, said to his brother-in-law: "If Julie has a baby in 9 months' time, you needn't think I'm its father; I am innocent."[38]

Freud does little to make sense of the atmosphere of incestuous longing in the Rat Man's family, and he virtually ignores it in his published interpretation. In the unpublished notes, he jotted down the suggestion that the

Rat Man's varying, conflictual attachments to his sisters provided the prototype for his habit of "always [having] several interests simultaneously," and that perhaps his recurrent hesitation between his lady and another woman replicated choosing between his sisters.[39] Beyond such remarks, however, nothing is made of the relationship with Julie. Even less attention is given to the fact that the Rat Man, well beyond the immediate aftermath of his father's death, had a sexual fascination with his youngest sister, Gerda. "Even in recent years," as Freud learned in the same session in which the Rat Man recalled his attacks on Julie, "when his youngest sister was sleeping in his room, he took off her bed-clothes in the morning so he could see the whole of her."[40] Gerda was 21 when the Rat Man, 29, began seeing Freud.

Since Freud was on the lookout for an event going back to the Rat Man's third or fourth year to anchor the later compulsions and guilt, he looked straight past the adult behavior in search of the elusive infantile antecedent. He never examined the continuum—or the continuousness—of the aggressive sexual advances that characterized the Rat Man's relations with his sisters and servants. Just as he had hidden the fault of the father in his self-analysis and in his rejection of the seduction theory, he pushed the Rat Man's misdeeds so far into the background that they could be deleted altogether in his published interpretation.

Freud's blindspots frequently rise straightaway from the prejudices of his time. His attitude toward Dora, as feminist critics have shown, was barely distinguishable from the crudest male attitudes toward rape: any behavior that a male acquaintance, perhaps even an anonymous male, might himself construe as seductive is an invitation to sex. The coercive conditions of domestic relationships—a husband's power to command sexual submission from a wife, or from a servant—did not figure in Freud's assessment of the pathologies that befall sexuality. At times his own sentiments and imagination seem seized by the appeal of male power and social prestige. Several commentators show, for example, that Freud conducted sessions with Dora as though he identified with Herr K. And his demonstrative admiration for the Rat Man may have led to his skewed representation of his character and actions.

Freud was also, of course, an incisive, frequently critical commentator on his society. He often set himself against the grain of its prevailing values and mores. But the flaws in his view of sexuality and gender significantly distorted just this capacity for social criticism. Freud's psychoanalytic writings as well as his great essays of cultural commentary make it abundantly clear that when he looked at the society around him, in effect, the bourgeois lifeworld, he saw a constellation of three kinds of social pathology:

(1) The stifling discretions and refinements of polite society, especially pronounced in a bourgeoisie still imitating aristocratic manners; (2) the inhibited sexuality of the women within this lifeworld, in particular, his own female patients; (3) the sexual practices of the men in this same lifeworld, who were prone, when not suffering from impotence, to enjoy their most intense sexual gratifications outside their marriages, with prostitutes, with maids, servants or employees and with adolescent girls, including their sisters, nieces or daughters. The *pater familias* glimpsed in Freud's writings does not so much resemble the Moses of the Bible as the John Huston of *Chinatown.*

Freud's social observations suggest the need to analyze the repressive features of the bourgeois lifeworld in conjunction with the social relations of men and women. Ultimately, the fault of the father is the patriarchal fault, the violence and coerciveness wound into the relations between men and women by virtue of the social power exerted by men over women. Freud discovered that the moral universe of heterosexuality was out of joint in his society, as it still is today. But when he actually set about to derive an account of individual pathologies from these social pathologies, he converted his tripartite social diagnosis into a bipolar scheme. He set forth the opposition between *sexual impulse* and *moral stricture.*

The social relations of men and women became irrelevant. Neither sexual coercion nor coercive sexuality finds a place in this conceptual scheme, except as part of "libido." Sexual violence becomes but a modality of libido, which Freud equated with the "masculine" and considered the *active* manifestation of eros, including aggressive and sadistic impulses. The life-history of the Rat Man, the exemplary Oedipal narrative it presented Freud, has stirred questions about power, identity and sexuality that exceed Freud's own frameworks. The dialogue between social thought and psychoanalysis will have to undergo yet another turn. It is a question of interrogating where psychoanalysis stands in relation to the lifeworld in which it intervenes. For this historically specific lifeworld has also shaped the horizons of psychoanalytic thinking as well as the lives of those who seek out the psychoanalyst.

6

Family, Community, Polis

PSYCHOANALYSIS SHARES with modern literature a penchant for discovering in the forms of personal suffering ciphers of a more general condition. When decked out metaphysically, these ciphers have become, variously, visions of the human condition or mythologies of violence and the sacred or even allegories of language. I am a partisan of another alternative, where exemplary forms of personal suffering become ciphers of the social relationships in which we wittingly and unwittingly participate. I therefore look to psychoanalysis to contribute to the cultural interpretation of the modern forms of individuality, and to help disclose the norms and the pathologies that typically occur in the making of the socialized individual in our society.

Psychoanalysis has generally left its ties to social theory fragmented and largely covert. Moreover, it tends to invert the relation between cultural forms and specifically psychoanalytic concepts, believing the latter to be purely descriptive of the psychic mechanism and then deriving the cultural forms from them. Psychoanalysis also tends to eschew historical questions by casting the historical context of life-histories as merely contingent elements in a universal structure.

Nowhere are these intellectual habits more deeply ingrained than in the Freudian theory of the Oedipus complex. The Oedipus complex is also perhaps the most developed figure of exemplary suffering that psychoanalysis has produced. The reference to Greek tragedy, with its ritual reenactments of the actions of ancient royalty, can be misleading. For psychoanalysis tells a very modern and very bourgeois tale. Freud's Oedipal theory was a search for the inner logic of the middle-class male's socialization into heterosexuality, marriage and vocation.

Freud's own life-history and its historical context were at the very origin of Oedipal theory. The basic concepts of psychoanalysis, including the rudiments of the "father-complex," were discovered in the course of the self-analysis whose traces Freud left in *The Interpretation of Dreams.* As Carl E. Schorske showed in his classic essay "Politics and Patricide in Freud's *Interpretation of Dreams,*" Freud's autobiographical self-reflection also reveals the "flight from politics" that marked Freud's painful shift from his youthful aspiration to politics as vocation to a safer, more sober decision in favor of science as vocation. He abandoned his plans to study law and eventually entered the medical profession instead.[1]

His dreams are shot through with images of political heroism in which he or his father struggles against the conservatism of the Habsburgs in the name of German, Hungarian and Italian nationalisms. The dreamed hero also triumphs over anti-Semitism. In the 1890s anti-Semitism was on the rise. Karl Lueger's anti-Semitic party won elections in Vienna, and there was anti-Jewish violence in Galicia. Many Jewish intellectuals, including Freud himself, encountered intensifying obstacles to their advancement in Austrian academic and professional positions. Freud encountered the "blocked ascendence" that Alvin Gouldner has identified as the motive that has historically driven intellectuals to become revolutionaries.[2]

The choice of science over politics changed the scene of his revolutionary ambitions. The phrase Freud chose from the *Aeneid* for the epigraph of *The Interpretation of Dreams* registered the displacement triumphantly: *Flectere si nequeo superos, Acheronta movebo,* "If I cannot bend the higher powers, I will stir up the river Acheron," that is, I will stir up hell, the demonic, the unconscious.

Unlike many of his contemporaries who witnessed the general breakup of liberalism at the end of the century, the young Freud did not repudiate his liberal father's beliefs. Instead, he sought, Schorske writes, "to overcome his father by realizing the liberal creed his father professed but had failed to defend."[3] Freud's long unhealed wound at the hand of his father was not some primal paternal castration threat but rather the dismay he felt as a child upon hearing his father tell of being bullied. He recounted the episode, which had figured in his self-analysis, in *The Interpretation of Dreams:*

> "A Christian came up to me and with a single blow knocked off my cap into the mud and shouted: 'Jew! get off the pavement!'" "And what did

> you do?" I asked. "I went into the roadway and picked up my cap" was his quiet reply. This struck me as unheroic conduct on the part of the big, strong man who was holding the little boy by the hand. I contrasted this situation with another which fitted my feelings better: the scene in which Hannibal's father . . . made his boy swear before the household altar to take vengeance on the Romans.[4]

Karl Lueger, Rome, Austrian aristocracy, the Catholic Church and the Habsburg regime do not disappear as antagonists to Freud's values and aims, but through his interpretation of his dreams he manages to transform them into merely the setting for the supposedly more fundamental antagonism of son and father. He then completes this intellectual maneuver by making the father the source of political and social power: "the father is the oldest, first, and for children the only authority, and from his autocratic power the other social authorities have developed in the course of the history of human civilization."[5]

The preeminence of the father as a symbol of authority and power takes the place of the real-life father with his unheroic submission to injustice and humiliation. By the same token, in the other register of Freud's imagination, he had transformed his own scientific vocation and his discovery of the unconscious—including the rudiments of the Oedipus complex—into acts of rebellion and retribution. "Patricide replaces politics," according to Schorske. "By reducing his own political past and present to an epiphenomenal status in relation to the primal conflict between father and son, Freud gave his fellow liberals an a-historical theory of man and society that could make bearable a political world spun out of orbit and beyond control."[6]

Turning the tables on Freud is never that easy. Schorske himself is caught square in a very Freudian paradox. For he argues his claim that Freud replaced political explanations with psychological ones by advancing, precisely, psychological rather than political explanations. Nevertheless, Schorske's reassessment has the virtue of not disputing the Freudian project so much as disclosing how its aims went beyond what Freud would, or could, actually articulate. The biographical revisionism points up the need for a theoretical reconstruction as well. Moreover, it would be wrong to conclude that Freud's family, vocation and politics were merely limitations on his thinking. These concrete circumstances were also its enabling conditions. Ultimately, my aim is to ask: How did Freud use conceptions of the family and the psyche to think out the historical processes that were transforming the forms of *community* and *polis* at the turn of the century? To what extent are Freud's concepts a mere rewriting of social and political processes in psychological terms? To what extent are they a discovery, however partial, of new forms of individuality accompanying new forms of sociality?

Carole Pateman has done much to rescue Freud's forays into anthropology and history from the obscurity they might deserve on account of their sheer inaccuracy—*and* from the astounding prestige they have enjoyed on account of structuralism. *Totem and Taboo* (1912-13), *Civilization and Its Discontents* (1930) and *Moses and Monotheism* (1939) focus on ancient and prehistoric societies, but they actually embody, according to Pateman, Freud's very relevant reflection on modern society. He draws the conceptual and narrative resources of this reflection, Pateman argues, from the tradition of social contract theory. His political fiction of origins surpasses other theories of the social contract by revealing what they systematically hide: namely, that a fundamental subordination of women by men lies behind the supposed founding moment of society in an agreement among equals. Male sex-right, in other words, precedes fraternal equality.

The Freudian story of the primal horde—of the rebellious sons who killed the tyrannical father to end his exclusive control over all the women of the horde and then created the rules that outlawed murder, guaranteed the just distribution of women among all the males and honored the dead father with idealizing symbols—this story may seem infinitely removed from the preoccupations of modernity. But modern society becomes Freud's real referent as soon as he takes up the task of explaining relations of equality established through an agreement upon rules. Like the social contract stories, Freud's primal horde story furnishes the backing for the kinds of equality associated with the economic, the legal and the political institutions of capitalism and the liberal state. His analysis is really designed to explain present-day society but is projected into the remote past as a narrative of origin.

Pateman credits Freud with giving the story of the emergence of civil society its true starting point. Fraternity is born with the subjugation of women. "The motive for the brothers' collective act," she writes, "is not merely to claim their natural liberty and right of self-government, *but to gain access to women*. . . . No man can be a primal father ever again, but by setting up rules that give all men equal access to women (compare their equality before the laws of the state) they exercise the 'original' political right of dominion over women that was once the prerogative of the father."[7] Even as social contract theorists challenged the justifications of absolute monarchy modeled on paternal authority, they left unchallenged the father-husband's rule. They interpreted it as a natural rather than political power. Contract theorists, like their antagonists the patriarchalists, asserted "first, that women (wives), unlike sons, were born and remained naturally subject to men (husbands); and, second, that the right of men over women was *not political*."[8]

Freud provides Pateman with the needed representation or mapping of the two domains of sociality that contract theory separated: the family and civil society. Pateman points out that what Freud meant by "civilization" is what she means by "civil society": "The fraternal social contract creates a new, modern patriarchal order that is presented as divided into two spheres: civil society or the universal sphere of freedom, equality, individualism, reason, contract and impartial law—the realm of men or 'individuals'; and the private world of particularity, natural subjection, laws of blood, emotion, love and sexual passion—the world of women, in which men also rule."[9] And indeed Freud's conception of "civilization" is at once broad in scope, covering labor and material culture, legal institutions and the state, cultural and ethical ideals; and distinctively modern in that the forms of equality he connects to the fraternal pact are those of the capitalist market, liberal jurisprudence and the constitutional state.

By the time Freud refined this version of the social contract in *Civilization and Its Discontents,* his Oedipal theory had acquired its achieved form. It was ready for use in those speculative exercises of applied psychoanalysis through which he read out complex historical processes and social institutions as libidinal economy. Like Pateman, I consider these exercises to be attempts on Freud's part to think out political and social questions in psychoanalytic categories. Such a reading has to begin by following out the movement of Freud's explicit claims regarding archaic societies or civilization in the abstract. His real referent can only be gained through a twist in the more immanent reading. Let us turn, then, to Freud's own terms.

Communal life as such, he postulates, has "a two-fold foundation: the compulsion to work, which was created by external necessity, and the power of love."[10] He proceeds on the basis of an axiom whose iron-clad gender roles he is at once exposing and naturalizing: "the power of love . . . made the man unwilling to be deprived of his sexual object—the woman—and made the woman unwilling to be deprived of the part of herself which had been separated off from her—her child."[11] The elemental form of sociality, therefore, combines the male desire to keep control over a woman for purposes of sexual gratification and the female desire to keep watch over her child.

Men's heterosexual desire and women's maternal love founded the sociality of the family. Civilization then developed not only by proliferating families but also by progressively distinguishing itself from the family. This does not, however, imply that civilization arises solely from the other anthropological foundation Freud identified, that is, the necessity to labor in concert. Love, too, builds civilization, but only in the guise of male desire. Men's sensual love leads them to find a mate and create new families, while their "aim-inhibited love" devotes itself to the whole range of sublimated attachments from friendships to a devotion to cultural or ethical ideals. Male desire divides, to use Eve Kosofsky Sedgwick's terms, into its homosocial and its heterosexual forms.[12] Freud credits both with enhancing civilization. Women's maternal love, however, hardly leads them further into civilization than their participation in the heterosexual couple; maternal love is otherwise what puts the family "in opposition to civilization," since it cements the family attachments that discourage family members from venturing "into the wider circle of life." In Freud's view, the evolution of civilization has steadily sharpened the sexual division of labor; men have become ever more extensively and exclusively preoccupied with civilization rather than family. "Thus the woman finds herself," Freud proclaims, "forced into the background by the claims of civilization and she adopts a hostile attitude towards it."[13]

Freud's mapping of the differentiation of family and civil society and their interaction is thus complete. He attributes the building of civilization to male homosocial desire; he attributes the civilizing reproduction of families to the combined power of male heterosexual desire and maternal love; and he attributes the conflict between family and civil society to the "retarding and restraining influence" of maternal love alone.

The libidinal economy of the family and civil society also turns out to trace the ideal path of male socialization. The son at first lives wholly within "the mode of life which is phylogenetically the older" to which he is attached by the bonds of maternal love. Growth will follow a trajectory beyond these bonds, as the little boy, under the pressure of the father's authority within the family circle itself, undergoes the splitting of his love into the homosocial and the heterosexual and, finally, under the impact of his complete individuation, becomes suited for vocation and marriage, that is, the roles which civil society and the family, respectively, demand of him. The cluster of childhood experiences that Freud considered crucial to the realization of this ideal defines the so-called positive Oedipus complex and its dissolution.

From the standpoint of Freud's intellectual career, these various mappings—civil society and family; male socialization; Oedipus—came in a particular chronological order. Oedipal theory emerged first, though fragmentedly and slowly, and with it a tacit model of male socialization, and then later Freud applied the model in works like *Civilization and Its Discontents* to society writ large. But the primacy accorded the psychological concepts is deceiving. As Schorske's interpretation suggests, Freud forged the initial psychoanalytic categories out of the political experiences of his generation as they impinged on his own social aspirations and vocation. And, as Pateman's interpretation suggests, a whole tradition of political thought furnishes the impetus and terms of Freud's conceptualization of the family as well as the distillation of gender roles which underpins psychoanalytic theory. Freud is caught up in that political discourse's imperatives from the outset, in particular the imperative of explaining and justifying the specifically modern form of patriarchy. It makes some sense, therefore, to consider Freud's thought a social thinking that was always shuttling back and forth between his mappings of civil society and the family and his mappings of the Oedipus complex.

These mappings suggest a way of looking at the kind of life-history that becomes exemplary for psychoanalysis without, however, taking up the psychoanalyst's own starting-point in the clinical picture presented by that life-history. Rather than starting with the symptoms, enumerated and categorized through the therapist's medicalized lens, let us use the Freudian map to ask, instead: What are the crises, the stumbling-blocks, the sources of suffering, that create this life-history's unsolved problems and unfinished tasks? The question is certainly relevant to Freud's self-analysis and his case history of the Rat Man, both of which contributed so crucially to the making of Oedipal theory.

Like Freud, the Rat Man was the son of a businessman who had made the great transition from rural life in a Jewish village to secular, commercial life in the city. The sons did not follow their fathers' footsteps into commerce, but pursued professions. Neither Freud's father nor the Rat

Man's reproduced his own religious upbringing in his son's life. Another son who had experienced how this generational divide made it impossible for the shape of his own life to equal his father's wrote: "It was much the same with a large section of this transitional generation of Jews, which had migrated from the still comparatively devout countryside to the cities. It happened automatically; only it added to our relationship, which certainly did not lack in acrimony, one more sufficiently painful source."[14] Like Freud and the Rat Man, this beleaguered son, a contemporary of the Rat Man's, was a child of the Habsburg empire. I have quoted from Franz Kafka's "Letter to His Father." For Kafka as for Freud and the Rat Man, the watersheds of maturity were *vocation*, science for Freud and law for the Rat Man and Kafka, and *marriage*. Like the Rat Man, Kafka faltered at both. His sparsely narrated life-history discloses the pressures that shape or interrupt or distort the path of male socialization as it traverses and connects the social spaces of family and civil society.

Kafka's "Letter to His Father" was written in 1919 when he was 36. It was never delivered, except to his mother. The letter painfully and painstakingly reveals how the son's response to his father's authority, marriage and vocation snuffed out his own capacity to value a vocation and ruined his own plans to marry. Kafka had been stopped dead in his tracks on the path of socialization. "I fled everything that even remotely reminded me of you," he writes. "First, the business."[15] He had acquired a double perception of his father's vocation, corresponding to the two-sided role of the dry goods wholesaler: he was an *entrepreneur* whose "magnificent commercial talents" and decisiveness his son admired, and he was the *employer* who despised and terrorized his employees, "shouting, cursing, and raging in the shop." Young Kafka acquired a sense of injustice at the store, but at the same moment his impulse to rebel in the name of justice was destroyed:

> You called the employees "paid enemies," and that is what they were, but even before they became that, you seemed to me to be their "paying enemy." There, too, I learned the great lesson you could be unjust; in my own case I would not have noticed it so soon, for there was much accumulated sense of guilt in me ready to admit that you were right. . . . it made the business insufferable to me, reminding me far too much of my relations with you.[16]

In becoming the imaginary class enemy of his father, he lost his hold on business as vocation; yet, confronted with a tyrant whose paternal recognition he nonetheless craved, he did not rebel but merely became ever more convinced of his own inadequacy: "you must, as I assumed, in the same way be forever dissatisfied with me too."[17]

Cut off from any expectation of his father's approval, he let his schoolwork and then his own choice of vocation become "a matter of indifference to me." "And so it was a matter of finding," he wrote, "a profession that would let me indulge this indifference without injuring my vanity too much. Law was the obvious choice."[18] Kafka's devotion to the law as vocation never got beyond his undistinguished position in the bureaucracy of a workers' insurance company.

While Kafka managed in his vocation to balance his indifference to social achievement against his remaining shreds of bourgeois self-esteem, he attained no such heights when it came to his marriage plans. His broken engagements to Felice Bauer, twice, and to Milena Jesenska were catastrophic proof of his failing at life. Marriage possessed a supreme value for Kafka: "Marrying, founding a family, accepting all the children that come, supporting them in this insecure world and perhaps even guiding them a little, is, I am convinced, the utmost a human being can succeed in doing."[19] This valuation led Kafka to desire and fear marriage with equal intensity.

Although his father had undermined the engagements by belittling the women Kafka chose and mocking Kafka's feeling for them, he does not blame his failings on the father's opposition. Instead, he uncovers a paradox in his own desires and aspirations, as they are mediated through his esteem for his father. For when he let himself imagine becoming a husband, it not only gratified a cultural ideal but also held out the utopian prospect of achieving parity with his father:

> I picture this equality which would then arise between us . . . as so beautiful because then I could be a free, grateful, guiltless, upright son, and you could be an untroubled, untyrannical, sympathetic, contented father.[20]

But "so much cannot be achieved," he laments, and dismisses his vision as a "fairy tale." He does not, however, then cast off this utopian expectation. On the contrary, he lets marriage recede beyond his reach because the equality of father and son seems unattainable. Why should he arrive at this bitter and yet absurd impasse? In part, of course, because of his virtually inexplicable lack of rebelliousness. But his own explanation looks elsewhere.

The uncanny lucidity characteristic of the "Letter to His Father" deserts Kafka when he turns to explain why the aspiration to be like his father has ultimately ruined the marriage plan which would indeed make him like his father:

> marrying is barred to me because it is your very own domain. . . . In your marriage I had before me what was, in many ways, a model marriage, a model in constancy, mutual help, number of children; and even when the children grew up and increasingly disturbed the peace, the marriage as such remained undisturbed. Perhaps I formed my high idea of marriage on this model: the desire for marriage was powerless for other reasons. Those lay in your relation to your children, which is, after all, what this whole letter is about.[21]

This passage does not gel with all that one gleans about the marriage from the "Letter to His Father" as well as Kafka's diaries and letters. All these virtues of constancy and helpfulness, as well as the burdens of the family's size and of restoring the peace the children disturbed, were the hallmarks not of the marriage but of Kafka's mother.

His attitude toward her adherence to these virtues, however, was hardly affirmative. A few pages earlier he saw in her kindness and desire for harmony the very instrument that destroyed his own ability to rebel against his father. Addressing his father the harsh disciplinarian, he wrote:

> Even if your method of upbringing might in some unlikely case have set me on my own feet by means of producing defiance, dislike, or even hate in me, Mother canceled that out again by kindness, by talking sensibly . . . , by pleading for me; and I was driven back into your orbit.[22]

Kafka achieves his idealization of marriage by taking those traits of his parents' marriage which he inadvertently reveals are his mother's contribution and attributing them to his father's power. His identification with his father and his valorization of the role of husband originate precisely in his admiration for his father's power. The father's rule is what makes him, rather than the mother, the author of the marriage. Kafka identifies with his father *in his power.* "When the primal horde gives way to kinship and marriage," Pateman remarks, "the father's legacy of sex-right is shared equally among all the brothers." It is this legacy of sex-right that Kafka covets, but he cowers at the thought of exercising it because he fears his real-life father. Lacan is certainly right to trace Oedipal pathologies to the dissonance the son experiences in apprehending his father as both a real-life individual like himself (a potential equal) *and* the representative of fatherhood itself. What is missing in Lacan, however, is the sense, so vivid here, that this very discrepancy feeds on the real-life father's double role as head of the household, where his sex-right *is* the basis of his tyranny, and as the bourgeois or citizen whom the son might encounter as an equal. It is his real-life power in the private sphere that supports his symbolic function. The patriarchal tyranny Kafka fled in the dry goods store he craves in his ideal of marriage. There is nothing paradoxical in this. Marriage promises him a masculinity and power like his father's—until he renounces it as a fairy tale that his own weakness does not permit him to hope for. The pathologies of the Oedipus complex are pathologies of patriarchal power.

Woven into the life-histories Freud typically encountered was the dense web of social relationships in which the family and its members participate. From these social relationships, Freud distilled the Oedipal triangle. He eschewed the questions of gender, community and power at play in the family and its links to civil society and the polis. They became, at most, the back-lighting of the Oedipal scene. Faced with the typical pathologies of modernity, the stumbling-blocks and unsolved problems in men's and women's life-histories, Freud looked through the medical lens to define symptomatologies solely with reference to the individual as an organism, never as participant in social and political relations.

Social and political relations are regulated by norms, and they require justifications and often evoke challenges. Freud's medicalizing, psychologizing stance apparently sidestepped the thorny problem of legitimating or criticizing norms and practices. Nevertheless, the clinical terrain he marked out itself still needed some kind of normative order against which to read the individual psyche's symptoms. What would a non-pathological outcome of the Oedipus complex really look like? Just as Freud's account of Oedipal pathologies diverted the elements of social diagnosis and cultural critique into a purely psychological symptomatology, he responded to the need to imagine a resolution or healing of Oedipal pathologies by projecting a psychological norm: a *dissolution* of the Oedipus complex.

This concept was not, however, readily available to Freud. It had to be wrenched from a confusing array of clinical experiences. Moreover, I am suggesting that this search for a psychological norm tacitly forced Freud to register the social and political relationships at play in the formation of the Oedipus complex. He therefore continued to refine Oedipal theory until it yielded a coherent conception of the dissolution as well as the formation of the Oedipus complex. The story of the pathogenic family drama had to be matched with a story of the individual male's resolution of its conflicts. It was not until *The Ego and the Id* (1923) and "The Dissolution of the Oedipus Complex" (1924) that Freud found an adequate formulation for the Oedipus complex's resolution, even though he had steadily pushed the Oedipus complex to the center of his theory of neurosis for two decades, gradually universalizing its role in psychosexual development.

As it turns out, the dissolution of the Oedipus complex—as opposed to its merely more or less unsuccessful repression—requires, first, that it be initially formed along the lines of the "simple positive Oedipus complex," that is, in the heterosexual form where the little boy has an erotic attachment to his mother and a (desexualized) identification with his father. Freud had in fact come to the conclusion that "a strong innate bisexual disposition becomes one of the preconditions or reinforcements of neurosis."[23] Lacking a notion of what Adrienne Rich calls *compulsory heterosexuality,* Freud misses the political interpretation this hypothesis suggests.[24] The simple positive Oedipus complex enjoys a privilege by virtue of the fact that it lies on the path to male-dominated heterosexuality: its every manifestation and nuance is socially validated and rewarded. The *normative outcome* it promises is nothing more than the *coercive appeal* it holds in an overwhelmingly homophobic and male-dominated lifeworld.

Once the Oedipus complex is appropriately formed, it can then be utterly dissolved, without any repressed residue, only if the son's rivalrous hatred of his father and his erotic attachment to his mother each end in a particular way. As regards the father, the route for the son to follow is already laid down by the heterosexual imperative. "What makes hatred of the father unacceptable is *fear* of the father; castration is terrible, whether as a punishment or as the price of love. Of the two factors which repress hatred of the father," Freud writes in "Dostoevsky and Parricide," "the first, the direct fear of punishment and castration, may be called the normal one; its pathogenic intensification seems to come only with the addition of the second factor, the fear of the feminine attitude."[25] As regards the mother in the simple positive Oedipus complex, the son's fear of castration is the motive for abandoning his erotic attachment. But what then is the fate of this love?

> Its place may be filled by one of two things: either an identification with his mother or an intensification of his identification with his father. We are accustomed to regard the latter outcome as the more normal; it permits the affectionate relation to the mother to be in a measure retained. In this way the dissolution of the Oedipus complex would consolidate the masculinity in a boy's character.[26]

Here then is Freud's real man. He is required, in sum, to have a weak bisexual disposition; he should abandon his hatred of his father out of fear rather than love; and, when he abandons his love for his mother in the face of the father's castration threats, he should end up identifying less with her than him. The only reassurance here is that, according to Freud, few ever attain this ideal!

The castration complex is the key to each moment of this ideal progress. But it is hard to see exactly how the castration complex can work very well in practice when it is so confused in theory. Lacanianism's elaborate distinction between the penis and phallus notwithstanding, the Freudian castration complex amounts to the notion that children's understanding of sexual difference comes down to their perception—judgment really—of having-a-penis-or-not. Freud's greater stress on bisexuality in the finalized version of Oedipal theory does not ultimately mitigate against this phallocentrism, since it is accompanied by his unwavering reference to the so-called "anatomical difference of the sexes." In fact, bisexuality and having-a-penis-or-not are closely linked concepts in the later Freud.

By bisexuality Freud sometimes meant that children's erotic wishes and love could be directed at men and boys or women and girls, and he sometimes meant that gratification could come through either active or passive aims (seeing/being seen, swallowing/being swallowed and so forth). In taking these senses of bisexuality into Oedipal theory, Freud introduced two questionable assumptions. First, he regards an "active" sexual aim as *masculine* (or inevitably or completely encoded as *masculine*), while a "passive" sexual aim is *feminine* (or is inevitably or completely encoded as *feminine*). Second, he believes the male child is constrained to picture himself in an *active* and hence *masculine* role with his mother, and a *passive* and hence *feminine* role with his father. Add to this that both *active/passive* and *masculine/feminine* are deemed to straightforwardly correspond to having-a-penis-or-not, and the apparently radical notion of innate bisexuality is completely assimilated to the whole Oedipal regime of compulsory heterosexuality and male dominance.

The phallic equations are in fact all that Freud has to make sense of the simple positive Oedipus complex, its formation and dissolution. Consider the fear of castration associated with the little boy's erotic attachment to his father, that is, the notion that he discovers that he would have to lose his penis to have intercourse with his father: since *father = masculine = active,* he himself would therefore become *passive = feminine = castrated.* Inversely, the consequence of having intercourse with his mother would be a punishment in the form of losing his penis, since *mother = passive = castrated,* making him *active = masculine = having-a-penis.*

All the basic equations are anchored in having-a-penis-or-not. But by Freud's own accounts the requisite "recognition" of castration, that is, the judgment that the "one thing" that makes women different from men is that they do not have a penis, is acquired only very late in the socialization process. If that is the case, then the elaborate emotional, libidinal relationships the child has with his mother and father, with other adults male and female, with other children, are obviously webs of passive and active erotic aims that have not been divvied up according to the phallic equations.

In a culture which produces images, symbols, narratives, jokes and slogans laden with these phallic equations, it is surely safe to assume that their impact will be crucially a part of male socialization, perhaps congealing in a more or less dramatic way in certain experiences or crises. But what is that impact? Freud's emergent ideal of male socialization—that is, the positively formed, completely dissolved Oedipus complex—would suggest that the impact of the phallic equations is mental health itself. This precisely ignores their belatedness and inadequacy in representing the wealth of relationships in which the child has participated. The phallic equations have to recode, and recalibrate, the intricacies of passive and active sexual aims, the love for same-sex and different-sex playmates, parents, relatives. Wouldn't it make more sense to expect the reign of the phallic equations to be a kind of catastrophe that befalls the layers of uncertain, remembered, ill-named experience? Contrary to Freud's hypothesis, shouldn't we suspect that the acceptance of phallocentrism delivers such a blow to the weave of passivity and activity that you can fall ill?

Freud's definition of health has to be turned upside down. What is pathogenic is the inadequacy of the simple positive Oedipus complex to represent erotic and emotional life. It is not merely a theoretical misrepresentation. When Freud suggests that the simple positive Oedipus complex "represents a simplification or schematization,"[27] he inadvertently points up the crucial unsolved question. For this is at once a theoretical and a social schematization.

The simple positive Oedipus complex is a social schematization in the sense that it is the distilled form of the models, directives, stories, values and so on through which our society tells the male child that he must grow up to be masculine and heterosexual in the ways valued by that society. The culture furnishes individuals with a construct for interpreting their relationships in keeping with the norms of compulsory heterosexuality and male dominance. This construct is the Oedipus complex viewed as a social schematization of experience, a disposition, a structure of feeling. The norms embodied in this construct are not the equivalent of the incest taboo; they operate a particular code upon it: I must not want my Father, *because* he is a man. I must not want my Mother, *because* she *belongs* to my Father. I look beyond loving my Mother out of fear rather than identification. I identify with my Father rather than my Mother because I aspire to his power. I identify with him rather than wanting to love him because I aspire to masculinity.

As a theoretical schematization, the simple positive Oedipus complex simplifies the child's multifarious attachments to this one heterosexual drama in an attempt to explain how the so-called bisexual male child, filled with contradictory ideas about the salient differences between his parents, uncertain of his own or others' gender and, *pace* Freud, rife with passive and active sexual aims toward both parents, reemerges on the other side of latency and adolescence merely a more or less neurotic heterosexual. The theoretical schematization plainly fails in this task. Even when Freud declared that the ideal was seldom if ever attained, he did not reinterrogate its claim to normativity but simply retreated to his theme that the undifferentiated process of civilization exacts impossible demands on the human organism.

Since Freud does not see that the Oedipal structure of feeling derives from specific social practices and cultural forms—compulsory heterosexuality, male dominance, patriarchal symbols, male fantasy—he does not acknowledge that the norms embodied in this structure are in need of moral-political justification. Nor of course does he acknowledge that those norms, particularly the phallic equations, are open to challenge. Even though the Oedipal schematization anchors an entire process of socialization and individuation, it appears to Freud beyond the pale of political reflection. He does, however, tacitly acknowledge that the phallic equations require a theoretical explanation. For they have to come from somewhere. Freud responds by producing another round of origin stories. I refer now not to the primal horde but to the primal scene. Following a pattern we have seen before, Freud's effort to furnish a theoretical explanation for an apparently psychological question will lead him covertly to engage the moral-political justifications used to legitimate specific social and cultural practices.

Freud gave his fullest account of primal scenes in the context of postulating that they most typically were not memories of actual events but rather fantasies whose "psychical reality" was just as decisive as it would be if they also had a "material reality." Freud enumerates the most prominent of these fantasies "in the youthful history of neurotics" as follows: "observation of parental intercourse, seduction by an adult and threat of being castrated."[28] The seduction scenes are most closely associated with Freud's women patients. When he decided to discount the stories he had been told early in his career by young women who had been molested in their childhood, usually by their fathers, he recast actual manifestations of abusive father-right into the Oedipal fantasy of girls' longing to marry their fathers. Male dominance became a female fantasy, but for that very reason all the more "real" in the sense of "psychical reality," and all the more legitimate and justified in social reality for being no longer an actual father's crime.

The primal scene of parental intercourse and the threat of castration, on the other hand, are the necessary props to the male Oedipus complex. The primal scene presents the child with a view of sexual intercourse in which the *father* is *active* and the *mother* is *passive*. Freud never wavers from his conviction that this is exactly how the child comprehends the sexual act. In fact, it goes beyond *active/passive*. The father performs an act of aggression against the mother. The primal scene is a rape. The phallic equation *father = masculine = active* is linked to an act of domination. The subjection of women is folded into the culturally validated representation of masculinity and its power.

According to the Freudian scenario, the father's violence next turns threateningly on the male child himself in the primal threats of castration. Because Freud always construes castration in terms of anatomy, he misses the fact, as feminists as varied as Simone de Beauvoir, Juliet Mitchell and Luce Irigaray have demonstrated, that having-a-penis acquires its special value because it "stands for" something valuable: prestige, privilege, power, property and so on. By the same token, the reason these goods get symbolized by *having-a-penis* is because they are monopolized by men. In having recourse to the anatomical distinction of the sexes, Freud hides and naturalizes this nexus of social relations between men and women.

There is another striking feature of the primal scenes. Unlike the seduction scenes, which were reported as actual events but construed by Freud as fantasies, the primal scenes of parental intercourse and castration threats were seldom remembered at all. In fact, his patients did not advance them as memories *or* as fantasies. Wherever Freud delved into a scene of parental intercourse it was inevitably because he was pressing this vision of the sexual act on his patient as a "construction."[29] The fact that these constructions frequently proved efficacious in the therapy, clarifying the vicissitudes of the patient's symptoms and development, bolstered Freud in his conviction that these "events" were the product of the patient's unconscious memory or fantasy.

There is, I believe, a more viable hypothesis to account for why Freud's constructions were so compelling. The primal scenes provide an origin for the psychic representation of the phallic equations, *masculine = active, feminine = passive.* Masculinity is fused with images of female subordination and male sexual dominance. These representations, I have argued, do not arrive at an appointed hour in the socialization process. They seep into it through the cultural forms the individual takes up to interpret and norm his desires and his identity. They are certainly not full-blown representations in infantile experience at all. They always arrive belatedly, sometimes catastrophically.

From the standpoint of the therapy's progress, the primal scenes supply the missing representation that links infantile with adult sexuality. From the standpoint of the individual's psychosexual development, they crystalize the cultural forms that have recoded remembered and fantasized experience retrospectively, on the model of the *Nachträglichkeit,* the delayed effect or retrodetermination. From the standpoint of the lifeworld, the primal scenes are a stylization of the structure of feeling that continually links the individual's life-history and the social-symbolic world he inhabits.

Freud's construction of these primal scenes plays the same role for the patient in therapy as the social contract story plays in politics. It represents the several elements of complex social relationships as though they were all created in a single action whose intentions and meanings it renders intelligible. An existing state of affairs is illuminated as though from the inside, aglow with coherence and purposiveness. But just there is the fatal flaw of origin stories and primal scenes. Their extraordinary power to justify—or criticize—some lived set of social and political relationships is purchased at a great cost in historical understanding.

Pateman offers an interpretation of the Freudian primal scene that unveils its social and political significance. The representation of parental intercourse as rape reflects the deep-seated ambiguity that political, legal and cultural norms have created regarding women's consent in sexual activity and in political activity. The child's fantasy flourishes in the politically significant zone of ambiguity where "there is widespread lack of ability to understand what consensual intercourse is."[30] In the politically structured relations of men and women, coerciveness is blended into ostensibly consensual interactions.

Pateman's critical reassessment of the social contract stories itself runs up against some of the same limits as the Freudian primal scene. The ambiguities and unanswered questions created by her appropriation of origin stories deserve reflection. Pateman's mapping of the family and civil society identifies the salient components in that complex of social and political relationships which she aptly calls modern patriarchal society: (1) Private and public spheres are separated according to gender. (2) Women are excluded from participation in civil society and are subordinated within its various institutions. (3) Masculine sex-right underlies and sustains the husband-father's real power within the family. The origin story Pateman deconstructs and reconstructs represents these various elements as though they were created by a single set of actions. They thereby become somehow more intelligible, grasped in a bold single stroke, but this newfound intelligibility raises other questions.

When Pateman takes over the Freudian primal scene to represent the origins of male sex-right and paternal power, she ends up having to puzzle out a new mystery. For she is led to ask, Did men subjugate women at the origin for the sake of sexual possession and power or in order to create and control offspring? Pateman endorses the former position but to make good on her choice she is driven to draw on the speculative excesses of Gregory Zilboorg:

> Mother-right was overthrown when, "one day [a man] became sufficiently conscious and sure of his strength to overpower the woman, to rape her." Taking issue with all the stories in which men's discovery of paternity is the driving force that institutes the patriarchal family and civilization,

> Zilboorg speculates that the primordial deed had nothing to do with paternity; "the act was not that of love and of anticipated fatherhood, nor of tender solicitude. . . . It was an assault. . . . It was a phallic, sadistic act."
>
> Zilboorg argues that the original deed was prompted purely by "the need to possess and master." The subjugation of women provided the example required to enable men to extend their possession and mastery beyond their immediate needs.[31]

Here is the problem: there are no grounds for accepting this interpretation over the alternative. Moreover, like all origin stories, Pateman's has to presuppose one of the things it had to explain. In projecting that men in the beginning took sexual possession of women for the sake of dominance, the story presupposes heterosexuality. But compulsory heterosexuality is another element of our current social order in need of illumination and critique.

And, finally, the origins of the politically structured confusion of consent and coercion are pictured as a purely coercive act performed by a male agent on a female victim; at the origin of the confusions over consent and coercion there is no confusion of consent and coercion, because the origin story expunges all forms of consent. It thereby fails to explain the very thing it was designed to explain. Moreover, women's agency, including their long history of resistance and opposition to male dominance, has no place in the representation itself. There is no female agency on the scene where women are said, primordially, to participate. The supposed scene of political origins is "over there" where female agency does not exist; consequently, women's agency in the sense of a feminist politics devoted to overcoming coercion and remaking consent remains unrepresented at the origins.

The radical-feminist gesture Pateman deploys goes insightfully to the root of modern patriarchal society, enumerating the many-sided forms of female subordination in modern social and political institutions. But in simultaneously setting up its critical standpoint outside the structures it criticizes, it loses touch with the actual processes of political change. Pateman sets radical critique against liberal critique, rather than looking to extend the liberal critique in the radical:

> The history of liberal feminism is the history of the attempts to generalize liberal liberties and rights to the whole adult population; but liberal feminism does not, and cannot, come to grips with the deeper problem of *how* women are to take an equal place in the patriarchal civil order.

> Now that the feminist struggle has reached the point where women are almost formal civil equals, the opposition is highlighted between equality made after a male image and the real social position of women *as women.*[32]

Such a thesis overstates the completedness of the liberal project and so underestimates its continuing relevance. Moreover, it does not fully appreciate how radical feminism builds upon the political gains of liberal feminism. Historically, it has been the panoply of reforms in women's political rights and economic roles and in the penetration of civil and criminal law into the male-dominated household that has *enabled* a critique of the gendered division of social and political space. We must be prepared to radicalize reforms and rights rather than transcend them.

Pateman is right to open a new path of political criticism by interrogating the mapping of society derived from social contract theory. Accordingly, the division of public and private on the axis of "civil society" and the "family" becomes for her the decisive terrain for a critique designed to cut to the bone of the social structure. However, Pateman too often slides into the view that the mapping and critique she develops produce the only politically relevant conception of civil society. While it is the mission of radical critique to go to the root, as Pateman surely does in showing how sex oppression pervades modern political life, the inequalities and injustices of contemporary societies have more than one root. Radical critique always needs to guard against projecting a single explanation of oppression and injustice. Put another way, there are *politically relevant* criticisms of our society's institutions which require other mappings, different conceptions of civil society and other avenues of critique.

7

Family Histories

WHEN CAROL PATEMAN sets forth the sense of civil society she deems relevant to feminism, she brushes aside an important alternative. This other mapping of modern society was developed by Hegel and distinguishes private and public on the axis of civil society and the state. While the Hegelian mapping may well obscure the path of feminist critique, it has at the same time illuminated the way for significant critiques of state socialism, on the one hand, and of the impact of imperialism on non-Western societies, on the other.

Should civil society be defined in opposition to the family or in opposition to the state? Pateman has no doubts that the force of the first definition has been in the course of Western political history the more relevant for the issues that concern feminism. In the following passage, she gives a cogent account of the alternatives, while asserting her thesis on behalf of understanding civil society as the public realm set off against the private realm of the family:

> The meaning of "civil society" in the contract stories, and as I am using it here, is constituted through the "original" separation and opposition between the modern, public—civil—world and the modern, private or conjugal and familial sphere: that is, in the new social world created through contract, everything that lies beyond the domestic (private) sphere is public, or "civil," society. Feminists are concerned with *this* division. In contrast, most discussions of civil society and such formulations as "public" regulation versus "private" enterprise presuppose that the politically relevant separation between public and private is drawn *within* "civil society" as constructed in the social contract stories. That is to say,

> "civil society" has come to be used in a meaning closer to that of Hegel, the social contract theorists' greatest critic, who contrasts the universal, public state with the market, classes and corporations of private, civil society.
>
> Hegel, of course, presents a threefold division between family, civil society, state—but the separation between the family and the rest of social life is invariably "forgotten" in arguments about civil society. The shift in meaning of "civil," "public" and "private" goes unnoticed because the "original" creation of civil society through the social contract is a patriarchal construction which is also a separation of the sexes.[1]

The risks of taking the origin story literally are apparent in the last sentence of this passage. Despite the scare-quotes in the phrase "'original' creation of civil society," the separation of public and private which social contract theory *represents* at the origin of society is taken by Pateman to really be the basis of modern society. But in fact the many-layered social and political relationships that make up the fabric of modern society were not invented whole cloth from just one set of inequalities.

It is true that social contract theory tells a powerful story about the political equality among men by disguising the political oppression of women, and it is true that it simultaneously tries to map the whole of social and political relationships on the public/private, civil society/family axis. Pateman's immanent critique of this mapping yields a rich vocabulary of feminist political criticism, but the Hegelian model of *civil society, family* and *state* has proved fruitful as well. On the one hand, the threefold distinction points up that the market, the household and the polis are not ruled by identical norms. And, on the other hand, the Hegelian mapping has itself been the object of immanent critiques that yield yet other valuable vocabularies of political criticism.

I now want to turn to a recent example of such an immanent critique. It will turn out to bear very directly on Freud and Pateman, even though its own immediate aim is to contest the imposition of Western political thought on non-Western societies. Partha Chatterjee has argued that when Hegel mapped the forms and institutions of social life he was intent on eradicating or subordinating any reference to *community* in the sense of the various forms of ethnic, religious or regional belonging that were in fact powerful aspects of social identity in 19th century Europe. The market called for separated individuals who would act in their own self-interest;

the modern nation-state called for subjects and citizens whose loyalty to the state superseded all other group solidarities. "Civil society," writes Chatterjee, "now became the space for the diverse life of individuals in the nation: the state became the nation's singular representative embodiment, the only legitimate form of community"[2]—or, more precisely, I think, the *overriding* form of community.

The imperatives of capitalist development set about to destroy the forms of "pre-capitalist community which, in various forms, had regulated the social unity of laborers with their means of production." What Marx called the "primitive accumulation" of capital set in motion the real destruction of communities and along with it an ideological revaluation that relegated community to the prehistory of capital, indeed, to the prehistory of modern times in general, and identified it "with medievalism in Europe and the stagnant, backward, undeveloped present in the rest of the world."[3] The "particularism" of community and communal identity henceforth appears regressive from the vantage of progressive European social thought.

However, capitalism meanwhile remained, "notwithstanding its universalist scope, . . . parasitic upon the reconstructed particularism of the nation."[4] The nation-state commanded a kind of loyalty that drew on the need for community, while the market gave root to individualistic self-interest. National identity fed on people's subjective capacity for shared feelings and mutual belonging. The market honed their individualism. In Chatterjee's view, nation and capital, polis and market, together set in motion the destruction of community.

Community was never really obliterated, of course, as the upheavals today from Yugoslavia to Central Asia attest. Chatterjee's point is that Western political institutions and forms of political identity are so individualistic and so linked to the "narrative of capital" that they have utterly failed to accommodate communities and forms of communal identity within a meaningful vision of justice, right and participation. Moreover, imperialism and neo-imperialism have imposed this European model on societies the world over under the fraudulent banner of universalism. The potential for "people, living in different, contextually defined communities [to] coexist peacefully, productively and creatively within large political units" in countries like Nigeria or India cannot be realized according to Chatterjee on the Western model of individualism and nationalism.[5]

On its own local terrain European political thought had to struggle with the survival of forms of community that did not readily boil down in the cauldron of the market and the state. Chatterjee suggestively, and insightfully, reads Hegel as devising a strategy for containing and overcoming the demands of community. Those attributes of community which are not absorbed into the nation-state Hegel sloughs off onto his account of *family*.

Consider Hegel's reflection on the meaning of family and love in the *Philosophy of Right* at just the point where he is concerned to establish the qualitative and unbridgeable distinction between the family and the state. The family achieves unity through the feeling of love, which is "ethical life in the form of something natural," in contradistinction to the state, in which "we are conscious of unity as law":

> Love means in general terms the consciousness of my unity with another, so that I am not in selfish isolation but win my self-consciousness only as the renunciation of my independence and through knowing myself as the unity of myself with another and of the other with me. . . . The first moment in love is that I do not wish to be a self-subsistent and independent person and that, if I were, then I would feel defective and incomplete. The second moment is that I find myself in another person, that I count for something in the other, while the other in turn comes to count for something in me. . . . Love is at once the propounding and the resolving of this contradiction. As the resolving of it, love is unity of an ethical type.
>
> The right of the family consists in the fact that its substantiality should have determinate existence. Thus it is a right against externality and against secessions from the family unity.[6]

Chatterjee reads here a deflected narrative of community. "Hegel's arguments on the family remind us," he writes, "of the irreducible immediacy in which human beings are born in society: not as pure unattached individuals free to choose their social affiliations (whether gender, ethnicity or class) but as already-ascribed members of society." He also notes the deep resemblance between Hegel's rhetoric and that "in which, even in this age of the triumph of individualism, all movements which appeal to the 'natural' solidarity of community speak. They claim precisely the right against externality and secession, they seek determinate existence precisely in 'property' and 'representation' through collectively recognized heads, they speak in the language of love and of self-recognition through the free surrender of individual will to others in the community."[7]

Freud's intellectual inheritance includes just this tendency to eradicate community from the mapping of society. The Hegelian topography of civil society, family and state reduced the relevant sites of social life to the market, the household and the polis. The values and attributes associated with community had to be absorbed either into the family or the state; failing that, they had simply to be suppressed. This pattern of thinking Freud shared with Hegel and a whole tradition of social thought from Marx to Max Weber and Georg Simmel.

But the deflection of what Chatterjee calls the "narrative of community" into the narrative of family was not merely an intellectual exercise. For it is also true that the bourgeois family inherited many of the norms and habits, feelings and needs, that had previously structured the religious, ethnic and regional communities which were breaking up, dispersing, migrating throughout the 19th century. The family was in reality as well as ideology a deflected site of communal identities and desires. The bourgeois household was a complex social space. Its inner relationships were determined by its material and symbolic relation to the market and the polis and also, more covertly, to community.

The liberal ideals of the 19th century foresaw a social world in which *men* were offered precise forms of individuality matched to the market, the family and the polis: namely, the identities of owner, husband-father and citizen (or citizen-subject). Liberalism envisioned a stable society whose institutions would centrally serve the realization of just these roles. The decades that stretch from Freud's birth to his major intellectual crises and theoretical innovations span the period during which Austro-Hungarian liberalism first flourished and triumphed and then floundered and shattered.

In 1857, the year after Freud's birth, Austro-Hungarian liberals unveiled their plan to rebuild Vienna. Streets, buildings and parks would fill the massive ring that had always separated the walled city of feudal, dynastic, Catholic Vienna from the suburbs where the lower classes were amassing. As Schorske shows in his study of the Ringstrasse, the liberals projected their ideal self-image into the new architecture and public spaces. The Ringstrasse was a secular city, a large-scale enterprise, a seat of national government, a center of education and the arts. The new Vienna rose up in the very buildings that housed its institutions of democracy, culture and rational administration.

The liberals built their political identity, including their ideals of citizenship, on their expectation that the individual, the male individual, would find fulfillment in his roles as owner, father and citizen. From the 1860s until the 1890s, Austro-Hungarian liberalism thrived on this set of assumptions and expectations. Social and political progress was envisioned as a peaceful process. The liberals, Germanic and bourgeois, believed their own ideals would be the model and beacon for the other nationalities and the other classes whom they expected to adopt this same style of citizenship and this same cultural identity on the way to becoming fuller partners in the civic enterprise.[8]

The expectations proved illusory and shattered in the 1890s. Not only did liberalism never fully liberate the polis from the crown and the Church, but its reforms failed to preempt class conflicts, nationalist and ethnic upheavals or the rise of right-wing Christian Socialism. When Karl Lueger led his Christian Socialist party to victory in Vienna on an anti-Semitic platform in 1895, liberal ideology was left in shambles. The ideological and political program that had progressed so far in remapping society on the model of civil society, the family and the state was in crisis.

Austro-Hungarian liberals, including Freud, had to face up to the recognition that the polis they had so assiduously helped to construct was in fact distorted and increasingly fragile. They also faced the fear that their vision of inevitable political equality and social harmony was mere illusion. How should they respond to the unhinging of the political identity that had anchored the liberal bourgeoisie's sense of its mission and of the future? Central European intellectuals—writers, social theorists, psychoanalysts—would in the next few decades attempt to comprehend the confusing pattern of change that had overthrown the cherished ideals of progress.

Freud, in my view, had inherited, and deeply adhered to, the ideal of individual self-realization that was generally the product of liberal and socialist thinking. The training for citizenship was to hinge, as we have already seen, on the achievements of vocation and marriage. Modern liberal political identity enabled, and reciprocally was reinforced by, men's undisturbed participation in their roles in the market and the family, their autonomous freedom in the market-mediated relations of a capitalist economy and their autocratic power within the household they headed. Citizenship, of course, is never merely a question of the individual's qualities or accomplishments; it also requires political foundations. The polis is not, as the ideal image suggests, the open yet protected space in which all the city's dwellers may gather to debate, deliberate and decide. It is distorted, a space of uneven participation, a structurally distorted space of unequal participation.

The crises that threw into doubt the ability of Austro-Hungarian liberals to master this political space challenged Freud to make an intellectual and professional response. I do not disagree with Schorske's conclusion that with Oedipal theory "Freud gave his fellow liberals an a-historical theory of man and society that could make bearable a political world spun out of orbit and beyond control."[9] But psychoanalytic theory and practice more actively sought to relocate an arena of mastery. Freud did not choose the family or the household as this arena; he chose, rather, the individual's *representations* of family relationships. His encounters with the autocratic power of fathers and the traumatic illnesses of their daughters had not only led him into crisis over the seduction theory but also made any kind of intervention in actual families seem impossible. Freud turned the "psyche" into that arena in which the relevant pathologies could be identified and their causes isolated. The psychoanalytic dialogue promised to put those pathologies under the individual's control. The problem, its origin and its cure became the province, once again, of the individual. Freud waded into the ruins of liberal individualism to rescue the individual, seeking to replace the damaged social and political underpinnings with an unprecedented experience of self-reflection and self-expression.

In order to make such inwardness the consistent reference-point of the theoretical language and the therapeutic techniques of psychoanalysis, Freud had to cope with the many social and political experiences that arose within the life-histories and the free associations of his patients. Such experiences had to be marginalized, effaced or absorbed into the Oedipal narrative. Revisionist critics who today want to foreground class or gender or nationality and religion in revaluations of Freud's work have to comb through the detritus of his case histories and his self-analysis, reaccenting the rich testimony of the unconscious to be found there.

Consider the nanny who suddenly reappeared in Freud's dreams during the crucial week he was first tempted to turn from the seduction theory to Oedipal theory. On October 3, 1897, Freud wrote Fliess that "the 'prime originator' [of my troubles] was a woman, ugly, elderly, but clever, who told me a great deal about God Almighty and Hell and who gave me a high opinion of my own capacities."[10] This woman, who was Czech and Catholic, had cared for Freud during his first three years, only to be expelled from the household and sent to prison for stealing from the family. "I asked my mother whether she still recollected the nurse," Freud reported to Fliess on October 15. "'Of course,' she said, 'an elderly person, very clever. She was always taking you to church: when you came back afterwards you used to preach sermons and tell us all about God Almighty.'"[11]

Religion and nationality are rendered tangential details in Freud's account. Yet, as Schorske shows concerning the crisis Freud was suffering in the midst of his self-analysis, "the Rome of his mature dreams and longings is clearly a love-object" but is fraught with ambivalence because it represents Catholicism and conservatism as well as "pleasure, maternity, assimilation, fulfillment."[12] The Czech nanny might well be read as a libidinal and symbolic nexus connecting Freud's deepest sense of himself to the historical context in which he was now having to make his life. Schorske rightly questions the tendency of Freud and his followers to identify "the Rome longing with the nanny as mother-substitute and oedipal love-object, reducing the Catholic and Czech attributes of Rome in Freud's dream-pictures to symbols of this primal tie, and interpreting the inhibition preventing travel to Rome as an expression of the incest taboo."[13]

Freud in fact was in the process of transforming the nanny from "originator" into substitute by means of an interpretive trajectory that has been carefully analyzed by Jim Swan and by Peter Stallybrass and Allon White. The self-analysis first disclosed (whether as memory or hypothesis is unclear) that the nanny had initiated him into sexuality: "She was my teacher in sexual matters and scolded me for being clumsy and not being able to do anything." But this history of seduction and the "memory of the old woman who provided me at such an early age with the means for living and going on living"[14] run counter to the Oedipal narrative then emergent in Freud's thinking. The dreams and recollections Freud revealed in his letters to Fliess put the nanny at the very core of his feelings of love and loss as well as his traumatic sense of inadequacy and guilt. But by the time these childhood scenes are retold in published form, Freud has turned the episode of the nanny's dismissal and imprisonment into a mere happenstance that backgrounded his anxieties connected with a brief separation from his mother and his jealousies toward his newborn sister.[15]

In tracing how "Freud wrote the maid out of the family romance," Stallybrass and White capture the dynamic of social class that is as central to the structuring of Freud's own experience as it is to the structuring of the Rat Man's divided desire for the Poor Woman and the Rich Woman or Kafka's divided identification with his father and his father's employees:

> Paradoxically, to desire one's mother, despite the incestuous implications, is more acceptable than to desire a hired help. And Freud seems to validate his emphasis upon his mother by the conscious adult reconstruction which opposes the "slim and beautiful" mother to the "ugly, elderly" nurse. Thus, Freud's grief (he cried "his heart out" for nurse and mother alike) is split between an acceptable and an unacceptable mother. . . . And in the concept-formation of the Oedipus complex, Freud effaces the "unacceptable" mother.[16]

The nurse was raising him, but she is refused the social recognitions accorded a mother. The place of honor, that is, of esteem, dependence and desire, had to be reserved for the mother herself. I find it tempting to speculate that here may lie the biographical origins of Freud's promotion of a symbolic mother in the Oedipus complex at the expense of the mother in her real activities and interactions. To the extent that it was the Czech nanny who performed the tasks of caring, teaching, playing, this *5th term* of the Oedipus complex gets completely eclipsed by the *2nd term,* that is, the symbolic mother who embodies the requisite social ideals.

The actual functioning of the bourgeois household made this kind of complication of desire a constant feature of everyday life. Yet Freud took such networks of desire and power, subservience and resentment, exploitation and retaliation, and distilled from them the Oedipal triangle of I—mother—father. He brushed out seduction by a servant in his self-analysis, just as he would brush out seductions of servants by the Rat Man, to keep the emotional family portrait free of all these unsightly, uneducated, immoral proletarians. That their actual presence was part and parcel of his patients' and his own experience never found theoretical expression.

Did mere Victorian reticence, or perhaps ruling-class arrogance, form this blind spot? I think it more to the point that Freud carried out the simplification to the nuclear family because it enabled him to contain the larger crisis of political identity in a more manageable form. The splintering of the promised synthesis of vocation, marriage and citizenship that was disturbing the lifeworld of liberal Vienna did not have to be confronted as a specific set of deep-seated social and cultural pathologies. The crisis it unleashed in individuals' life-histories could be read, instead, as the misadventures of instinct coming into conflict with civilization.

The historically evolved and now threatened norms of male socialization could be rewritten as a psychic norm which could henceforth serve as theoretical and therapeutic benchmark. The puzzle of the individual's integration into market, household and polis could be solved on an utterly new terrain. Diagnosis could be accomplished by a remembering of family history and a repeating of filial loves and hatreds in the dialogue with the analyst, and the cure could be achieved by the working through of an individual myth and private history.

Freud's intellectual and therapeutic tactics were thus following in the tracks of the social process that had already displaced onto the family the hopes and problems of community. Community, too, is therefore suppressed whenever the clinical picture acquires too much social density. The Czech nanny's importance was also connected to her Catholicism. The visions of heaven and hell with which she inspired Freud the toddler resonated in his dreams forty years later because of the professional pressures and anti-Semitism that had slowed his career. In the midst of his intellectual doubts, his career crisis, his mourning of his father and the political crisis in Vienna, Freud was haunted by dreams that questioned his Jewish identity and utopianized complete assimilation and conversion.

The temptation to convert to Christianity tugged at the unconscious and conscious thoughts of Jewish families in the Habsburg empire and in Germany. Schorske shows how Freud's dreams in the critical weeks of 1897 pulled him between two heroic models both of whom he had often yearned to imitate and who were associated with his own most complex dream symbol, Rome: Hannibal, the Semitic general and politician who had failed to reach Rome, and Johan Joachim Winckelmann, the scholar who conquered Rome intellectually but at the cost of renouncing Judaism for Christianity.[17] Politics versus science, Jewishness versus conversion, rebellion versus accommodation.

My point is not to highlight Freud's conflicts of cultural identity. The point to be made is that these kinds of questions of cultural identity, community, belonging and estrangement are thoroughly a part of the forming of desires and identities. Freud himself always remained very clearheaded about his affiliations, especially in times of greatest political stress and uncertainty. In 1926, for example, he explained in an interview the effect of rising German anti-Semitism on his sense of self: "My language is German. My culture, my attainments are German. I considered myself German intellectually, until I noticed the growth of anti-Semitic prejudice in Germany and German Austria. Since that time, I prefer to call myself a Jew."[18]

In the household in which Freud himself was raised, the visible distinctions between social classes and the clash of values between rural Catholics and urban secular Jews were indelible aspects of his earliest, most formative experiences. So much so that when he faced the dangers of anti-Semitism and the doubting of his intellectual achievements at 40 it was the Czech Catholic nanny who came back in his dreams. But Freud's emergent interpretive procedures were destined to subordinate and dispel just this tangle of cultural identities and social relationships. He had made the family his interpretive reference-point, that is, the psychic representation of the family simplified to I—mother—father, and forced all else to the wings.

The interpretive displacement from community to Oedipal family completely governs Freud's handling of the Rat Man's religious experiences and of the marriage plan that precipitated his illness. The Rat Man's mother and father had approached matrimony strategically, in striking contrast to what would become their son's nine-year courtship of his "lady." The Rat Man's illness had been precipitated by his mother's plan that he should abandon his courtship and marry her relative's daughter and thereby secure a position in the Rubensky family's business. It is this plan which replicates the father's history, since he had attained a position with the Rubenskys upon marrying the Rat Man's mother. This account, which makes its way into Freud's published version of the case, barely touches the essential facts.

The mother herself had been raised by the Rubenskys from childhood. She apparently stood to inherit little or nothing from them, however, and as a woman she had no place in the family business. The Rubenskys, it is safe to assume, had decided to continue their support for her by offering her fiancé a job, thus guaranteeing his livelihood and her welfare. Freud does not reveal in the published version of the case that the Rat Man's father and mother were themselves first cousins, just as he does not disclose that the Rat Man and his "lady" were first cousins. And even in the clinical notes he does not explain exactly how they were related. If the father was himself related to the Rubenskys, their offer amounted to an effort to aid two relatives not just one; the family could consolidate its resources by lowering the incest barrier a bit, extending employment to a relative with few prospects, profiting from his contribution to the business and assuring the security of their foster-daughter besides.

Whether or not he was a Rubensky relative, the father's decision to marry strategically put money and social advantage above love. The mother had not hid her resentment over the years that before his engagement to her the father had been "the suitor of a butcher's daughter."[19] And even though she did not look back fondly on her life with the Rubenskys—she "was brought up by the Rubenskys as an adopted daughter, but was very badly treated"[20]—she nevertheless strongly advocated the proposed match between her son and the Rubensky daughter. Her motives seem to have been thoroughly pragmatic, just as her disapproval of the Rat Man's "lady" centered on her family's lack of wealth.

The matrimonial strategies that the Rat Man's parents practiced with a hard-bitten sense of necessity gave rise to confusions in the next generation. The Rat Man and his sister Julie openly displayed an affection for each other that others considered incestuous. Not only was the "lady" the Rat Man courted their first cousin, Julie herself went on to marry another cousin (Bob St.). What amounted to the extended family's strategies for survival and growth had become, in the nuclear families which those strategies had spawned, something like a suspicion or fear of outsiders. The family's ferocious pride often expressed itself as contempt for others. "'After all, the Lorenzes are the only nice people,' one of his sisters said."[21] The family also deemed personality a direct effect of inheritance. Again quoting the clinical notes: "He gets everything that is bad in his nature, he says, from his mother's side. His maternal grandfather was a brutal man who ill-treated his wife. All his brothers and sisters have, like him, gone through a great process of transformation from bad children to worthy people."[22]

Freud pursues very little of this. Did the first cousin who is his "lady" come from the bad side of the family? Were his mother's objections to her an expression of contempt for a side of the father's family or of her own? Are the Rubenskys, and therefore the other cousin he is urged to marry, from the good or bad side? All we know is that when the Rat Man was presented with the plan that would have him, just like his father, marry into the Rubensky family at the expense of his true love, he became more and more ill, beginning with his chronic postponements of the legal exams he needed to pass before he could take his position within the Rubensky business. And the suggestion that his father had married for money drove him to violent dreams and fantasies directed against Freud. We also know, of course, that his true love itself was fraught with mortifying ambivalences as well as violent swings of temper and feeling.

When the question of the Rat Man's religiosity arose, Freud straightaway suggested a connection to the marriage plan. Did his fantasy of converting to Christianity provide a ready out to avoid the marriage plan, since the Rubenskys were religious Jews? However, since the Rat Man's "lady" was also Jewish, his impulse to convert does not seem a viable fantasy for resolving his marital choice. Freud might have pursued other avenues of interpretation. He did not because he avoided connections that might enmesh the Rat Man's symptoms in a set of relationships and processes that were as much political as psychological. The Rat Man's episodes of religiosity have meanings whose connections and shadings cannot really be determined since the relevant analytic work on Freud's part is missing.

Nonetheless, the key episode is worth examining. It shows how thoroughly the pressures of assimilation weighed on the Rat Man's family and community at a historic juncture where family was assuming the burdens and expectations of community:

> In the Spring [?1903] he felt violent self-reproaches (why?). A detail brought the answer. He fell on his knees, conjured up pious feelings and determined to believe in the next world and immortality. This involved Christianity and going to church in Unterach after he had called his cousin a whore. His father had never consented to be baptized, but much regretted that his forefathers had not relieved him of this unpleasant business. He had often told the patient that he would have no objections if he wanted to become a Christian. Might it be, perhaps, I asked, that a Christian girl had appeared just then as a rival to his cousin? "No." "The Rubenskys are Jews, are they not?" "Yes, and professing ones." Indeed, if he had become a Christian it would have meant the end of the whole R. scheme. So, I replied, his kneeling must have been directed against the R. scheme and he must therefore have known of this plan before the scene of the kneeling. He thought not but admitted that there was something he wasn't clear about. What he definitely remembered was the inception of the scheme—his going with his cousin (and future brother-in-law) Bob St. to visit the R.'s where the plan was mentioned of their being established near the Cattle Market, St. as a lawyer and he as his clerk.[23]

Freud might have pursued the significance for the Rat Man of his father's lament that his own ancestors had not converted. Such a sentiment is a barely disguised repudiation of the marriage that brought the Rat Man himself into the world. In fact, the Rat Man had revealed in a session the week before that his own birth was unwanted. He had dreamed that his dead father returned home, and "He thought they would have to cut expenses down after all, as there would be an extra person living in the house now. This thought was in revenge against his father who, he had been told, was in despair over his birth, as he was over each new baby."[24]

From yet another angle, Freud might have explored the links between the Rat Man's temptation to Christianity and the obsessive thoughts and rituals that permitted him to relate to his father as though he were alive. Belief in an after-life and personal salvation (or damnation) may have held out a socially acceptable way of gratifying his need to keep his father alive, whether motivated by his own guilt or his aggression. The failure to accept death, the death of the father, was in any case a crucial part of the Rat Man's symptoms. Did Christian conversion and the repudiation of Jewishness represent an imitation of his father (who had lamented not being baptized) or a rejection of him (since conversion would keep him from marrying as his father had) or an impossible combination of the two (in keeping with the Rat Man's contradictory identifications with his father)? The question remains unanswerable.

Freud might have pursued another path as well. Assuming, as seems likely, that the Rat Man's immediate family was not religious, he may have longed for a substitute for the rituals of remembrance and the affirmations of the community's historical continuity that are so central to Judaism. His father's death may have made this loss of community palpable. How would he keep faith with the past? How would personal memory take over the tasks previously fulfilled by communal rituals of renewal? If these were the problems that weighed on him, then his inability to accept his father's death would have been most directly linked to a crisis of Jewish identity. Such a possibility would invert the Oedipal interpretation according to which the Rat Man's efforts to affect his father beyond the grave were a retaliation against the father's inhibitions on his pleasures, archaically associated with the childhood biting episode. Indeed, from another angle still, the Rat Man's conflicts and symptoms may have been shaped from the beginning by the lure of complete assimilation, whether motivated by a desire to find a new level of social acceptance or to break with his own family and community.

None of these interpretations can be adequately developed and then evaluated in the absence of a therapeutic procedure that would have left these royal roads to the unconscious open.

As Sartre argues so forcefully in *Search for a Method,* an individual's life-history cannot really be comprehended unless the life is also apprehended in history. Significant pieces of historical process flow through the father-son relationship. Generational differences in modern societies are forged from the upheavals of civil society, communities and the polis. While Freud, Ricoeur and Lacan occasionally take a nostalgic glance back at some supposedly steadier kind of patriarchy, paternal legacies have not really survived modernity or modernization. They are ultimately regressive benchmarks for understanding the modern family. When it comes to models of the father-son relation, the continuity that primogeniture gave to the aristocratic transfer of titles and property is as irrelevant as the romanticized ideal of the peasant or villager handing down the tools and skills of a whole way of life.

Freud's father was a textile merchant who moved his new wife and older children from a Jewish village in Moravia to Vienna, perhaps escaping the memories of his first wife's death and of the mysterious, unacknowledged second wife whose fate became the family's buried secret. What Freud acquired from his father's devotion and generosity were a gymnasium education, a German cultural identity and the vocation of science rather than commerce. Kafka's father—a contemporary of Freud chronologically, but of his father sociologically—was a village peddler who married a wealthy brewer's daughter and became a dry goods wholesaler and retailer in Prague. Kafka so identified with and yet repudiated this crude and cruel autocrat that he not only avoided commerce but squandered his legal education, lived timidly at home and wrecked engagements to two women he deeply loved.

The Rat Man's father used marriage into a family of wealthy Viennese industrialists to overcome youthful poverty and nearly dishonorable military service. Like the scientist Freud and the lawyer-bureaucrat Kafka, the Rat Man sought refuge from commerce in a profession. Having started down his own path vocationally, however, he nearly squandered his independence in a stratagem of failure that was designed to keep himself from following in his father's matrimonial footsteps; he postponed his law exams to avoid a marriage with his rich cousin and continued to court his poor cousin, though in hesitating between two women he in fact was imitating his father's erotic history after all. On the verge of a nervous breakdown at the end of his military maneuvers, he was frantically attempting, all at once, to repay and replicate the debt his father had incurred at the end of his military career.

All three fathers blazed a trail from the community of the Jewish village to the secular city where they encountered and began to cope with new forms of economy, power and learning. The sons were all thrown into crisis in having to consolidate this process of secularization and assimilation begun by their fathers. In the Rat Man's neurotic struggle with Christianity and in Freud's own unconscious turmoil over his cultural identity and vocation, this historical process became a personal, intergenerational ordeal.

Kafka, who eventually developed interests in Zionism and made efforts to preserve Yiddish cultural forms, expresses outrage at the shallowness and hypocrisy in his father's failure to pass Judaism on to him in his childhood or youth:

> it would have been thinkable that we might both have found each other in Judaism or that we might have begun from there in harmony. But what sort of Judaism was it that I got from you? . . . As a child, I reproached myself, in accord with you, for not going to synagogue often enough, for not fasting, and so on. . . . Later, as a young man, I could not understand how, with the insignificant scrap of Judaism you yourself possessed, you could reproach me for not making an effort (for the sake of piety at least, as you put it) to cling to a similar, insignificant scrap.[25]

According to the liberal ideals that guided bourgeois aspirations, vocation and marriage were the steps young men were to take on their way to becoming owners, citizens, fathers. The life-histories of the Rat Man, Freud and Kafka suggest that the watersheds of vocation and marriage were rife with conflicts that arose from the changing forms of community in which these men and their families participated, from the clash of cultural values attached to the professions versus business and from conflicts between economic exigencies and erotic values. Moreover, all three suffered their vocational or matrimonial crisis in a context where the very forms of citizenship on which their ideals and ambitions had been staked were unraveling around them.

Freud neutralized all these links between history and life-history and tried, instead, to recover the liberal ideal in his model of an ideal route to the formation and dissolution of the Oedipus complex. A young man had only to overcome his incestuous and aggressive impulses toward his mother and father to step into his roles in civil society, the family and the state. When Freud then turned to explain why this ideal maturation was typically derailed or complicated or compromised, he set aside the historical dimension altogether. He attributed Oedipal pathologies to nothing more tangible than an insufficient fear of the father and a sexual constitution that failed to be singularly masculine and heterosexual.

The limitations of Freud's view were by no means an intellectual fabrication or a mere error. Pressures within and upon family life, do indeed make the I—mother—father relationship into an emotional stencil laid over the individual's relation to the world. It is not therefore a question of examining society and politics *instead of* family relationships. Rather, it is a question of grasping the social and political processes that, variously, shape or dictate or interrupt family life or are reflected or refracted or veiled by family relationships.

Freud absented himself from this task by calibrating his theoretical and therapeutic work to an ideal of male socialization which naturalizes compulsory heterosexuality and male dominance as "psychic" norms. As I have also been arguing, this psychic norm was used to ground the mapping of the family, civil society and the state at the very time that the political underpinnings the liberal mapping really required were collapsing. Historically, a new structure of feeling had crystallized as communal needs and aspirations were shifted onto the family, as public and private were distinguished and encoded anew and as the male owner-citizen-father role emerged and was valorized. Even as this structure of feeling took root in everyday experience it was fraught with conflicts and a capacity for pathology. And it was in the midst of a particularly intense crisis at the precise moment of Freud's most significant discoveries.

The Oedipus complex is dotted with pathogenic zones. They correspond to the conflicts and crises to which the bourgeois lifeworld proved vulnerable. What erupts at these zones are the pathological effects, within an individual's life-history, of compulsory heterosexuality, male dominance, economic exploitations and tyrannies, the clash of public, private and communal and the vicissitudes of citizenship. The cultural pathologies find expression in the individual myth. This should not suggest a simple, one-way causality between history and life-history. The imperatives or the crises of particular social institutions or cultural practices have a very wide range of effects on the contingencies of an individual life. The point is to grasp them in terms of one another. The Oedipus complex is an *individual* myth but each of its joints, each of its points of articulation, links with cultural pathologies as well.

From his earliest work with hysteria in women, Freud uncovered the tremendous pathological potential created by the dynamics of male authority in the modern middle-class household. In the end he cut himself off from seeing it in those terms. As a consequence, he tended thereafter to misread the pathologies of paternal authority when he encountered them anew in the Oedipus complex. His self-analysis failed to uncover, as Balmary shows, the extent of the disturbance created in his own desires and identity by the aura of wrongdoing that compromised his father's standing and authority.

When Lacan interprets such a discrepancy between the real-life father and the symbolic father as though the former is entangled in "society" while the latter basks comfortably at the center of "culture," he misses the fact that the father's capacity to represent the paternal symbols is rooted in his real power as head of the household. Ultimately, that is, his power over his wife. Kafka's "Letter to His Father" reveals just how seductive the prospect of such power is to a son. By the same token, the father's authority finds its legitimation in symbols of a beyond-desire-and-effort which his real life palpably and emphatically contradicts. Freud's father, therefore, could fall under suspicion of being a Bluebeard embroiled in some scandal of sex and death. The Rat Man's father's social ambition and economic shrewdness could appear to his son as broken promises to a faithful friend and a deserving woman. And Kafka, of course, encountered his father's desires and efforts directly and painfully in the guise of the tyranny he exercised over family and employees. In each of these cases the inner contradiction in the father's role—the discordance between the symbolic and the real-life father, between the *3rd term* and the *4th term* of the Oedipus complex—comes back to haunt the son precisely because he is summoned to identify with the father, to aspire to his power, his sex-right, his patriarchal privilege.

The discord between the *3rd* and *4th term* is thus one of the pathogenic zones of the Oedipus complex. Another is the discord which psychoanalytic theory ignores in the figure of the mother. The *2nd term* of the Oedipus complex is created from a discourse of male fantasy and patriarchal symbols: this is the mother as ideal object, as possession of the father, as taboo, as mother/whore. As is so striking in Freud's case histories as well as his self-analysis, the Oedipal mother lacks reality. Little or nothing of the mother's real life figures in the psychoanalytic interpretations, giving rise to the suspicion that a *5th term* lies hidden behind the *2nd term* of the Oedipus complex, obscured in the Oedipal cultivation of desire.

The discrepancy between the *2nd* and the *5th term* evokes a range of social and political relations. In Freud's self-analysis, the discrepancy touched on relations of social class, ethnic and national identity and religion, since the obscured *5th term* is actually the nanny whose love and misdemeanors so profoundly affected Freud but who gets eclipsed by the *2nd term* in the person of Freud's idealized, symbolically charged mother. In the case of the Rat Man, the Oedipal mother is fabricated from his identifications with his father. The polarity of Rich Woman and Poor Woman became the grid through which the Rat Man's heterosexuality divided just as his father's had. The real-life mother is relegated further into the shadows the more Freud's interpretation foregrounds the Oedipal nature of the Rat Man's desires. Because of a paradox at the heart of psychoanalytic theory, Freud makes the mother the basis of the Oedipus complex at the very moment he ignores mothers altogether.

Freud thereby secured a foundation for Oedipal theory in the sense that he sealed mother-son, mother-father, husband-wife relationships off from any concerted attention to the social relations of men and women. Questions concerning male dominance, the sexual division of labor and the male control of wealth, the inequalities rooted in the modern separation of public and private, the restraints on women's citizenship—these sorts of questions are kept at bay so long as the mother in the Oedipal triangle of I—mother—father is the fabricated *2nd term*. So long as the whole of the mother's real existence and activities and relationships were rendered irrelevant to an understanding of her formative role for her child, psychoanalytic theory fit into the society's patriarchal imperatives like a hand into a glove.

Part Three

Oedipus: Individual Myth and Cultural Pathology

8

Like Father, Like Son

BOTH RICOEUR AND LACAN have placed the crucial connection between the family and the marketplace in the son's encounter with his father as a counterpart to himself—a potential equal. The individual myth maps this encounter through the *4th* and *3rd terms.* The son's task of attaining his independence and maturity, that is, his autonomy, must pass through his identification with his father.

Ricoeur and Lacan clearly envision autonomy as a man's achievement. They define autonomy, normatively, as the ability to sustain relatively harmonious relations of equality in one's social transactions with others, and consistently to feel one's identity confirmed in the rewards and goods one receives for one's efforts and labor. Ricoeur and Lacan part company when it comes to assessing how thoroughly modern society fulfills this promise of autonomy.

Ricoeur considers the son's likeness to his father the transition from a fantasmal fear of the father as rival and castrator to a genuine experience of autonomy. The son's identification with his father is his training in the forms of equality associated with the market and the polis. As an experience of equality between *men,* the father-son relationship prepares the son for possessive individualism and citizenship.

Lacan sees the same linkages of family, market and polis but concludes that the son's recognition of himself in his father disturbs the achievement of autonomy and equality. The father's presence as a counterpart or equal (the *4th term* of the individual myth) conflicts with his representation of the father symbol (the *3rd term*). In designating the father *begetter* and *name-giver,* the individual myth establishes the son's symbolic debt of existence to his father. He owes his father his life. Meanwhile, maturation calls for the son to become independent in the sense of henceforth owing his existence primarily to his own activities and the rewards they yield. The son is called upon to resolve this tension between symbolic indebtedness and juridical-economic autonomy.

The son's identification with his father as model social agent is vulnerable to disturbances in several directions. It can embroil the son in an impossible attempt to achieve independence by eradicating or canceling the symbolic debt. As with the Rat Man, the son can then find himself recapitulating the *father's* actions in place of performing actions that could count as his own. Or the father's perceived deficiencies or faults, his failure to embody the father symbol, can compromise the son's efforts to model himself on him. As with Kafka, recognizing the father as he really is can unhinge the son's ability to see himself performing the very tasks that would define his autonomy and maturity.

How then does Lacan understand the social or cultural pathology that consistently thwarts the son's endeavor to stabilize his identity at this intersection of family, market and polis? Lacan sensed a deep-seated crisis in the shaping of individuality in modern society. He became in fact a cultural critic of modernity. Modern society had lost, in his view,

> all those saturations of the *super-ego* and the *ego ideal* which are realized in all sorts of organic forms in traditional societies, from rituals of everyday intimacy to the periodic festivals in which the community is revealed. . . . Moreover, in abolishing the cosmic polarity of male and female principles, our society knows all the psychological influences characteristic of the modern phenomenon of the so-called *battle of the sexes*.[1]

In place of rituals, festivals and cosmologies of community, modern society produces a form of naked individuality:

> it is clear that the promotion of the *self* [or "ego," translating *le moi*] in our existence ends up, in keeping with the utilitarian conception of man which supports it, realizing man ever more completely as an individual, that is, in an isolation of the soul ever closer to his original helplessness.[2]

These statements anchored Lacan's thought throughout the 1950s. They blend a radical critique of the Enlightenment with a barely disguised masculine protest. If there were no battle of the sexes, men would enjoy unquestioned authority. If there were communally binding symbolic representations of the super-ego and the ego ideal, men would enjoy unquestioned authority. And if intimacy were ruled by traditional rituals, men would enjoy unquestioned authority.

Kant established the normative principle of maturation as autonomy in the opening lines of his essay, "An Answer to the Question: 'What is Enlightenment?'":

> *Enlightenment is man's emergence from his self-incurred immaturity. Immaturity* is the inability to use one's own understanding without the guidance of another. The immaturity is *self-incurred* if its cause is not lack of understanding, but lack of resolution and courage to use it without the guidance of another. The motto of enlightenment is therefore: *Sapere aude!* ["Dare to be wise."] Have courage to use your *own* understanding![3]

It might be argued that Lacan did not so much reject Kant's values as severely question whether the direction of modern society was capable of actually realizing them. He does in fact draw on just this opposition of maturity and immaturity when he characterizes the modern predicament as a regression of the individual to "his original helplessness," that is, to infancy.

Lacan's meditations on modernity are in general a feature, the pay-off, really, of the theory of the mirror-phase he was developing at this time. In the infantile mirror-phase experience, I recognize my own image and identify with it as a *Gestalt* or fully formed body image. This self-recognition contrasts sharply with my body sensations and lack of coordination. In my movements and sensations I experience my body as beyond my control, even fragmented or torn, while in the mirror-image I experience my body whole.

According to Lacan, these contradictory experiences of the body and self condition the structure of identity. I identify with my self as another in the imaginary register in contrast to my uncoordinated, fragmented body. My own image or that of another with whom I identify in the same way can therefore provoke extreme delight—of recognition, of anticipated mastery, of the promise of growth—or a depressive reaction in which I fall back on the feeling of being torn and fragmented or an aggressive reaction in which the fear of being cut in pieces is directed back at the threatening image itself, an image which is ambiguously me or another.

In the essay "The Neurotic's Individual Myth," Lacan suggests the mirror-relation between self and other oscillates between anticipated maturation—that is, a promise of autonomy—and wrenching anxiety. The aggressive or depressive response to the other is "a kind of original experience of death": "what is revealed in all imaginary relationships is an experience of death: an experience doubtless inherent in all manifestations of the human condition, but especially visible in the life of the neurotic."[4]

Like Freud, Lacan considered mental illness the key to ordinary experience. In his essay on "The Mirror Stage as Formative of the Function of the I," Lacan wrote, "The sufferings of neurosis and psychosis are for us a schooling in the passions of the soul."[5] Thus, this "original experience of death" in an unmediated terror or hatred of the other is, in Lacan's view, not only a moment in the child's early development and a crux of neurosis but is also "something that goes far beyond the formation of the neurotic, specifically the existential attitude characteristic of modern man."[6]

It is in this way, then, that the theory of the mirror stage articulates a theme that is part and parcel of Lacan's radical critique of modernity. The mirror stage provides a vivid drama, a fable perhaps, of the ordeal of loneliness and helplessness that can afflict the modern individual and the anxiety and aggression that can dominate interpersonal relations. The emphatic experience of the neurotic serves as the intermediary between a diagnosis of modern society and a supposedly empirical description of the experience of the preverbal child.

Typical of Lacan and many of his followers, the theoretical certainty in which the formulations about childhood experience are couched lends weight and authority to the conjectures about society and culture. This aspect of Lacan's influence has been especially pronounced in discussions of the mirror stage. Later commentators have not, however, renewed the early Lacan's lament over the loss of pre-modern community and cosmology. They have drawn, instead, on the later Lacan's notion that the imaginary relations of self and other have to be overcome in the symbolic relations established by language and by the paternal Law. The imaginary dyad has to be replaced with the symbolic triad: self/other by I/other/language, and I/mother by I/mother/father.

Lacan's anti-modernity drops out of this second version of the imaginary and the symbolic, or appears to. But the whole problematic of the dissonance between the *3rd term* and the *4th term* of the individual myth drops out as well. The father reigns supreme again in the familialism of the new orthodox Lacanians. The heterosexual couple regains its theoretical and normative preeminence in a decade in which fewer and fewer children are raised by their biological parents. The worry over the loss of community and ritual evaporates in a celebration of compulsory heterosexuality as the lifeblood of culture.

In Stuart Schneiderman, for example, the individual myth loses its specificity. It ceases to be an individual's mapping of a particular set of relationships, contexts and difficulties. Instead, the individual myth reverts to the static Oedipus complex, which is equated with the symbolic and credited with superseding the imaginary:

> Being structured, the elements of the child's prehistory hold together in much the same way that the child perceives his image in the mirror as being together. In fact, the symbolic should come to replace the imaginary as structuring.
>
> In psychoanalytic work the symbolic manifests itself in the form of the family romance or the mythic structure of the Oedipus complex. This discourse is the conjuncture into which the subject was born, and it determines the success or failure of his maturation and development.[7]

By attributing the success or failure of maturation to the Oedipus complex, Schneiderman effaces most of "the conjuncture into which the subject was born." Community, market and polis disappear as the family becomes the single institutional context for understanding maturation.

Compulsory heterosexuality becomes the paradigm of the structure of culture itself in the work of Ellie Ragland-Sullivan. The male-dominated household and the heterosexual couple are accorded the status of an indelible mental inheritance, virtually wired into the very possibility of mirroring or speaking:

> At around eighteen months of age, the identificatory representations that compose an infant's incipient *moi* undergo a transition from perceptual "presence" to repression. The *moi* had its origins as a break in the "natural" consciousness, a mirror-stage, secondary structure built into a gap in being. In a structurally similar way, the phallic signifier (which gives rise to the Law of the Name-of-the-Father) imposes a scission in the *moi*. Mathematically speaking some third term (usually the father, but possibly the mother's brother or someone else) appears to the infant as an obstacle to symbiotic unity with the mother. It therefore requires three persons to teach the infant that the mother and itself are not one but two beings. This intervention initiates the true passage from nature to culture in ternary or Oedipal terms.[8]

Whereas the early Lacan saw in the presence of uncles or stepfathers in the individual myth a clue to its four-term structure and the discord in the function of paternity itself, Ragland-Sullivan resolves their presence back into the triangular frame. For her what counts is the Father. She simply affirms fatherhood's power within the family structure and the psyche to set the child within culture, language and sociality.

Because this sociality is put under the simple sign and reign of the father, psychoanalytic theory loses any access to the actual institutional contexts of modern society. In Schneiderman and Ragland-Sullivan, the various economic, legal, political, ethnic and religious forces that come into play in the child's relation to the father are simply obliterated. As I will try to show in a discussion of the name-of-the-father (Chapter 10), Lacan turned away from his initial dialogue with social theory as soon as he equated the father with the law, with culture, with language. The end result in posthumous Lacanian orthodoxy is a social conservatism disguised as philosophy of psychoanalysis.[9]

What I have called Lacan's second version of the imaginary and the symbolic—they became the Imaginary and the Symbolic—established a fixed order of transcendence. The symbolic supersedes the imaginary. As a result, Lacan's original conception of the imaginary and the dynamic of identification has gradually been simplified and depleted. It has acquired a negative charge: the self is an illusion; identification is misrecognition, since the self forms in the subject's identification with an image.

The Marxist appropriation of the mirror stage went precisely in this direction, beginning with Louis Althusser's very influential essays. Althusser sought to empty the notion of consciousness in the tradition of Hegel, Marx and Lukács of any title to agency or action in history, whether as spirit, labor or class consciousness. Likewise he sought to unseat the concept of the subject. Only bourgeois individualism could view the individual as an inviolable or an initiating social agent. The subject is in reality an effect of structure; the subject is summoned (interpellated) by various ideologies to play out its roles according to the laws of "culture" (language, kinship, gender) and the dynamics of the relations of production (social class). The subject's self-recognition, on the other hand, is a *misrecognition*. As in the mirror stage, it is by means of an imaginary identification—an identification with an image—that you see yourself as a full-fledged agent. Only in the imaginary do you see yourself as an autonomous individual perceiving, believing, knowing and acting on your own. Hence, Althusser's central thesis: "Ideology is a 'representation' of the imaginary relationship of individuals to their real conditions of existence."[10]

Althusser, like Schneiderman and Ragland-Sullivan, emphasizes only one moment in the mirror stage, namely, the illusory aspect of the identification with an image. The sharpened contrast between the imaginary and the symbolic makes this emphasis inevitable. The imaginary is then fixed as the illusion of self, and the symbolic is fixed as law. The complexities of individuality and autonomy are quickly dismissed in the opposition between an illusory self and the law of culture or of society.

An alternative sense of the imaginary and the symbolic can, however, be extrapolated from Lacan. He implicitly locates two distinct and contrary *promises of autonomy* in a child's development. One comes from the mirror stage, the other from the acquisition of language. Moreover, each *promise* of autonomy is matched to specific risks. I want to stress this polarity between promise and risk in both the imaginary and the symbolic registers to show that the mirror stage and language learning are ordeals traversed in various ways rather than fixed steps in the child's development or fixed points in the psychic structure.

The first promise of autonomy arises from the mirror experience. My identification with my body image not only enhances my orientation in space but also establishes my orientation in time. For when I apprehend my own or another's *Gestalt* over against the uncoordinated sensations of my body, my identification with the image is also an expectation of growth and eventual mastery. The first promise of autonomy, therefore, takes the form of an *imaginary self-sufficiency.*

The early Lacan also stresses the humanizing power of the mirror relation. The moment of alienation in identifying my self as another also teaches me to identify another as someone like myself. Mutual recognition in the form of mirroring, orientation in space and time and the prospect of self-sufficiency—these make up the mirror stage's promise of autonomy. The risk of this experience of identification lies in the vacillations between violence and fear, aggressions and depressions. Those responses to the menacing face of another's mastery or completeness always threaten the gains in mutual recognition or in one's own mastery.

The acquisition of language establishes a second promise of autonomy: namely, *the capacity to participate on a par with others in symbolically mediated interactions.* From the standpoint of language and discourse, mutual recognition takes on new dimensions that distinguish it from the mirror-relation's form of mutual recognition. Now recognition of another means acknowledging his or her reciprocal place in the dialogue. Second, recognition does not here preclude, as it does in the mirror-relation, the recognition of differences between self and other. And, third, the recognition of another through his or her "image" becomes in the context of dialogue provisional and revisable; while the mirror-relation tends to congeal and stereotype the roles of self and other (ugly/beautiful, awkward/graceful, victim/victimizer), the dialogue encourages the interlocutors to modify their perceptions of one another on the basis of their continued interaction.

Such an "ideal speech situation" is not a given or premise of discourse. It is a *promise* in the sense of a tacit or implied norm. It can be appealed to when challenging your exclusion from the dialogue or the misrepresentation of what you are saying. As this sense of norm or ideal should imply, the entry into language and dialogue is fraught with risks. If dialogue tacitly promises participation, it also actively enables exclusion and maneuver. It is a field of power relations as well as communicative acts. Moreover, if dialogue implies the possibility of mutual understanding, it also opens the way to using language to distort, conceal, lie and deceive self or other.

These risks of the symbolic are no less potent than the risks of the imaginary. Likewise, the second promise of autonomy does not merely or purely supersede the first promise of autonomy. Most commentaries on Lacan miss the persistence of the mirror-relation *in* the dialogic relation, for the participants cannot recognize one another or establish their own presence as participants without the imaginary form of recognition. Recognizing someone by their face, voice, walk or silhouette is a recognition congealed through an image, a stereotyping, an alienation. Identifying someone by a single act they committed or a handful of stories about them also belongs in the imaginary register. But these sorts of recognitions and identifications enable dialogue just as they can stifle it.

Conversely, the fact of dialogue does not guarantee a higher form of mutual recognition; it makes it possible. The imaginary and the symbolic do not line up as illusion versus law, since they can also embody, respectively, respect versus lie. The mirror stage and the acquisition of language are, from the standpoint of development, trials in which the individual encounters new potentials but also new risks or threats. These crucial childhood scenes of instruction do not, it seems to me, lend themselves to direct translation into political allegories of the kind found in the early Lacan's anti-modernity, Schneiderman and Ragland-Sullivan's social conservatism or Althusser's authoritarian brand of Marxism.

These concepts of autonomy at work in Lacan's imaginary and symbolic are nevertheless extremely relevant to the question of modernity and its forms of individuality, and in turn to the question of the father-son relation as conduit and barrier to the son's maturity within the relevant practices and institutions. Lacan's anti-modern stance obscured the forms of individuality at issue by lumping them under a category of simple loss of community. Modernity, it seems to me, has produced different forms of individuality and autonomy. They cannot be easily subsumed under a single label, whether positive or negative.

In the polis, political modernity has produced the individual as citizen and as rights-bearer. Societal modernization, through the extension of industrialism, capitalism and bureaucracy, has forged the possessive individual, the wage-earner, the "organization man," the professional, the welfare client and so on. There has been a proliferation of forms of individuality within this domain of economy and power. Moreover, these individualities often do not mesh with the political role of rights-bearing citizen: the welfare client is generally deprived of the security and leisure that are preconditions to actively fulfill the duties and exercise the rights of citizenship. Moreover, citizenship is still not universally granted even in the oldest Western democracies. And inequalities between men and women traverse each of these categories.

A third face of modernity is what I will call, following Jürgen Habermas, cultural modernity. It touches on the themes evoked by Kant. In the whole domain of knowledge and learning, modernity does witness the decline of tradition and community as the bearers of identity-confirming knowledge. The modern individual is called upon to have the resolution and courage to use one's understanding *without the guidance of another.*

The polis, the market and communities are all, simultaneously, involved in shaping the forms of individuality. And every individual inhabits more than one of these forms. It is this order of social reflection that needs to be increasingly integrated into psychoanalytic theory. Family relationships do not, by themselves, generate the forms or the paths of individuation. The revision of Oedipal theory I am advocating is designed, in part, to show how the variegated spaces of social and political life in fact intersect with the family in the individual myth or Oedipus complex.

Let us come back once more to an instance of the discrepancy between the real-life father and the father symbol to clarify, and keep open, the dialogue between Lacanian psychoanalysis and social theory. Lacan's introduction of the *4th term* in effect broke the intrafamilial boundary Freud had so carefully set for the Oedipus complex. The son's recognition and understanding of the real-life father requires, among other things, seeing him in his role as the family "breadwinner," whether as worker, entrepreneur or bureaucrat. What the individual myth therefore represents through the *4th term* is the intersection of the family and the market.[11] The real-life father is at once "father" and an individual whose individuality and agency are shaped by the market and polis.

In capitalist society, the market-mediated individuality of employers and employees is shaped by a model of autonomy as self-sufficiency. Now, this self-sufficiency is imaginary in the sense that the individual's experience of being on one's own or going it alone rests on a self-perception that obscures the webs of coordination and cooperation that actually make a modern economy work. In short, the possessive individualism mandated by the workings of the economic system at once represents and misrepresents the individual's role within that system. The fact that the movement of capital rather than the decisions of the participants dictates the dynamics of the market produces the individual's image of self-sufficiency.

It is this dynamic of social representation—ideology—that enters the individual myth to the extent that the son gathers the particular narratives of his father's involvement in market-mediated practices and institutions. Those narratives furnish the son with his first evidence of capitalist social relations and with his primary model of autonomy as imaginary self-sufficiency. He begins to anticipate the modes of self-identity, mutual recognition and autonomy that await his own entry into this field of social practice.

Certainly the ambiguities of this identification with the father owe their dynamic to the archaic mirror-relation, which Lacan described in just these terms as fostering an "illusion of autonomy" and "self-sufficiency of consciousness."[12] By the same token, however, it is the father's particular social context that will determine the shape of the son's crisis and the meaning of his responses. The crisis provoked for the Rat Man in recognizing his likeness to his father had a specific content, which nonetheless is hardly anomalous in the life-histories of the bourgeoisie: his father appeared to him a social climber, a cheat, a figure more ambitious than successful, calculative in courtship and dishonest in love and friendship. The son's compulsion to identify, to have to accept the father's model to learn his own roles, leads him into a series of trying experiences which cannot be interpreted with reference merely to the father as symbol or the mirror stage experience. It is at bottom a moral-political ordeal filled with the specific contents of social experience and represented, in however refracted a form, in the individual myth.

9

"Mother/Whore"

NOTHING IS MORE BASIC to the Oedipus complex than the little boy's incestuous yearning for his mother. It is the first axiom of Oedipal theory. But this axiom has not survived close scrutiny. When the incestuous attachment returns after the latency period, it supposedly inhibits the adolescent's initiation into the adult form of male heterosexuality. But Freud's own clinical materials suggest, instead, that male heterosexuality, in all its social and cultural elaboration, is part and parcel of the Oedipal formation in the first place.

Indeed, what is "the first place"? For the primacy of the mother-son bond to the formation of the Oedipus complex is itself in question. The son's incestuous attachment to his mother looks more like the complex's effect than its cause. Freud and Lacan ultimately give so much weight to the father-son relation in creating the Oedipus complex that the Oedipal wishes seem nearly independent of the mother. Yet how could you claim that there is something more primary than the mother-child bond?

Nothing of course actually comes before their intimacy and the child's dependence on her love and care. At issue, rather, is the nature of that intimacy, love and care. The skepticism I have directed at the Oedipal mother is aimed, precisely, at the Oedipal mother. I am questioning whether the primary relationship that mothering establishes between mother and child is Oedipal at all. (Later I will also question whether it is "pre-Oedipal.") My skepticism has arisen in response to a surprising lacuna in all of Freud's writings and Lacan's; the more they foreground the Oedipus complex the less they discuss the actual history of any mother and son.

The resulting vacuum is often quickly filled by the most fanciful interpretations. Disciples of Freud and Lacan have been especially quick to conjure up the missing mother. They endow her with motives, traits and actions. They seem never to suspect the stereotypes they employ. Consider two recent commentaries on the case of the Rat Man, one by Stuart Schneiderman, a guardian of the new, posthumous Lacanian orthodoxy, and the other by Patrick J. Mahony, vehement anti-Lacanian and adherent of object-relations theory. As we saw earlier, Freud uncovered precious little about the Rat Man's mother and gave her no role whatsoever in the patient's infantile sexual development, despite the centrality of his Oedipal interpretation. My commentary drew on the unpublished notes to discuss her pragmatic, strategic approach to marriage and the role the Rat Man himself gave her as the keeper of his inheritance even as he neared thirty years of age. Schneiderman and Mahony convince themselves that she is the root of the Rat Man's disorder, a pathogenic mother whose influence overflows the required patriarchal barriers.

Schneiderman's portrait draws on the crudest formulations of Oedipal theory, those which suppose that the mother's emotional power and significance simply compromise autonomy, growth, masculinity. Schneiderman gives this dogma free rein in a context where Freud's lack of interest in the real-life mother has left the interpretive field wide open. Schneiderman takes a pseudo-Lacanian approach to the mother's desire as the benchmark of the Rat Man's own desire—desire is the desire of the Other—and invents a role for her. From Freud we know of the mother's sensitivity to the fact that her husband may have married her for her money even as he was still in love with another woman, but Schneiderman skips over the many different connotations such sensitivity might have and concludes that the Rat Man's mother wanted "a man who [would] be all for her." In assessing the son's confusion over the meaning of autonomy, love and power in relation to masculinity, he likewise ignores all the contradictions in the father-son relation in this case and blames the mother:

> Since her husband is not up to this calling, she has attempted to fabricate such a man in the person of her son. To do so is not the easiest task, for it implies necessarily a destruction of desire, not only of her son's desire but also of her husband's. She will even go so far, as is seen in other clinical examples, as to encourage her son in the activity of destroying and denigrating his father's desire, and this is the pathway to the son's not having the phallus that will signify his desire. If the son cannot go to his

> father for the phallus he can go nowhere . . . except perhaps to the psychoanalyst.[1]

Such an inept blaming of the mother might simply be laughable were it not for the fact that it is a practicing psychoanalyst who makes these sweeping assumptions. He ignores the complexities glimpsed in Freud's sparse commentary on this woman's circumstance and personal history and merely portrays a shrew.

The Oedipal axioms play just as easily into the hands of misogyny in Mahony, in whose text the Rat Man's mother arises as in a vision:

> Her controlling nature, entrenched miserliness, ambivalent attitude toward neatness, and lack of the outbursts so characteristic of her husband and son indicate an obsessional personality with restrictive traits. If she was family-conscious, concerned about the comfort of her house, and even protective of her son against her violent husband, she could yet be critical, controlling, and dangerously seductive and phallic.[2]

None of this characterization can be reasonably drawn from Freud's text. Where then does it come from? Oedipal theory gives these analysts a very limited framework for surmising what actually motivates a patient to follow out certain lines of psychosexual development. Because they assume that the mother-son relation must be at the source of the later pathologies, Mahony and Schneiderman are unconstrained in their hypotheses about the kind of woman the Rat Man's mother would have had to have been to create his particular pathologies. Faced with the Rat Man's deadened feelings, his antagonism to his mother's marriage plan and his propensity to replicate his father's romantic history, Schneiderman thus interpolates an appropriate maternal source: "Here we might say that this mother awaited from her son the same attentions that she assumed her husband would have bestowed on the lady who was his true love."[3] The voracious, affection-starved and manipulative mother of Schneiderman's and Mahony's imagination is a figment of Oedipal theory.

When psychoanalytic thought obscures the real-life mother and replaces her with the Oedipal mother, theory is merely following blindly in the paths of male dominance and modern patriarchy. For it is these institutions which produce the elaborate social-symbolic construction that transforms a son's relation to his mother into a desire molded by compulsory heterosexuality. Because psychoanalytic theorists fail to see that the Oedipal mother is a product of specific social practices and cultural forms, they have to naturalize her presence and embody it "in the first place" in the woman from whom the patient was born. My alternative hypothesis needs the backing of the Freudian notion of *Nachträglichkeit*. The complex temporality Freud traces in sexual development suggests, I have argued, that the adolescent boy's adaptation to the compulsory forms of heterosexuality happens along with a retrodetermination of his attachments to his mother. In this movement back to the future, the Oedipal fixation on the mother is created retroactively as the adolescent's heterosexuality and masculinity are being created in his anticipatory fantasies and his actual "object-choices."

The forces shaping a son's Oedipal relation to his mother are not any universal or archaic condition of the mother-child relation, but rather the cultural codes and representations which derive from the historical and collective relations between men and women. The psychogenesis that Freud sought to explain the pathological and the normal tendencies of male heterosexuality has to be reframed in terms of the social genesis and cultural genealogy of the pathologies and norms themselves. The "mother/whore" representation is a linchpin of the Oedipus complex and a nodal point in the cultural representations and symbols that legitimate the social domination of women by men.

Even though Freud considered the "mother/whore" dichotomy an essential component of the Oedipus complex and a feature of the virtually universal pathological tendencies of modern male heterosexuality, he could not see the relevance of the social relations of male dominance. Nor could Lacan, despite his emphasis on the tendency of male heterosexuality to split the "female object" in two, as in the Poor Woman/Rich Woman in the Rat Man. It is once again necessary to reconstruct Freud's clinical interpretations—this time those that bear on the intrinsic pathologies of male heterosexuality—in order to rethink the link between a cultural pathology and the psychosexual pathology of individuals.

Two years after the article "A Special Type of Choice of Object Made by Men," Freud returned to the "mother/whore" figure in the second of the *Contributions to the Psychology of Love,* "On the Universal Tendency to Debasement in the Sphere of Love" (1912). His topic is "psychical impotence" in men, and he moves from a discussion of its etiology to the claim that the essential features and dynamics of this pathology are well-nigh universal in male heterosexuality. He concludes the essay with a speculation on civilization and the instincts that sets the pattern for later works like *Civilization and Its Discontents.*

The clinical picture presented by men who suffer psychical impotence is, Freud reports, remarkably uniform. Moreover, this complaint was the reason men most frequently gave for seeking therapy from Freud and his psychoanalytic colleagues.

> This singular disturbance affects men of strongly libidinous natures, and manifests itself in a refusal of the executive organs of sexuality to carry out the sexual act, although before and after they may show themselves to be intact and capable of performing the act, and although a strong psychical inclination to carry it out is present. The first clue to understanding the condition is obtained by the sufferer himself on making the discovery that a failure of this kind only arises when the attempt is made with certain individuals; whereas with others there is never any question of such a failure. He now becomes aware that it is some feature of the sexual object which gives rise to the inhibition of his male potency, and sometimes he reports that he has a feeling of an obstacle inside him, the sensation of a counter-will which successfully interferes with his conscious intention.[4]

Almost invariably, according to Freud, the woman with whom the individual is impotent possesses "some feature, often an inconspicuous one," which becomes the obstacle and is itself associated with his mother or sister. The woman then acquires the mantle of the incest taboo at the same time that she is the recipient of the man's esteem and affection.

Freud's whole approach to the etiology of male impotence rests on a distinction he makes between two "currents" in the psyche. "Two currents whose union is necessary to ensure a completely normal attitude in love have, in the cases we are considering, failed to combine. These two may be distinguished as the *affectionate* and the *sensual* current."[5] Already differentiated in the psyche in infancy, these currents make up the two slopes of the child's libidinal-affective relations with others. Affection is said to arise from "the interests of the self-preservative instinct" or "the valuations made by the ego-instincts" in the sense that the child's extreme dependence on particular individuals, especially the mother, imbues them with intense emotional value. "From the very beginning [the affectionate current] carries along with it contributions from the sexual instinct—components of erotic interest—which can already be seen more or less clearly even in childhood and in any event are uncovered by psycho-analysis later on."

This erotic slope is said to arise because the acts of caring for the child's needs simultaneously stimulate and gratify the "component instincts," and because the family members treat the child as "an erotic plaything."

During latency the sensuality that was originally mixed with affection "is diverted from its aim." Not until the psychophysiological changes of puberty is the boy's "affectionate fixation" on his mother again "joined by the powerful 'sensual' current which no longer mistakes its aim. . . . Here, however, it runs up against the obstacles that have been erected in the meantime by the barrier against incest." It is not just the barriers that have been constructed in the meantime but also, as I have argued earlier, the forms of heterosexual desire themselves. The mother cannot be loved Oedipally except through the many mediations that intervene between the son's original relationship with her and the unfolding of adolescent sexuality. Freud, however, does not see that a refashioning of the other, of the maternal object, is likewise in process. He sees the determination of the future objects but not the retrodetermination of the past object. The sensual current, he asserts, "will make efforts to pass on from" the "objects of primary infantile choice" to others who are unaffected by the incest taboo: "These new objects will still be chosen on the model (imago) of the infantile ones, but in the course of time they will attract to themselves the affection that was tied to the earlier ones."[6]

The recombination of the affectionate and sensual currents is the path Freud postulates for the psychologically normal outcome of the adolescent crisis. The sexual aim will first be redirected toward females who are not family members, and then the affection and esteem the boy formerly reserved for his mother and sisters will follow along. By the same token, this is the critical point at which the two currents are vulnerable anew to splitting. The etiology of psychical impotence in men lies, according to Freud, in just such a splitting. If too much frustration "opposes the new object-choice" or if too much attraction is still exercised by the "infantile objects," then "the libido turns away from reality, is taken over by imaginative activity (the process of introversion), strengthens the images of the first sexual objects and becomes fixated to them."[7]

The force of the incest taboo then prevents these libidinal attachments from becoming conscious. The individual's erotic capacities are henceforth inhibited. When the maturational crisis of adolescence takes this turn, the adult male will, according to Freud, find himself able to love a woman only so long as his sensual desires are not implicated as well. Esteem and affection become incompatible with pleasure. Some women become his "mother," others are "whores." Freud expressed the sexual economy of men suffering from psychical impotence in the well-known formula: "Where they love they do not desire and where they desire they cannot love."[8]

I question the adequacy of the clinical picture and etiological scheme just detailed to situate and explain "the universal tendency to debasement." Freud does not hesitate to assume that the affectionate and sensual currents exist separately and as such before the individual accepts or adopts the "mother/whore" representation in adolescence. He thus also assumes, conversely, that this representation is ready and waiting as a meaning-structure to which the individual's two psychical currents can fit themselves. The currents precede the representation and flow directly into its dichotomy of "mother" and "whore."

Freud's clinical observations, however, misguide his theoretical reflection, for they seem to warrant the assumption of an archaic differentiation of affection and sensuality. The sexual impasse a man encounters when his love for a woman becomes stymied because of the traits she shares with his mother is often overcome Freud had observed when the man seeks out a "debased sexual object":

> The main protective measure against such a disturbance which men have recourse to in this split in their love consists in a psychical *debasement* of the sexual object, the overvaluation that normally attaches to the sexual object being reserved for the incestuous object and its representatives. As soon as the condition of debasement is fulfilled, sensuality can be freely expressed, and important sexual capacities and a high degree of pleasure can develop.[9]

Debasement refers to the moral, aesthetic and social valuation by means of which the man deems a woman his inferior and on this basis finds her desirable. The debased sexual object is "a woman who is ethically inferior, to whom he needs attribute no aesthetic scruples, who does not know him in his social relations and cannot judge him in them. It is to such a woman that he prefers to devote his sexual potency, even when the whole of his affection belongs to a woman of a higher kind."[10]

The theoretical model takes its cue from the sequence of behaviors through which a man's psychical impotence manifests itself. He first suffers the inhibition of erotic capacity. He then recovers this capacity with women he considers debased morally, aesthetically and socially. And, ultimately, he falls prey to the bifurcation of heterosexual experience into incompatible forms of "love" (with those who figure as "mother") and "desire" (with those who figure as "whore"). In this view, psychical debasement is the solution, albeit pathological, that the "mother/whore" representation offers to the young man's libidinal-existential dilemma.

It is a mistake, however, to assume that the "affectionate" and "sensual" currents are independent of the "mother/whore" representation and its accompanying forms of debasement. It makes more sense to suppose that the representation enables the differentiation to start with. In the earlier essay on the "special type of choice of object," Freud in effect showed that the "mother/whore" representation is part of the *formation* of the Oedipus complex. "Overvaluation" and "debasement" are already linked in the adolescent boy's incestuous fantasies. His mother has to be reembodied as Mother and Whore to become the object of Oedipal desire. Debasement has already helped make male heterosexuality in its bifurcated form, before it can be called upon as a "protective measure" *against* the bifurcation of male heterosexuality.

Freud does not acknowledge the contradiction between the two essays, but he does respond to it. He revises the first essay in the guise of a simple clarification:

> We can now understand the motives behind the boy's phantasies mentioned in the first of these "Contributions," which degrade the mother to the level of a prostitute. They are efforts to bridge the gulf between the two currents in love, at any rate in phantasy, and by debasing the mother to acquire her as an object of sensuality.[11]

It is in fact quite clear in the first essay that the "mother/whore" representation does not bridge but creates the gulf between esteem and sexuality. It marks the intrusion of a moral regime that opposes respect and pleasure and a symbolic-institutional regime that projects this division onto women in the opposition between housewife and prostitute. This binary, this impoverishment of the language of desire, becomes the idiom in which the adolescent boy expresses his feelings toward the real and imagined women in his life.

Freud's first essay carefully distinguished two movements of this symbolic process. First, the dichotomous force of "mother/whore" dubs the real-life mother the esteemed and therefore asexual "mother" opposed to the "whore"; second, the boy's often tormented recognition of the mother's sexuality—

which is itself mediated through his understanding that his father possesses her—re-dubs the real-life mother a "whore," a "mother/whore" who is then and only then the object of the son's *Oedipal* desire. The so-called *2nd term* of the Oedipus complex is this "mother/whore." Contrary to Oedipal theory, this is not a "primary" object at all. It is a highly mediated one, having been worked up through the eyes of the father and through the symbols, institutions and roles of the society. Nor therefore is the son's incestuous attachment to the mother at all immediate, given, axiomatic. It emerges through the cultivation of male heterosexual desire. It is not a natural desire in need of taming by the paternal powers of civilization; it is a civilized desire produced by paternal power.

Freud's evocation of the "universal tendency to debasement" signals a pathology at the very heart of the prevailing forms of male heterosexuality. He does not look to the social relations between men and women in his search for an explanation. None of men's monopolies over social goods and power becomes a focal point. The institutions of modern patriarchy never become relevant. Instead, Freud advances an early, though already refined, version of his story of the conflict between civilization and instinct. He treats instinct as natural impulse and civilization as barriers against impulse. He misses how the forms of impulse are themselves cultivated, and how the institutions and norms of civilization are varied and changing. His mode of social diagnosis and cultural critique forgoes specifying the institutional and symbolic processes that are formative of male heterosexuality.

Where Freud should have looked for the cultural pathologies of the Oedipus complex he saw only the pathology of civilization. The Oedipal pathology in question is quite sharply delineated by Freud. He defines psychical impotence as a scale of symptoms. At one extreme "the whole of a young man's sensuality becomes tied to incestuous objects in the unconscious, or to put it another way, becomes fixated to unconscious incestuous phantasies. The result is then total impotence."[12] At the other end of the scale are men who are "psychanaesthetic: men who never fail in the sexual act but who carry it out without getting any particular pleasure from it—a state of affairs that is more common than one would think."[13]

Between these extremes lie the symptoms which Freud presented at the outset of the essay, that is, men who end up impotent with women they esteem, potent with women they deem inferior. The constant across the whole spectrum is the tendency to debasement organized around the "mother/whore" dichotomy, whether the debasement is confined to fantasy or actually determines object-choice. "We cannot escape the conclusion," Freud asserts, "that the behavior in love of men in the civilized world to-day bears the stamp altogether of psychical impotence."[14]

Encumbered by his hypothesis of an archaic differentiation of affection and sensuality, Freud concludes that civilization discourages the requisite coalescence of the two currents. The polymorphous components of sexuality remain intractable to the denials and sublimations exacted by civilization. The conflict is exacerbated by the cultural ideals and social norms that direct male heterosexuality toward marriage to a woman who can be esteemed in light of prevailing moral, aesthetic and social standards. And the social constraints that typically postpone sexual experience well beyond puberty cause the adolescent's sensuality, nourished only in fantasies, to remain fixed on his mother. However relevant all these factors may be, Freud's account leaves out the essential: it is not the simple fate of affection and sensuality that is at stake here, but rather the cultural forms that actually embody such feelings in particular types of relationships.

In the frequently cited conclusion to the essay, Freud tacitly acknowledges the one-dimensionality of his own cultural criticism:

> Thus we may perhaps be forced to become reconciled to the idea that it is quite impossible to adjust the claims of the sexual instinct to the demands of civilization; that in consequence of its cultural development renunciation and suffering, as well as the danger of extinction in the remotest future, cannot be avoided by the human race. This gloomy prognosis rests, it is true, on the single conjecture that the non-satisfaction that goes with civilization is the necessary consequence of certain peculiarities which the sexual instinct has assumed under the pressure of culture. . . .
>
> It is not the aim of science either to frighten or to console. But I am myself quite ready to admit that such far-reaching conclusions as those I have drawn should be built on a broader foundation, and that perhaps developments in other directions may enable mankind to correct the results of the developments I have here been considering in isolation.[15]

However much Freud is willing to allow that there may be actual or potential countertendencies in modern society—the "developments in other directions"—his own theoretical model in fact leaves him at a dead end. The limitation to the "single conjecture" regarding sexuality and culture has emerged from the most basic premises and procedures of his social reflection. And it remains ingrained in the whole of his approach to the Oedipus complex.

To reinterpret the role of the "mother/whore" in the Oedipus complex requires a shift in focus. Instead of supposing its psychogenesis out of affection and sensuality, it is necessary to look at this representation's *social genesis* and *symbolic genealogy*. Where does the meaning-structure "mother/whore" come from?

The most compelling response to this question has come from Silvia Bovenschen, a German feminist and cultural critic, who has offered a genealogy of the "mother/whore" representation that reaches back to the dichotomy of *saint* and *witch* in the late Middle Ages and, behind that, to the distinction between white and black magic in premodern practices of witchcraft. In a speculative, programmatic essay—"The Contemporary Witch, the Historical Witch and the Witch Myth: The Witch, Subject of the Appropriation of Nature and Object of the Domination of Nature"—Bovenschen argues that the persecution of witches in the late 15th and early 16th century reflected an anxious reassertion of male dominance in the midst of massive social upheaval. The result of Bovenschen's reflections is a feminist genealogy of morals. She provides a way of resituating the Freudian theme within a longer history of social transformations and symbolic transvaluations.

The survival of pagan magic in the Christian Middle Ages amounted, Bovenschen suggests, to the persistence of a prepatriarchal heritage in a patriarchal society. While women's very practice of magic reflected the deep-seated, transepochal division of labor which assigned women a distinct and subordinate role, these practices also confirmed that women enjoyed "an extremely authoritative and intimate relation to nature" and corresponded to "their actual power in prepatriarchal times": "Despite the fact that women were so far removed from all actual and political power, they still played an important role in the still intact agrarian society within the realm of magic."[16] Women's social subordination was able to coexist with their privileged relation to nature.

It was just this stable coexistence that began to break down in the 15th century. A complete transvaluation of women's magical practices, inaugurated by the Church, spread through wide segments of society. The distinction between white and black magic had previously expressed the ambivalence of the forces of nature for an agrarian world, "the good harvest and the destructive drought, the healing herbs and the lethal mushroom." But with the persecution of witches this *ambivalence* was refashioned into the *dichotomy* between the "saint" and the "witch." The destructive "natural-demonic" potential of nature was transfigured into the "eschatological-demonic" potential of women.

Not only did women's special knowledge of nature cease to be the counterweight to their social subordination, it now justified repression and violence:

> the Church at that time made women responsible for only the evil effects of nature. . . . The "black" principle was from then on the witch in the service of Satan, the apostate Angel; the "white" principle was Mary, handmaiden of the Lord, the denatured, desensualized woman of the immaculate conception. . . . The ambivalence towards appraising women's status—at an earlier time the evaluation fluctuated between magical awe and fear—now appears ideologically displaced in the two distinct images of the "virgin" and the "witch."[17]

Whether or not one accepts with Bovenschen the claim that perhaps a million women died in the campaigns against witches, it is certainly true that the persecutors believed that "*every* woman was a potential witch." Femininity was being reimagined, embodied in new symbols and confined to new social roles. Among the explanations Bovenschen advances for this transvaluation, two are particularly persuasive.

First, neither popular mythologies nor Church doctrine proved capable of interpreting the social transformations and upheavals unleashed in the waning of the Middle Ages. The Church's cosmological picture of stable social hierarchies was thrown into question by "inflation, famine, the dissolution of the guilds, the development of new means and techniques of production, an increasingly monetary economy . . . and the pauperization and brutalization of large segments of the society."[18] The popular imagination tended to interpret the general turmoil as the malevolent force of nature. The Church modified its official denunciations of magical practices and beliefs and now granted those beliefs in altered form. Witches became instruments of the devil, and their destruction promised the populace a return to social stability at the same time that it shored up the Church's social and ideological authority.

Second, Bovenschen argues that circumstance turned witchcraft into a challenge to male dominance. In the context of general social upheaval, the institutions of male dominance that would fit the emergent social structure were yet to be invented. In the interim, the social changes that were rendering the "magical" interchange with nature obsolete were simultaneously revealing the antagonism to male dominance in women's healing and hexing practices and in the accompanying forms of association among women. Uncertain of its authority and its future, male-dominated society attacked the prepatriarchal inheritance still preserved in witchcraft. The subjugation of women took the form of organized, socially sanctioned violence.

The new institutionalizations of male dominance, the modern patriarchal order, would ultimately find their anchor in the male-headed household. The bourgeois family would reorganize the sexual division of labor and transvaluate once more the dichotomous symbol of femininity. "Mother/whore" replaces saint/witch:

> the dualism of body and spirit, of witch and saint, continued to prevail in the bourgeois world. In the typifications of mother and prostitute this dualism took its institutionalized form. The mother and the prostitute were embedded in a stable social structure; external force was no longer needed to subdue them. Mary, the saint, was secularized into the housewife and mother (who was given the duty of mastering a larger repertoire of virtues), the witch became the prostitute, the assertive woman. . . . Both the mother and the prostitute were definitely of this world and under the control of men. But towering above these bourgeois typifications there hovered the ideological feminine ideal. The witch and the saint became myth. The idolatry and demonification of femininity—flip sides of the same coin—were cut off and distinct from the empirical woman. . . . the modern myth of femininity distanced itself further and further from reality.[19]

Bovenschen's genealogy of morals helps illuminate the Oedipal pathologies Freud encountered in the erotic life of men. His patients' symptoms were effects of the socialization process and the forms of intimacy dictated by the new institutionalizations and symbolizations of male dominance. Housewife and whore are institutionally secured roles women have been constrained to accept in order to survive; these roles place them in relations of subordination, dependence and inequality to men. As symbolization, "mother/whore" governs the forms of male heterosexuality and intimacy; men's idolatry and demonization of women persist not only in mythopoetic images of femininity but also more tangibly in the valuations that are decisive in the formation of the Oedipus complex.

The genealogy of "mother/whore" includes the moral-aesthetic-social valuation of women according to the dichotomy of *esteem* and *debasement* as well as the distinction in male heterosexual experience between *affection* and *sensuality*. The Oedipal structure of feeling embraces all the various moments in this genealogy. Male heterosexuality tends to take a form in which "affection" and "sensuality" are posed as opposites impossible to reconcile; in which women are rendered unreal through the dichotomy of "overestimation" and "debasement" and the stereotypes of "mother" and "whore"; and in which the symbolic genealogy "saint" and "witch" is recapitulated even as its violent history is disguised in valuations of intimacy.

The *2nd term* of the Oedipus complex is the figure of the mother produced by the modern institutions and symbolic genealogies of male dominance. Recall Freud's own tracing out of the making of the Oedipal mother. First, "mother" is one semantic pole of the "mother/whore" representation; the mother is designated "mother" because misperceived as a desensualized being. The son designates his mother "mother" to the degree that he denies her sexuality and so misrecognizes her. In the second step, the mother is designated "mother" and "whore" at the same time. The son recognizes her sexuality in the doubly distorted form of her debasement (she's no better than a "whore") and her subjugation to the father (she belongs to him). These distortions of the mother's sexuality and personhood follow upon the original misrecognition and fabulation of her. From the one designation ("mother") to the next ("mother/whore"), the real-life woman is eclipsed by the cipher which represents her. This cipher is itself a product of the discourse of male dominance and male fantasy.

Psychoanalytic theory successfully isolated the Oedipal mother and placed her within the son's individual myth, unwittingly uncovering the process of her construction. Psychoanalytic theory also, however, confused this figure with the real woman engaged in childrearing. It is necessary, therefore, to distinguish this symbolic mother from the real-life mother, just as Lacan distinguished the real-life father from the symbolic father to show how the individual myth was a structure with four not three terms. It is in fact a structure with five terms. The *5th term* is the real-life mother whose experiences and practices were completely obscured in Freudian and Lacanian theory.

The symbolic mother is the *2nd term* in the nomenclature of classical psychoanalysis: I—mother. The father has been called the *3rd term* because his authority supposedly limits the mother-son relation and breaks its dyadic exclusiveness: I—mother—father. Lacan showed that this *3rd term* was symbolic, the force of the name-of-the-father or the designations of fatherhood in culture, and had to be contrasted to the real-life father whose life and actions inadequately embody the symbolic function. Entering the individual myth as a kind of double, reflecting the son in the father himself or some substitute, the discordant presence of the real-life father became the *4th term* of the individual myth. The real-life mother I am calling the *5th term*. She is eclipsed in the individual myth and obscured in psychoanalytic theory by the Oedipal or symbolic mother. There is therefore more than a hint of paradox in the fact that psychoanalytic theory's *2nd term* is really a refabrication of the *5th term*.

The project of redirecting psychoanalytic theory by recovering the mother's real practices and relationships has been largely defined by the work of Nancy Chodorow, Carol Gilligan and Jessica Benjamin. They have examined how the mother's primary, central role in childrearing affects the child's gender-identity, value orientations and emotional and moral capacities. They argue that a mother's interactions with a daughter will tend to differ markedly from her interactions with a son. It is more than a matter of simply conveying or inculcating the culture's prevailing understandings of masculinity and femininity. Since the primary task of raising children has historically been assigned to women, usually to the exclusion of participating in other, highly valued spheres of social activity, the mother's very activity of mothering becomes charged with the social meanings of gender. The practical, emotional and communicative habits of tending to the son or daughter become a drama of gender-identity.

According to Chodorow, children thus encounter the paths of gender-identity expected of them and the socially sanctioned traits of masculinity and femininity from the mothering they receive right from the first months of life. The mother's role in the sexual division of labor determines the entire range of the child's capacities, forms of experience and self-understandings according to gender:

> Mothers tend to experience their daughters as more like, and more continuous with, themselves. Correspondingly, girls tend to remain part of the dyadic primary mother-child relationship itself. This means that a girl continues to experience herself as involved in issues of merging and separation, and in an attachment characterized by primary identification and the fusion of identification and object choice. By contrast, mothers experience their sons as a male opposite. Boys are more likely to have been

> pushed out of the preoedipal relationship, and to have had to curtail their primary love and sense of empathetic tie with their mother. A boy has engaged, and been required to engage, in a more emphatic individuation and a more defensive firming of experienced ego boundaries. Issues of differentiation have become intertwined with sexual issues. This does not mean that women have "weaker" ego boundaries than men or are more prone to psychosis. Disturbances in the early relation to a caretaker have equally profound effects on each, but these effects differ according to gender. The earliest mode of individuation, the primary construction of the ego and its inner object-world, the earliest conflicts and the earliest unconscious definitions of self, the earliest threats to individuation, and the earliest anxieties which call up defenses, all differ for boys and girls because of differences in the character of the early mother-child relationship for each.
>
> Girls emerge from this period with a basis for "empathy" built into their primary definition of self in a way boys do not. Girls emerge with a stronger basis for experiencing another's needs or feelings as one's own (or of thinking that one is so experiencing another's needs and feelings). Furthermore, girls do not define themselves in terms of the denial of preoedipal relational modes to the same extent as do boys. Therefore, regression to these modes tends not to feel as much a basic threat to their ego.[20]

Carol Gilligan, who introduced the reflection on gender into the theory of moral development proposed by Lawrence Kohlberg, makes a claim parallel to Chodorow's revision of psychoanalysis. Gilligan argues that girls develop an "ethic of care" in their moral orientations. Unlike boys they are therefore more oriented toward the reciprocal recognition of needs and responsibilities than rights and obligations. Drawing on George Herbert Mead's terminology, the "concrete other" figures more prominently than the "generalized other" in girls' moral reflections and decisions. Boys tend to adapt, instead, an "ethic of right" and suffer an atrophy of their capacity for competently interpreting another's needs, concretely recognizing another's situated viewpoint or evaluating interactions according to norms of responsibility, bonding and sharing.[21]

Chodorow in effect has drawn out the unanticipated consequences of Freud's final insight into his Oedipal theory. Since the source of their earliest emotional bond for both little girls and little boys is their mother, the formation of the (heterosexual) bond of the Oedipus complex is asymmetrical in the two sexes. Unlike the little boy, the little girl has to abandon her first love, her mother, and replace it with an Oedipal love for her father. Persuaded by the work of Jeanne Lampl-de Groot, Freud concluded in the last decade of his life that girls maintained their pre-Oedipal attachment to their mother longer than boys. He was constrained to admit that in fact the whole model of the Oedipus complex did not really apply to girls' development at all.

Since the Oedipus complex is gender-specific, Chodorow argues for a wholesale rethinking of the psychoanalytic approach to the psychology of women. She nevertheless still grants Freud's account of the Oedipus complex as an accurate picture of male psychosexual and moral development. In fact, she typically confirms her own hypotheses about women's experience by drawing a meaningful contrast to the male model.

It has been my project and argument to challenge Freud's Oedipal theory itself. For once critics like Chodorow herself expose how thoroughly gender-specific Freud's account is, it becomes necessary to question his theorizing of males. The fundamental concepts of the Oedipus complex were forged precisely under the illusion that human sexual and moral development followed a universal pattern so deep-seated in civilization as to be a second nature. The gender critique shows that the Oedipus complex does not arise from the inner logic of desire and the biological necessity of sexual reproduction, but rather from the imperatives of social reproduction, the cultural forms of gender differentiation and compulsory heterosexuality. The male model, too, therefore, is thrown in question.

The Oedipus complex remains immune from Chodorow's critical reflection, I believe, for two reasons. On the one hand, there is her justifiable intent to establish a radically new problematic within psychoanalysis, which has been so hostile to feminism and to questions of gender. She therefore pursues a strategy of immanent critique—as I have—in order to transform rather than abandon the psychoanalytic project. On the other hand, she simultaneously privileges the heterosexual, that is, heterosexualizing, form of the Oedipus complex; she takes for granted the triumph of the "simple positive Oedipus complex," even though Freud himself openly admits that this supposedly normal and normalizing outcome seldom occurs.

Her motives are not homophobic. Rather, Chodorow employs such a rigid model of social reproduction that she assumes that the normative force of the "simple positive Oedipus complex" is ironclad. In the arguments of

The Reproduction of Mothering, institutions reproduce themselves through the psychic structure of individuals, which in turn replenishes the institutional forms unchanged from below. The cycle of causality is seamless. The Oedipus complex is the gridwork through which mothering produces the gender-differentiated psyches that will reproduce the patriarchal institutions that have produced the sexual division of labor and the concomitant forms of mothering. I have argued, instead, that the masculine Oedipus complex is the individual's mapping of his primary family relationships as they intersect with cultural meanings and social institutions. The points of intersection, however, should be thought of as pathogenic zones where the dynamic conflicts and pathologies within society flare up in the individual's life-history.

I want also to stress that Chodorow has introduced the crucial revision into Freud's Oedipal paradigm. By juxtaposing the divergence in male and female development, she brings to light that the formative—and deforming—moment on the Oedipal path arrives when the little boy must renounce his identifications and sense of merging with his mother in order to define himself as different by way of his masculinity and as possessive by way of his heterosexual, Oedipal love for the mother herself. Those capacities of nurturance, empathy and bonding which he has encountered in his mother tend to become "selected out" of his own repertoire of capacities, frequently being denigrated as feminine in the process, and he is drawn toward those capacities and styles of treating others that will be rewarded and valued in the male-dominated spheres he is increasingly being summoned to enter.

This last statement is a weakened version of Chodorow's thesis. But it is more defensible. It aims to avoid her reproduction hypothesis. Personal destiny is not a mere instrument of the reproduction of social structures. At issue, rather, are the typical trials that individuals in our culture face in the course of their growth and development; the resources that are provided them or withheld by the practices and norms of their family, community and polis; and the patterns of conformity or rebellion or pathology that result. Social structure and personality do not mesh so perfectly. I also therefore ultimately reject Chodorow's psychic determinism. For she supposes that the pattern of desires and identifications laid down in a person's childhood, in the Oedipal and especially pre-Oedipal periods, determines the whole scope of one's later interactive capacities, identifications and desires.[22]

How then can the connection be made between the asymmetries of gender in the Oedipus complex and the special role of women in childrearing without recourse to Chodorow's psychosocial determinism? I read Jessica Benjamin's *The Bonds of Love* as an attempt to do just that. She expresses her debt to Chodorow and Gilligan without engaging any direct criticism of their work. But the crucial difference can be seen in the approach to the problem that is my concern in this chapter: namely, How is the real-life mother transformed in the libidinal and moral economy of the Oedipus complex into the *2nd term,* the symbolic Oedipalized mother?

Benjamin, like Chodorow, comes to assess the moment at which "The boy does not merely disidentify with the mother, he repudiates her and all her feminine attributes."[23] In the Oedipus complex, the price of masculinity and heterosexuality is a repudiation of the experiences and traits hitherto unique to the son's interactions with his mother:

> the boy's repudiation of femininity is the central thread of the Oedipus complex, no less important than the renunciation of the mother as love object. To be feminine like her would be a throwback to the preoedipal dyad, a dangerous regression. The whole experience of the mother-infant dyad is retrospectively identified with femininity, and vice versa.[24]

I want to keep the stress on the boy's *retrospective* perception that his interactions with his mother threaten engulfment or confusion. Benjamin comes closer than other psychoanalytic revisionists in grasping the *Nachträglichkeit* of the Oedipal experience. It transfigures the history of the mother-son relation into the insignia of regression. How does this transvaluation of values take place?

Benjamin keeps an acute double awareness of the values embodied in the Oedipus complex. They are at once the values that the society imprints on the process of male socialization and individuation—and are therefore real elements of men's life-histories—*and* they are ideological blindspots in Oedipal theory itself. At issue here is the meaning of separation and autonomy in the supposed transition from the mother-son dyad to the mother-father-son triangle. As a matter of theory and ideology, Benjamin challenges the longstanding psychoanalytic notion that the father must liberate the son from the swamp and haze of maternal dependence:

> The other here seems to play no active role in bringing the child to reality. In this polarized scheme, the mother exercises the magnetic pull of regression

> and the father guards against it; he alone is associated with the progression toward adulthood, separation, and self-control. The problems start, I suggest, when we take the symbolic figures of father and mother and confuse them with actual forces of growth or regression. There is no denying that unconscious fantasy is permeated with such symbolic equations. But even if the father does symbolize growth and separation—as he does in our culture—this does not mean that in actual fact the father is the one who impels the child to growth.[25]

When the symbolic equations take hold of the theory, they systematically obscure two crucial dimensions of the mother-child relation. First of all, the pre-Oedipal child is in fact at various stages eager to pursue new paths of engagement with the people and world around him or her. Since "infants take pleasure in interpersonal connection and are motivated by curiosity and responsiveness to the outside world, we need not agree to the idea that human beings must be pulled by their fathers away from maternal bliss into a reality they resent."[26] Second, the very notion that mothers are primarily or inevitably opponents of the child's independence is simply a fabrication. "Real mothers in our culture, for better and worse, devote most of their energy to fostering independence. It is usually they who inculcate the social and moral values that make up the content of the young child's superego. And it is usually they who set a limit to the erotic bond with the child, and thus to the child's aspirations for omnipotent control and dread of engulfment."[27]

These theoretical fabrications nevertheless are not mere sand castles, for the ideological elements they contain also play a role in the socialization-individuation process itself. The events and pressures that bring about the Oedipal crisis are themselves shot through with the symbolization "mother/whore," the new valuations of desire as heterosexual possession and new identifications with patriarchal forms of power. These conspire to revaluate the son's more complex attachment to his mother, and motivate him to disavow it:

> Now her nurturance threatens to re-engulf him with its reminder of helplessness and dependency; it must be countered by his assertion of difference and superiority. To the extent that identification is blocked, the boy has no choice but to overcome his infancy by repudiation of dependency. This is why the oedipal ideal of individuality excludes all dependency from the definition of autonomy.[28]

Classical psychoanalysis saw the repudiation of femininity as a normal part of masculine personality formation, even as it considered the purported corollary, women's penis envy, to be an illness. But as with so many of the supposed outcomes of the Oedipus complex the repudiation of femininity is in fact pathological. For, as Benjamin writes, "the damage this repudiation inflicts on the male psyche is indeed comparable to woman's 'lack'—even though this damage is disguised as mastery and invulnerability."[29]

What, though, is the relation between the mother who is repudiated and the desired, tabooed mother of the Oedipus complex? I have distinguished them as the *5th term* and the *2nd term,* the real-life mother and the symbolic mother. Thanks to Benjamin, we can now see that the son, in repudiating the real-life mother, is invited to reimagine his affections and identifications with her as a dreaded engulfment. Contrary to Benjamin, I have argued that the Oedipalization and transfiguration of the mother do not happen at age five or six, where classical psychoanalytic doctrine places the Oedipus complex. Rather, this retrodetermination of the mother-son relation occurs in the wake of early adolescence when the son has had worked up within him the cultural tropes and values and the paternal identifications and male fantasies required to refashion the mother as taboo and model object.

I think my argument about the *Nachträglichkeit* of the Oedipus complex is ultimately consistent with the core of Benjamin's own revision of Oedipal theory. It is a question of squaring the notion that the Oedipus complex causes the son to repudiate the mother even as he makes her the (forbidden) object of heterosexual desire with the notion that the Oedipus complex retroactively transfigures the mother into a tabooed and model object.

Benjamin disputes the dyad/triad conception because it ignores the autonomy-enhancing practices of the real-life mother's nurturance and overblows the unique role of the father's authority in "separating" the child from mother. The Oedipal triad is, in short, a fiction. Benjamin departs from Freudian and post-Freudian orthodoxy when it comes to the pre-Oedipal dyad. Reinterpreting the work of Margaret Mahler and other developments in object-relations theory, Benjamin shows that the intersubjective world of infants includes not only their complex interactions with their mother but also their various strivings for independence and active relationships with others, including the father in the household of the nuclear family. There is a whole many-layered history of interactions with mother *and* father that does not derive from the Oedipal configuration.[30]

Therefore, the reduction of the pre-Oedipal to the dyadic relation of mother-son is as misguided as the reduction of the mother-son relation to a pre-Oedipal dyad.

In place of the classical picture of the I—mother dyad being supplanted with the I—mother—father triangle, Benjamin strives to show how the patterns of parent-child interaction keep undergoing transformations and crises. When these ordeals culminate in the Oedipal crisis of adolescence, the adolescent boy, as I have tried to show, is wrenched from his attachments and identifications with his real-life mother insofar as he must now desire her according to the scenarios of male fantasy, ambiguously following and avoiding his father's footsteps. The real-life mother is misrecognized. She is christened anew as the *2nd term* of the Oedipus complex (the Oedipal mother), and the reality she has had for the son is transformed into images of a dreaded oceanic oneness.

The "Oedipal mother" and the imagined "pre-Oedipal mother" are in this sense created at the same moment. They are of course contrary representations: the mother to be possessed and the engulfing mother. And the Oedipal mother is further contradictory in being the "mother/whore" or, in another register, the tabooed and the model object at the same time. The real-life mother is, as it were, lost twice over in the formation of the Oedipus complex. The son's nonrecognition of her occurs along two slopes. To become the object of his newfound heterosexual desire, her mothering must disappear behind the myth of oceanic oneness. And, even as the mother is brought into the field of heterosexual desire, her own desire and will go unrecognized. "Realizing that mother belongs to father, or responds to his desire, is not," Benjamin writes, "the same as recognizing her as a subject of desire, as a person with a will of her own."[31]

The very concept of the pre-Oedipal is misleading, despite its considerable appeal and heuristic value. It emerged in response to the limitation imposed on psychoanalysis by Freud's insistence that the Oedipus complex was the central event of psychological life and the key to the formation of neurosis as well as the benchmark of normative psychosexual growth. Melanie Klein, object-relations theorists, Jacques Lacan and others struggled against the limitation by examining the many phenomena that could not be subsumed under the Oedipal paradigm: principally, the earliest effects of the mother-child relation; the experiences of affection, fear, gratitude and dependency that bind a child to others; and the wealth of powerful imagery in dreams and fantasy that have to do not with possession, rivalry and genital desire but rather with engulfment and separation, merging and abandonment. All these phenomena become "pre-Oedipal" by default, because the overriding assumption remains that they are part of a phase on the way to the Oedipal. Moreover, it is wrongly assumed that the Oedipus complex is formed and dissolved at age five or six, leaving the "pre-Oedipal" associated with early childhood.

Benjamin's arguments as well as mine throw these assumptions completely into doubt. Significant "Oedipal" elements are already in the "pre-Oedipal" relation of mother and child to the extent that the mother brings to her mothering the whole of her own experiences, relationships, fantasies and desires. Moreover, mothering includes schooling the child in separation, autonomy and independence, all of which cannot therefore be subsumed under the paternal tutelage of the Oedipus complex and yet are not "pre-Oedipal" in the conventional sense. Much of what psychoanalytic theorists consider "pre-Oedipal" about the maternal relation—oceanic body, semiotic *chora,* precommunicative flux—are images of dubious origin which come to designate the mother retrospectively, retroactively. Such images of merging and unboundedness are surely important, culturally encoded benchmarks of happiness or dread, and they certainly resonate with, among other things, our earliest experiences. But that does not mean that they or the trajectory of their meanings comes from the mother. Finally, since the Oedipus complex is in no way completely formed or fully effective at the age psychoanalysts have traditionally placed it, it cannot be the sole or key entry into experiences of independence or rules or language or symbols.

The retrodetermination of the Oedipus complex is a crisis whose effects and pathologies radiate out into the adolescent boy's sense of self and others. The meaning of his relationship with his mother, reaching back beyond the reach of memory, becomes a cacophony of "mother/whore," taboo, ideal, oceanic immersion. This powerful, yet incomplete de-realization of the mother feeds and is fed by the heterosexual forms of his desire and the difficulties of recognizing women as "equal independent subjects."[32] His masculinity, as Chodorow and Gilligan in effect show, becomes tied to suppressing or abandoning capacities for empathy, care and dependence. He is prone to associate need for another with loss of self, just as he is prone to interpret autonomy as self-sufficiency.

As I have argued before, all of these elements of the Oedipus complex are bound up with the father-son relation, including the dissonance between the symbolic and the real-life father. It is via the identifications with the father and the promises of patriarchal power that son experiences the transformation of his relation to his mother—the eclipsing of the *5th term* by the *2nd term.* Yet it would be wrong to say that the Oedipus complex marks the intrusion of the father into the mother-son relation. That is too close to the cliches of the classical doctrine.

The Oedipus complex forms, rather, in the interplay and conflict between two intersubjective fields: *mothering* and *fatherhood.* I use the terms mothering and fatherhood to stress that "maternity" and "paternity" are asymmetrical terms. The practices that make up mothering are not parallel to those that create fatherhood. However rich the dramas psychoanalysis stirs up regarding Mother and Father, it has had recourse to the crudest ideological allegories when trying to account for the conflict between mothering and fatherhood. Lacan occasionally figures maternal love as the "natural" slope of the child's experience, while fatherhood is the "cultural" slope. Ricoeur likewise juxtaposes the pathogenic mother and the cultivating father, untamed maternal fixation and paternal symbolism.

The ascendancy of fatherhood over mothering in the Oedipal crisis marks the power of patriarchal institutions and symbols over the social-symbolic practices of women's nurturance. In the context of our society's sexual division of labor and still patriarchal households, boys encounter this ascendancy of fatherhood over mothering at the most decisive point of their maturation. Their socialization and individuation is at that moment imprinted with the effects of compulsory heterosexuality and male dominance. Their responses vary enormously, which is why even the Oedipus complex is not a simple instrument of social reproduction. Nevertheless, those responses always can and need to be read back against the oppressive cultural and social structures that shape them.

It is worth heeding a warning Benjamin made in her reflection on Oedipal theory. It is crucial not to mistake our culture's symbolic figures of mother and father for the "actual forces of growth or regression." That warning against the equation of father with liberation and mother with regression applies quite directly to classical psychoanalysis. But it also raises a question about Benjamin's procedures and about my own.

Benjamin presents her scenarios of growth and regression in the form of typical dramas between the child, carefully distinguished as boy or girl, and the mother and the father. Her material includes Mahler's observations of children and parents, some clinical observations of her own and the case histories and examples of other theorists. She has then taken the trends she sees in this material and recast them into the behavior patterns of certain ideal types (mother, father, son, daughter) and then personified these in her psychological scenarios of patterns of growth or regression. Unlike Chodorow, she does not draw the circuits of causality too tightly between these family dramas and the relevant social and cultural processes. She also, importantly, tries to cast the typical behaviors as moments where more than one outcome is possible. After all, we are discussing the ordeals of growth, self-identity and desire which individuals do not live out according to script. And yet the sense of a script remains, a feeling that the complexities of families and contingencies of individuals are being remolded to a theory.

My own arguments are vulnerable to the same questioning. The whole project of linking cultural interpretation, social criticism and psychoanalytic theory is, it seems to me, inevitably caught up in this problem. It does not admit of a theoretical solution. Rather, it requires a vigilance and skepticism about your own generalizations, and a constant effort to cross-check your conclusions with disparate materials, from case histories to biographies, from self-analyses to novels.

There is an advantage I think in approaching the Oedipus complex as an *individual myth.* The classical Oedipus complex delineated three roles to be fulfilled by three people: child, mother, father. Oedipal theory stylizes the supposed behavior of empirical individuals, threatening to stereotype the particular experiences encountered in therapy and to enforce covert ideological patterns through theory. The individual myth, by contrast, is understood as one's *representation* of one's relation to mother and father. Furthermore, the institutional-symbolic context of these empirical relationships—male-dominated monogamy, compulsory heterosexuality, the sexual division of labor, patriarchal culture, public and private spheres, community and polis—is variously inscribed within the individual myth. I have been identifying those "joints" or points of articulation between the parental relationships and the larger social and cultural context by explicating the significance of dissonances between the real-life and the symbolic mother and father.

Those points of articulation are also the typical pathogenic zones of the Oedipus complex, the sites of crisis in the process of socialization-individuation. From this standpoint, the concept of the individual myth focuses the conflicts and pathologies of the Oedipus complex, rather than supposing its regularity as a means of social reproduction. The latter view of the Oedipus complex is common to Ricoeur, who celebrates its normative validity, and to Chodorow, who criticizes it. Ricoeur therefore sees the Oedipus complex as the culmination of the making of modern individuality and patriarchy, while Chodorow sees it as the crux of a relentless social mechanism.

Neither can see it as responsive to or wracked by historical change. Yet, as I have tried to show in situating the origins of Freud's thought in its historical context, the Oedipus complex and Oedipal theory took shape in the midst of social and political change and registered those changes in the life-histories of individuals. The social spaces crucial to the formation of the Oedipus complex—household, community, market, polis—do not in fact mesh into a fitted whole, whether the Hegelian synthesis of spirit and flesh evoked by Ricoeur or the neo-Marxist, functionalistic totality evoked by Chodorow. The Oedipus complex is permeated by the conflicts that shape and disrupt these different social spaces.

A significant change in our lifetimes has been the challenges mounted by the women's movement to male dominance and the erosions of the legitimacy of patriarchal authority. Benjamin speculates that the debate over the supposed demise of the Oedipus complex signals an important historical change in the social relations between men and women. Writers like T. W. Adorno and Max Horkheimer and Christopher Lasch she reads symptomatically. Their lament over the waning of strong fathers and internalized authority reflects the fracturing of men's power over women.

Benjamin suggests that political and social changes are reshaping the experiences mapped out by the Oedipus complex. Theorists like Adorno and Lasch reacted defensively, as men do in their everyday lives when confronted with challenges to male authority. It is time, instead, she argues, to take stock of the cultural pathologies being exposed by these very changes:

> The breakdown of paternal authority and the resulting search for a different route to individuation are the context for the controversy over Oedipus and Narcissus. . . . But this does not mean that the decline of authority has "caused" the demise of a once successful form of individuality; rather, it has revealed the contradiction once hidden within that individuality: the inability to confront the independent reality of the other. Men's loss of absolute control over women and children has exposed the vulnerable core of male individuality, the failure of recognition which previously wore the cloak of power, responsibility, and family honor.[33]

The "inability to confront the independent reality of the other" I have traced in this chapter with respect to the misrecognitions that arise with the repudiation of mothering and the Oedipalization of the mother. The erosion or turbulence in the habitual structures of male dominance have not of course overturned these structures. We are historically in the midst of significant battles over the future of modern patriarchy. It is all the more important, then, to approach the Oedipus complex as a structure of feeling that registers or resists social changes. I have also traced the ascendancy of fatherhood over mothering in the Oedipus complex, for in fact that remains a shaping dimension of our childrearing practices. The symbols of fatherhood—the *3rd term* of the Oedipus complex—remain a powerful though contested dimension of contemporary life.

10

The Name-of-the-Father

ILL-GOTTEN GAINS usually inspire the usurpers—and their heirs—to offer recurrent justifications. They live out an acute moral dilemma, even as they struggle not to acknowledge it. It is the kind of dilemma Claudius faces right after Hamlet has caught the conscience of the king in "The Mousetrap," the little play that confronted him with the image of his own crimes. Claudius has killed his own brother and then taken his brother's wife to wife. He now suddenly burns to repent. But he cannot fathom losing what he has gained:

> My fault is past. But, O, what form of prayer
> Can serve my turn? 'Forgive me my foul murder'?
> That cannot be, since I am still possessed
> Of those effects for which I did the murder,
> My crown, mine own ambition, and my queen.
> May one be pardoned and retain th' offense?[1]

Claudius contemplates how "above" his inevitable confession will be wrung from him, too late to save him. Not so here below:

> In the corrupted currents of this world,
> Offense's gilded hand may shove by justice,
> And oft 'tis seen the wicked prize itself
> Buys out the law.[2]

Crime pays, especially when the crime gives you the throne. The injustices done can be made to appear the rightful laws of the realm. Even as torment drops Claudius to his prayerful knees, he cannot finally bring himself to come clean because he cannot give up his crown, his power or his queen.

Men have a problem. For much like Claudius they can scarcely fathom the loss of ill-gotten gains, the immeasurable material, psychological and political advantages they enjoy because of the dominance they have historically exercised over women. But they do not encounter their victim merely in the ghostly theatre of bad conscience. For men not only enjoy the fruits of dominance over women, they also typically owe their profoundest experiences of love to women—through their mothers, sisters, lovers, wives, daughters. When Freud uncovered men's tendency to fuse esteem and degradation in their most compelling images of women, he grasped just one consequence of the fact that the victims of male dominance are also the objects of filial, heterosexual and paternal love.

Like other usurpers, men have been compelled historically to furnish explanations and justifications for their dominance. These justifications tease out the divine designs, biological imperatives, social necessity, moral rightness—in short, the *laws* in all senses of the term—behind those arrangements that embody male dominance and female subordination. The modern discourse justifying male dominance frequently has an added imperative, namely, to obscure or disavow the fact of dominance altogether. Social and political theorists, as well as psychoanalysts, craft the slogans of disavowal. Inequalities are just differences. Subordination is natural inferiority. Obedience is affectionate reciprocity. Anatomy is destiny.

One of Lacan's most innovative contributions to psychoanalytic theory, the *nom-du-père,* is at the same time yet another attempt to interpret patriarchy while disavowing the reality of male dominance. The *nom-du-père* or name-of-the-father is Lacan's reworking of the *3rd term* of the Oedipus complex, the Father. The name-of-the-father is a symbolization. It is the cluster of cultural meanings associated with fatherhood. Picking up on Ricoeur's argument that fatherhood is a series of designations, I have proposed that the names-of-the-father include such designations of fatherhood as *begetter, name-giver, law-giver, castrator, provider, protector, redeemer.*

These designations enter the individual myth as its *3rd term;* they also have an organizing power in certain discourses that regulate social interactions. Lacan's own use of the concept includes a kind of working definition of the patriarchal dimension of culture, for he stresses the symbolic identity between the figure of the Father and the Law: "It is in the name-of-the-father that we must recognize the base of the symbolic function, which has identified his person with the figure of the law since the dawn of historical time."[3]

I will be challenging Lacan's understanding of "the law" and his ahistorical, undifferentiated conception of the name-of-the-father. Like Ricoeur, Lacan provides an affirmative hermeneutics of fatherhood. He ultimately accepts patriarchy as a fact of culture. In arguing for a socially critical interpretation of the symbolizations of fatherhood, I will show how the name-of-the-father supplies the symbolic legitimation of specific forms of male dominance in modern society. This legitimating function has eroded and become increasingly contested the more modern society has evolved a complex set of norms for regulating social interaction. Lacanian theory will have to be evaluated as a response to the erosions and the contestations that beset the paternal symbols.

Let us begin, however, by summarizing how Lacan brings the name-of-the-father to bear on the Oedipus complex. The name-of-the-father is enmeshed in a fabric of cultural representations and brings those representations into the life of the family and its members. As with the Penates in Ricoeur, the name-of-the-father connects household to the larger culture. The cultural designations of fatherhood are distinct from the man playing the role of father in the family. The concept of the name-of-the-father, according to Lacan, "permits us in a particular analysis to distinguish this function from the narcissistic and even the real relations the subject maintains with the image and actions of the person who embodies this symbolic function."[4] The son's relation to his father's image and actions is thus the *4th term* distinguished here, as in "The Neurotic's Individual Myth," from the symbolic *3rd term.*

Lacan grants the symbolic a kind of autonomous efficacy in family life. The paternal symbol operates independently of the parents' actual behaviors or intentions. It is a "structural" element of the parental complex, coming into play in the "contingencies" of an individual's life-history. Such a statement might be construed simply as saying that when particular individuals undertake the role of parent they participate in a background of practices and symbolizations that pre-form their own actions and may have effects on their child however exactly or completely they perform their roles. But Lacan also distinguishes the symbolic from the real more sharply. He asserts that the real-life father in the modern family always falls short in carrying out the archaic cultural imperatives of fatherhood: "When represented by a single person, the paternal function concentrates in itself imaginary and real relations that are *always more or less inadequate* to the symbolic relation which constitutes that relation *essentially*."[5]

Such distinctions between the symbolic and the real father are unobjectionable as they stand. They have proved useful in interpreting the role of the father in the case history of the Rat Man and in Kafka's autobiographical writings. But, as I have argued with respect to the *4th term*, Lacan falters when he tries to forge a social diagnosis of the modern family and modern society on the basis of the dissonance of the symbolic and the real in the father-son relation.

On the one hand, his historical perspective is reduced to the idea that the modern family is inadequate to its cultural task because the weakened real-life father cannot uphold the symbolic mantle of fatherhood. Premodern culture takes on the aura of a vanished glory from the standpoint of modern society. And, on the other hand, the primacy Lacan grants the symbolic over the real holds good only from the standpoint of the clinical focus on individuals. As regards this or that particular family, yes, the roles concrete individuals assume come with a cultural script. From the standpoint of collective life, however, the "real" has to be understood more amply as social relationships and institutions. The symbolic does not have primacy over the real in this sense.

Such confusions in Lacan's thinking not only turn his social diagnosis of the family into a vague lament against modernity, but also prop up his affirmative hermeneutics of fatherhood. He ends up viewing the paternal symbols and their ordering of cultural representations as intrinsically valid. In fact, the more discordant modern life seems with regard to those symbols and representations the more valid they appear.

Against Lacan, I will argue that the psychoanalytic interpretation of fatherhood should be joined to the social critique of male dominance. How do the symbolizations of fatherhood work in relation to the institutions and practices of male dominance? The Lacanian problematic is skewed from the beginning insofar as it defines the name-of-the-father solely in terms of the father-son relation and not the husband-wife relation or by extension the social relationships between men and women.

The paternal symbols are linchpins of the legitimation of male dominance in modern society. I am using the terms dominance and legitimation in Max Weber's sense. Male dominance comprises the real, socially organized power which men, collectively and individually, exercise over women. It is organized through various economic, political and cultural practices and institutions. Like all forms of dominance, it maintains itself by force and the threat of force; these are still ubiquitous aspects of male dominance in our society. At the same time, male dominance requires legitimations; it seeks to justify itself through discourses and to secure the agreement or acquiescence of those subjected to it.[6]

How do men, collectively and individually, seek to justify their domination of women by appealing to binding symbolizations of fatherhood? Ricoeur has helped differentiate among these symbolizations. I will focus on three sets of paternal symbols—*begetter* and *name-giver; law-giver* and *castrator; provider*—in order to reconstruct the elements of Lacan's own reflection. For he tacitly evokes just these particular meanings in discussions of the name-of-the-father.

Lacan first establishes the designation *begetter* in the name-of-the-father. Men's role in procreation only attains social recognition or significance, he argues, through language. Fatherhood *is* symbolic: "the attribution of procreation to the father can only be the effect of a pure signifier, of a recognition not of the real father but of what religion has taught us to invoke as the Name-of-the-Father."[7]

The formulation melds two distinct facts. First, any individual male's role in procreation is open to uncertainty, at least in his own eyes and his community's. He is therefore acknowledged to be the father only in being designated the father, in contrast to the recognition of the mother's role in pregnancy and childbirth. Second, in patrilinear societies a child receives its name from the man who has been designated the father. Fatherhood is established in a double designation: *begetter,* which gives social recognition to a man's role in procreation, and *name-giver,* which delineates generational ties via patronymics.

Begetter carries another semantic valence as well, namely, the father's death. Lacan, like Ricoeur, views the most elementary symbolization of fatherhood as a designation of the dead father. Since the father's name orders the generations, becoming a "father" is to take one's place in a lineage that not only reaches back to the dead father but also points ahead to one's own death and succession by others. It is the fate Laius feared. And the link between death and fatherhood is especially pronounced in primitive societies where the tribe's paternal heritage resides in its ancestral originators.

It is at the next level of interpretation that Lacan connects the designation of the dead father as *begetter* to the designation *law-giver*. The connection is already in Freud. According to Lacan,

> the whole thrust of his reflection led him to connect the appearance of the signifier of the Father, as author of the Law, to the Father's death, indeed his murder—thus demonstrating that if this murder is the fecund moment of the debt through which the subject is tied for life to the Law, the symbolic Father, insofar as he signifies this Law, is indeed the dead Father.[8]

This represents Lacan's extrapolation from *Totem and Taboo*. Freud had identified the totem as a symbol of the tyrannical father whom the sons had killed and then revered as the origin of the prohibition against murder and incest. Lacan accepted Freud's linking of *begetter* and *law-giver* under the sign of death, but he also realized the need for a more reliable anthropological grounding than the "primal horde." He therefore turned to Claude Lévi-Strauss's theory of primitive kinship exchange.

From Lévi-Strauss he takes the conception of "the Law" which he presupposes must be represented by the Father. In Lévi-Strauss's model of primitive societies, *the fundamental rules of social organization* reside in the bonds and exchanges governed by kinship and marriage. These rules Lacan construes as the Law. To the extent that the paternal symbols give order to the kinship bonds and exchanges, the Law can meaningfully be said to depend upon the name-of-the-father.

Lévi-Strauss showed that this Law could be reduced to the regulated exchange of women by men, an exchange whose mainspring is the prohibition of incest. In primitive practices of kinship exchange, women serve as gifts exchanged by men. Daughters, sisters or cousins are given to the men of other families or clans by their fathers, brothers or uncles. The men are the agents of exchange, the women are the signs and wealth exchanged. The sexual contact a man is forbidden with his own female relatives is compensated by the sexual access he acquires as the result of some other man's gift.[9]

A seamless web joins the general laws of social organization and the patriarchal symbolization of the Father as *begetter, name-giver* and *law-giver* in societies of this type. Lacan's appeal to Lévi-Strauss may well seem an improvement on the primal horde, but it raises fresh problems. The primitive social organization is founded upon male dominance. The theoretical significance of this historical fact will not, however, become apparent unless the two seamlessly connected aspects of primitive kinship are analytically distinguished, that is, the social practices of exchange and the patriarchal symbolizations which accompany them:

(1) The social practices of the tribe make men the *agents of exchange* while women serve as symbolically charged *wealth*. There accrues to men, by virtue of this role, an array of rights, privileges and powers which are unavailable to women. The status of women is that of the object on whom those exclusively male rights, privileges and powers are exercised. As Gayle Rubin has observed in her commentary on Lévi-Strauss, men exercise their *rights of bestowal* by giving their female relatives to one another, and they enjoy an *aura of sociality* because of their exclusive power to enact and affirm the bonds of the tribal community.[10]

(2) As regards the patriarchal symbols, men and women participate in the tribal community's normative discourse asymmetrically. In the pragmatics of this discourse, a man becomes *someone speaking* by virtue of being placed as the *referent* of the paternal symbols which govern the social practices of exchange themselves. The authority to speak derives from one's status as an actual or potential father. A woman, by contrast, is *something spoken* by virtue of being placed as the *sign* which the authorized male agents of exchange circulate among themselves.

It should now be easier to see that the specificity of the primitive social formations Lévi-Strauss describes lies in the peculiar relation between the form of male dominance and the mode of its symbolic legitimation.

On the one hand, the male dominance institutionalized in kinship exchange is isomorphic with the rules of social organization *as a whole*. Jürgen Habermas gets at this aspect of the Lévi-Straussian model in the following terms: "The primary roles of age and sex form the organizational principle of primitive societies. The institutional core is the kinship system, which at this stage of development represents a *total institution;* family structures determine the *totality of social interaction.*"[11]

On the other hand, the patriarchal symbolizations of kinship legitimate male dominance in a distinctive manner in this type of society. Kinship is the *sole* binding discourse of the tribe, and the *paternal* symbols determine the relation of *both sexes* to the discourse of kinship. As a consequence, any reference to a normative principle in the conduct of social relations is subordinated to those paternal symbols. They are the hinge of sociality itself.

Because Lacan relies on the Lévi-Straussian model without distinguishing the social practices of exchange from the patriarchal symbols, he does not see that those symbols are legitimations of male dominance. He will consequently make two false steps in the domain of social theory that haunt his entire reflection on the name-of-the-father.

(1) Lacan invalidly infers from the centrality of patriarchal symbols in primitive society that they are endemic to human language and culture as such:

> The primordial Law is that which in regulating marriage superimposes the reign of culture on the reign of nature left to the law of copulation. . . .
>
> That law has been adequately understood as identical to an order of language. For, without the nomenclature of kinship there would be no capacity to institute the order of preferences and taboos which braid and weave the thread of lineage through different generations.[12]

What does the claim that the Law expressed in paternal symbols is "identical to an order of language" really mean? So far two viable propositions about language and kinship can be advanced. Patriarchal kinship depends upon an order of language in the sense that there could be no socially recognized fatherhood without designation. Second, patriarchal kinship is itself an ordering of language—or, more accurately, of discourse and the pragmatics of speech—in the sense that the paternal symbols place the sexes asymmetrically in relation to the normative discourse of the tribal community.

It does not follow, however, that the paternal symbols of kinship are coterminous with the order of language. This *non sequitur* guides much Lacanian theory. Lacan takes the normative-legitimating discourse peculiar to primitive societies as the model for language per se. He will therefore tend to treat the connection between the Father and the Law as intrinsic to the very order of language and hence of culture, regardless of the social formation in question. Here, then, is the source of his erroneous insistence that the "symbolic" has primacy over the "real," and that culture is in principle patriarchal.

(2) Lacan extrapolates from primitive to modern society on the untenable supposition that paternal authority is a social-linguistic requirement intrinsic to human culture. He makes the name-of-the-father the one element within the rule-governed field of language which signifies the rules governing social interaction. In Lacan's own words, the name-of-the-father is "the signifier which, in the Other as site of the signifier, is the signifier of the Other as site of the law."[13]

He further assumes that the modern socialization of the individual is structured by the same seamless connection between paternal symbols and rules of social interaction as in primitive societies: "Isn't it evident that a Lévi-Strauss, in suggesting that the structure of language and the aspect of the social laws governing kinship imply one another, is already conquering the same terrain where Freud has placed the unconscious?"[14]

It is evident only if one disregards two crucial differences between primitive and modern social formations. First, kinship exchange, including its specific forms of male dominance, is no longer isomorphic with the rules of social organization as a whole. It is absurd to assert that the social-symbolic rules of kinship are the Law for modern societies. Second, the symbolizations of fatherhood do not therefore provide the sole normative discourse for modern societies. The designation of the father as *law-giver* does not subsume all the economic, moral, political, bureaucratic norms and rules of modern social life.

These theoretical confusions seriously mar Lacan's reflection on the modern family and socialization. He remains blind to the myriad forms of male dominance in modern society and their impact on the process of socialization-individuation. Because he does not acknowledge that the name-of-the-father legitimates male dominance, he also fails to critically interrogate the dysfunctions and challenges to which this legitimating symbolization has become vulnerable in modern societies. Instead, he misconstrues these historical rumblings as indications of the shortcomings of modern institutions relative to the supposedly permanent imperatives of culture. Finally, Lacan remains satisfied that the heightened discrepancy between the real and the symbolic father in the modern restricted family is the one problem of patriarchy that might serve as the paradigm for a general social diagnosis. As social critic, he is left to intone that the institutions of modern life do not live up to the culture's indelible paternal symbols.

Modern patriarchy does indeed have its own patterns and conflicts. The paternal symbols are themselves vestiges of earlier social formations and provide modern society with a language in which to legitimate male dominance. But the modern forms of male dominance are exercised within social and political spaces that are simultaneously subject to other norms and rules. The market, the polis and the household are sites of complex, contradictory norms.

Women have suffered, and continue to suffer, economic oppression because of their unequal and subordinated place in the division of labor;

compelled or channeled into certain forms of labor and deflected or barred from others, they have fewer opportunities and receive smaller rewards than men. These inequalities are continually legitimated with reference to the names-of-the-father, but they are also challenged by appeals to equality, comparable worth or affirmative action and by reinterpretations of women's capacities, aims and values.

Women have systematically been denied access to political and bureaucratic power and to political and cultural public spheres. These inequalities are continually challenged by women's appeal to rights of participation and by the cultural and moral innovations that attempt to transform the meanings of participation, power or publicness. So, too, the so-called private sphere of the household is rife with male dominance. Tradition, habits and laws secure men's power over women in the resolution of marital disputes and family conflict and in the control over reproduction and the shape of erotic life. The name-of-the-father still exercises supreme force in the domestic space, but even there the personal and the collective challenges that women undertake appeal to a spectrum of norms and rules—legal understandings of battery, reproductive rights, cultural understandings of sexuality, love, obligation, freedom and so on.

In all of these social and political spaces, the paternal symbols are powerful but not exclusive expressions of the governing norms or rules. Such symbols attempt to legitimate male dominance and secure acquiescence to it. But there is no seamless connection between the patriarchal discourse and the social practices as a whole or between the patriarchal symbols and discourse as a whole. Acquiescence is not coterminous with participation, as in the Lévi-Straussian model.

The social and political spaces of modern patriarchy have become conflictual. The social and political relations between men and women have likewise become conflictual, and their future open and undecided. Nor are the challenges uniform. As I have tried to signal in enumerating the kinds of responses mounted against the modern forms of male dominance, the norms thrown against the patriarchal norms are varied. Ethics of right as well as ethics of care are appealed to. Sometimes equality, sometimes difference is the linchpin of the transvaluation of patriarchal hierarchies. Critique sometimes appeals to already existing, deeply entrenched intersubjective norms; sometimes it reinterprets the interactions and rules altogether and seeks to create a new norm or new overriding value. The intricacies of women's movements and feminist politics are a reminder of how absurd it is to try to theorize gender relations or their fate within household, market, community or polis from any single vantage-point.

Yet that of course is exactly what psychoanalytic theory has tried to do, especially as regards the domain of marriage, family and childrearing. The household surely remains the most intense focal point of patriarchal power and symbolism in our society. The significance of the *3rd term* in the Oedipus complex or individual myth attests to the significance of that power and symbolism in the socialization of children. How, then, to grasp the insistence of patriarchy in the unconscious while recognizing that in fact it does not fully control the relationships over which it presides?

A displacement of the psychoanalytic emphasis is required. The parent-child relationship at the heart of the Oedipus complex is at the same time the child's relation to a husband-wife relationship. Ricoeur acknowledged this when he argued that the outcome of the Oedipus complex depends upon the son's perception of mother-father as wife-husband. However, Ricoeur was unwilling to see that the husband-wife relationship is constructed from multiple, potentially conflictual social norms. He indignantly repudiated Kant's discussion of the juridical-contractual dimension of marriage in favor of the Hegelian picture of marriage as a carnal-spiritual bond.

Lacan exhibits the same blindness. He attributes significance to just one normative aspect of the husband-wife relation, namely, the status of fatherhood. He is then able to isolate fatherhood as the key to the *mother's* role in the socialization of the child. All-important in the Lacanian scheme is the mother's willingness to refer in her dealings with her child to the *nom-du-père,* that is, in the pun that arises because "nom" is pronounced just like "non": the name-of-the-father and the Father's "No." According to Lacan, the child's very entry into a symbolic-moral order hinges on how the mother "esteems [the father's] word [*parole*], his—let's say it—authority, that is, the place that she reserves for the Name-of-the-Father in the promotion of the law."[15]

Having made paternal authority the decisive basis of socialization, indeed, of entry into the symbolic order as such, Lacan is reduced to evading the crucial question even when he himself poses it:

> The fact that the Father can be taken to be the original representative of [the] authority of the Law requires us to specify under what privileged mode of presence he is maintained beyond the subject who is actually led

> to occupy the place of the Other, namely, the Mother. The question is therefore postponed.[16]

How, in other words, is the mother in her capacity as the child's primary caretaker led to establish the privileged authority of the father in her own interactions with the child? The question need not be postponed once it is recognized that the name-of-the-father is already at work within the husband-wife relationship itself as a legitimation of male dominance.

Consider first how the father's authority legitimates the very division of labor in the husband-wife roles. The mother's primary caretaking role casts her as "the subject who is actually led to occupy the place of the Other." It is primarily through interactions with her that the child begins to acquire the competencies and capacities for interaction with others in general. She is the first person to embody the community to which the child will belong. The father's authority enters into this maternally centered scene of instruction.

The mother's evocation of the father as *law-giver* conveys the social value placed on their respective activities. His "privileged mode of presence" lies in just those values, which invert the value the mother and father's activities have had for the child. The mother must refer to his authority and superiority if he is gradually to appear in the child's eyes as the head of the household, the decision-maker, the breadwinner. In designating the father *provider* the wife establishes the social perception that his paid labor or income or profit is more valuable than her own role as the child's primary provider. The ascendancy of fatherhood over mothering thus legitimates the forms of male dominance embodied in the sexual division of labor and the gendered mapping of private and public, household and market.

Since Lacan will hear nothing of male dominance, he ignores the legitimating function of these names-of-the-father and instead opts for the standard psychoanalytic stylization of family relationships. He reduces the social practices of mothering to the "mother's love," which embodies "the irrefutably *natural*" bond in the conjugal family. Meanwhile, the father, whose real-life power he ignores, is said to embody *culture* and performs the civilizing mission of taming maternal love and maternal attachments:

> the father is the representative, the incarnation, of a symbolic function which concentrates in itself those things most essential in other cultural structures: namely, the tranquil, or rather, symbolic, enjoyment, culturally

> determined and established, of the mother's love, that is to say, of the pole to which the subject is linked by a bond that is irrefutably natural.[17]

Mother = Nature, Father = Culture—through these mythic equations Lacan bends Lévi-Strauss's investigations to support the very ideology whose reproduction within the modern family I have just described. These equations also express the underlying symbolic assumptions that Hegel and Ricoeur employ in picturing marriage as "carnal-spiritual" institution. For the synthesis they really imagine is between the maternal body and patriarchal spirit. The name-of-the-father is in practice a legitimation of male dominance. In Lacan's hands, the theoretical concept of the name-of-the-father does not merely fail to illuminate this fact but attempts to rationalize it.

Having failed so dramatically to recognize the mother's social and cultural practices, Lacan cannot distinguish the pathogenic from the socializing effects of the mother-child relation. He has recourse to the grossest abstractions. The mother-child relation is a "natural," quasi-incestuous bond that must be broken with the intervention of "culture" in the form of the Father's "No." The Lacanian position is finally deserving of the same criticism that Jessica Benjamin has leveled against Max Horkheimer and T. W. Adorno, who also reduce the mother-child relation to mere autonomy-robbing dependency. The neo-Freudian view, whether Lacan's or Horkheimer and Adorno's, ultimately "implies that the child has no spontaneous desire to individuate, to become independent, nor the mother to encourage independence—therefore the father's intervention is required to save civilization from regression. . . . Above all this view is problematic because it denies the possibility of a maternal nurturance which encourages autonomy. But what is nurturance if not the pleasure in the other's growth? if not the desire to satisfy the other's needs, whether it be the need to cling or the need to be independent."[18]

How then to describe the dynamic of dependence and autonomy in the mother-child relation without assuming that the father's authority, the *3rd term,* is a sufficient—or even necessary—condition for the child's socialization-individuation? I want to couch the beginnings of a response in Lacan's vocabulary even though he cuts himself off from even entertaining the question. My intent is to keep open a dialogue with the Lacanian problematic, a dialogue that can then be pursued in the next chapter, devoted to the work of one of Lacan's most innovative followers, Maud Mannoni.

The Lacanian dialectic of desire is always stated in genderless form: *There is no satisfaction of human desire except when mediated by the desire and labor of others.* In the family setting psychoanalysts take to be paradigmatic, the infant so completely depends upon the mother's love and labor that she in effect stands for "others." The child's autonomy will require that the mother's wishes and fantasies, gestures and actions, not become the exclusive field from which the child draws his or her own wishes and fantasies, gestures and actions. The more exclusive the mother's care, the greater the tendency, arguably, for her not only to stand for "others" initially, but to take their place ultimately, that is, to present herself as the Other.

Contrary to Lacan, this does not imply that paternal authority—or, in classical Freudian terms, the designation of the father as *castrator,* that is, the agent of the separation of the child from the mother—must or does serve to guarantee the child's individuation and autonomy.[19] What counts, rather, is that the mother refer to norms and rules of interaction that apply, in an increasingly reciprocal manner, to the relation between herself and the child and to the expanding set of intersubjective relations the child participates in. Her desire must not be the exclusive reference-point for the child's desire. The norms that regulate how the child's desire mediates or is mediated by the desire of others must be established as a *3rd* term vis-à-vis the mother-child relation itself.

Lacan confuses this dimension of the dialectic of desire with the practices of modern patriarchy. The reference to norms and rules, that is, to an extradyadic *3rd term,* tends to be usurped by the reference to paternal authority in the modern male-headed household. There is no intrinsic necessity for "law" and paternity to be linked in this way. The linkage is the product of the historical evolution of male dominance and the modes of legitimating it.

Since the name-of-the-father cannot, moreover, be considered the standard of the norms and rules of social interaction in modern society, its "privileged mode of presence" still needs to be explained. I suggest turning around the meaning of a central Lacanian concept, namely, the idea of the *paternal metaphor.* Fatherhood does not become a metaphor for the norms and rules of interaction because it adequately summarizes them. It is in fact inadequate and is frequently countermanded by them. The paternal metaphor commands its position, rather, because it fulfills the legitimation requirements of male dominance.

Moreover, far from enabling or enhancing the (male) child's path to autonomy, the name-of-the-father brings him to a second threshold of nonautonomy. There are pathological effects of the reference to paternal authority. The name-of-the-father legitimates the forms of male dominance embodied in the husband-wife, mother-father relation. Its supposed positive force in the little boy's moral development has to be weighed against its role in inducing the child of either sex to accept male dominance as a normative condition of social life. It induces the child to seek his or her gender-identity in patterns of desire and labor that tend to replicate those same relations of domination.[20] And, finally, Lacan's protestations notwithstanding, the mother's references to the authority of the Father are plainly references to the real-life father's power and social standing; they offer the son the prospect of masculine privilege and power in exchange for obedience and thus instigate the moral distortions of male privilege and female debasement which are at the pathogenic core of the Oedipus complex.

11

Mothering and the Promises of Autonomy

I HAVE CRITICIZED Freud, Ricoeur and Lacan for failing to understand the role the mother plays in socializing children. When they identify the mother with the *2nd term* of the Oedipus complex or individual myth, they ignore the practices, experiences and relationships that actually shape a mother's interaction with her child. They are left, instead, with a symbolic construct fabricated in male discourse and fantasy in accord with the "mother/whore" dichotomy. This construct is indeed central to the formation of the Oedipus complex. But typically it is through the son's pathogenic identifications with his father's desire and power that he finds the symbolic construct and refashions his mother within the economy of his own desire. Just as the son's nonrecognition of his real-life mother is an effect of this Oedipalization of desire, so too the theorists have latched onto the *2nd term* of the Oedipus complex at the expense of recognizing the *5th term* at all.

I have also criticized psychoanalytic theorists for further obscuring the role of the real-life mother through their interpretations of the *3rd term* of the Oedipus complex, the names-of-the-father. Freud, Ricoeur and Lacan all grant the father the unique power of separating the child from the mother, of representing the moral imperatives of social life at large, of embodying the essentials of culture. Such patriarchal assumptions thoroughly obliterate the mother's role in educating the child into mastery, morality, learning and expressiveness—except by means of her references to the father's authority. But the name-of-the-father is neither in fact a sufficient nor in principle a necessary force in the socialization-individuation of children. Since the theorists have refused to acknowledge the socializing effects of mothering, they have also remained blind to the pathogenic effects of the name-of-the-father.

To recover the *5th* term against these various theoretical and political tendencies is a many-sided task. It is necessary to give an alternative account of those dimensions of the mother-child relation that can in fact foreclose the child's autonomy. It is necessary to reinterpret the social meaning of the maternal obstacles to autonomy. And it is necessary to specify how the mother-child relation, how maternal nurturance, actually fosters autonomy, growth and learning and establishes norms and rules of interaction which are distinct from the name-of-the-father.

Nancy Chodorow's important work on mothering and psychoanalysis has proved an invaluable guide to uncovering the narrative of mothering hidden in psychoanalytic reflections and, in turn, linking mothering to larger social processes. However, as I argued earlier (Chapter 9), Chodorow makes too tight a fit between mothering, gender-roles and the imperatives of social reproduction in contemporary society. The specificity and contingency of mother-child relationships is lost; the ordeals of maturation are deprived of their uncertainty, variability, individuality. Jessica Benjamin has significantly overcome the mechanicalness of Chodorow's model. She has loosened the strands of causality enough to grant a range of outcomes in the ordeals of socialization and individuation. But her description of the practices, experiences and relationships that a mother brings into her mothering needs to be supplemented by further clinical explorations.

I am therefore going to draw on the remarkable work of Maud Mannoni to further flesh out a psychoanalytically informed, socially critical inquiry on mothering. Mannoni was an early participant in the Lacanian movement and brought to it many of the preoccupations of the anti-psychiatry movement. She undertook a pioneering study of retarded children and their families. The results of fifteen years of clinical work were published in 1963 under the title *The Backward Child and His Mother.*

Mannoni encountered two distinct, mutually illuminating situations in her practice. When a child's retardation has an organic origin, Mannoni concerns herself with the meaning that the child's being "retarded," "ill" or "handicapped" acquires for the parents—in their fantasies and anxieties, in their own histories, in their recognitions of the child. Mannoni is especially interested in how this meaning can then rebound on the child and overlay his or her retardation with neurotic or psychotic effects. The second situation Mannoni devotes herself to concerns families in which a child's retardation has in fact been created to support the parents' own anxieties and fantasies.

The boldness of Mannoni's project lies in her attempt to conduct full-blown psychoanalytic therapy with retarded children, in sharp contrast to the traditional analyst's requirement that a potential client be endowed with more than average intelligence. Moreover, her work, like that of R. D. Laing and David Cooper in England, took place in institutional settings. She drew psychoanalysis into an unprecedented, often conflictual relation to medical, educational and social authorities. At many crucial junctures in her work, therefore, the social meanings of clinical relationships and the politics of therapy are brought sharply into focus.

Mannoni achieved in practice as well as theory what I consider the most valuable aspect of Lacanian psychoanalysis, namely, the effort to reconstruct psychoanalysis along intersubjective rather than intrapsychic lines, and to reflect upon psychoanalytic therapy as dialogue. Mannoni had always to intervene in an ongoing family crisis, and she was led to experiment in conducting analysis with child and parent at the same time. The intersubjective world of the retarded child came to the fore along with the dialogic potentials of psychoanalysis.

What, though, can a focus on retardation, psychotic reactions, maternal neuroses and family illnesses actually illuminate? Like Freud, Mannoni theorizes from the standpoint of pathological rather than normal processes. She seeks to disclose the normative, in all its fragility, from the standpoint of the most abject forms of human suffering and inhibition. There does emerge from her work the clear, normative conception of autonomy that is otherwise latent at best in Lacanian theory: namely, the socialized individual's capacity to participate actively and on a par with others in a widening network of interactions.

The competences required for such autonomy are strikingly damaged in the children Mannoni studied. There are two forms of competence she stresses in keeping with her Lacanian orientation. An integrated body image is required to develop a capacity for bodily expression, movement and activity. And, second, the acquisition of language is required as a medium of reciprocal relations with others and of the capacity to relate to one's own history.

A general pattern seemed to emerge from Mannoni's cases. The mother's identity or self-recognition, including her acceptance of the social role she has chosen or been compelled to assume, has typically come to hinge on her child's dependence upon her and on fantasies nourished by the child's incapacitating traits. The prospect of the child's autonomy, and every step toward its realization, poses an unarticulated threat. Since the child's birth, the expectation of "being a mother" or "having a child" has become laden with meaning as a substitute for something missing or something lost in the mother's own history.

The awaited birth becomes the signification of the mother's unexpressed wounds or the symbolic, compensatory gratification of her unaddressed dissatisfactions and sufferings. The child's existence is to answer, and answer for, these wounds and sufferings. While Mannoni usually looks back to the mother's own childhood experiences, her detailed clinical accounts reveal that the mother's wounds are a record of her life in a society of sexual inequality and female subordination. Mannoni summarizes as follows the situation that typically oversaw the birth of the child she would eventually encounter in a state of abject incapacity, mentally retarded and neurotically or psychotically disturbed:

> For the mother, whether she is the real or the adoptive mother, there is an initial state, bordering on the dream, in which she wants to have a "child"; at first, this child is a sort of hallucinatory evocation of something from her own childhood, something that has been lost. This child of tomorrow is first created out of the trace of a memory that includes all the wounds she has experienced, expressed in a language of the heart or of the body (thus the mothers of psychotics experience the different stages of the embryo on the Imaginary plane as the development of a partial body within themselves). When this child, so ardently desired, finally arrives—that is, when the request is answered—the mother experiences her first disappointment: there he is, this being of flesh and blood—but he is *there,* separated from her, while at an unconscious level, what the mother really dreamed of was a sort of fusion.
>
> And it is from this moment, with the child separated from her, that she will try to reconstruct her dream. Upon this child of flesh and blood will be superimposed a fantasy image that will serve to assuage the mother's fundamental disappointment (a disappointment that has its origins in her own childhood).
>
> From now on, a deceptive relationship will be built up between mother and child—the child, in his materiality, always being for the mother a signification of something else.[1]

The most extensive of Mannoni's case histories is that of Isabelle, a neurotic child suffering from severe dyslexia and related learning disorders. Mannoni first interviewed her when she was seven and began psychoanalysis with her two years later. At seven, Isabelle was unhappy and ill-behaved. She had not mastered everyday communication and suffered complete spatial disorientation. She had an IQ of 71. She told Mannoni, "'The most beautiful thing that could happen to me . . . is for a fairy to make me dead. I'm too bad to live.'"[2] Mannoni's recommendation of psychotherapy was rejected, and Isabelle spent the next two years following "a course of orthophonic re-education, which enabled her to read while leaving unchanged her refusal to learn in school and her difficult behavior."

When Isabelle came back to Mannoni for treatment at the age of nine, "she was a frightened child, crying all the time, clinging to her mother, aggressive, friendless, and without any contact with her father, who seemed to ignore her completely." She had learned to read but "still refused to give a 'meaning' to reading—she could read, certainly, but it was no use expecting her to read either for pleasure or to increase her knowledge. Instead, in order to impede any possible progress, she became unreceptive to figures, and in this sphere one was up against a brick wall: she refused to have anything to do with sums."

I have earlier distinguished two promises of autonomy. The first, coming from the mirror phase, is the promise of *imaginary self-sufficiency*. The second is the promise of *participation on a par with others in symbolically mediated interactions*. Mannoni's work documents how the mother-child interaction can preempt these promises of autonomy and impede the child's acquisition of an integrated body image and a full capacity for speech.

Consider the mirror phase's promise of autonomy. Long in advance of the psychomotor development that will enable the child to experience his or her own body as completely distinct from others, the mother is called upon to accept that her newborn is separate from her. When the fantasies that are securing her identity as a mother repudiate this separateness, she and the child will "form, at times, a single body, the desire of the one merged in that of the Other, so that they seem to live one and the same history. On the fantasy plane, this history has as its support a body bearing, shall we say, identical wounds that have assumed a signifying mark."[3]

The child will in a sense miss the mirror phase experience of recognizing and identifying with the fully formed image of its own body. The mother's fantasy spares the child from the experience of alienation in which the recognition of oneself as another juxtaposes the body's inner disharmony and its harmonious image. By the same token, the child is robbed of the ordeal of countering this alienation with the sense of anticipation that the mirror phase also affords, the anticipation of growth and mastery and self yet to come. "The main danger confronting the feebleminded child is the inability to confront trials or ordeals."[4]

The anticipation of growth can become a source of anxiety for the child, an anxiety that reflects the mother's. At a fairly advanced point in her analysis, Isabelle told Mannoni a story that reflected her hesitant preparations for independence:

> The mother, in Isabelle's story, said to the little girl, "I don't want you to grow up, I'll always punish you for your faults, I don't want the sun to like you." "In ten years," Isabelle explained, "I'll be all alone, but Mummy tells me, 'If you grow up, I'll have no one to look after. When I was a little girl, my Mummy did everything and said everything for me.'"
>
> To grow up is to make Mummy die of sorrow, so the child hesitates to make Mummy die.

Isabelle's incapacity and dependence had become the meaningful, necessary core of her mother's own existence. Because Mannoni's methods make the mother's history as well as the child's a part of the analysis, this knotting of meaning in the threads of their two lives has to be unraveled for both the mother and the child.

Isabelle's mother had not wanted the pregnancy. Her first two children, twins, had just reached school age. "The birth of Isabelle was the turning point in her life: with this birth, she gave up her own personality to assume the anonymous role of wife and mother—anonymous because she herself did not recognize it." Isabelle was born prematurely and great effort was required to keep her alive. The mother had, in her own words, "to fight for the baby to be fed." At four months the infant was normal and the doctor ordered she be weaned, setting off an anorexic period which lasted until she was eighteen months, "practically at the age at which the child attained motor independence and was able to escape the mother 'and do silly things.'"

As Isabelle reached this first threshold of independent movement and unsupervised activity, accompanied by an inclination to eat grownup food, a second stage of the mother's relation to her took shape:

> from four to eighteen months she had been given considerable doses of phenobarbital, and, according to her mother, "didn't seem to be there."
>
> This "absence" was quite obviously linked to the suffering of the mother, who had still not adjusted to her new condition. It was when the child's absence appealed to the mother that the mother emerged from her own suffering to concern herself with her daughter's.
>
> The more difficult Isabelle became, the more the mother became fond of her and discovered in herself a sense of duty as a mother and housewife.

The mother was accepting her role in the victimized mode of duty. She was prompted not by Isabelle's first signs of health and independence but rather by her difficultness and her incapacity. From this point on, Isabelle and her mother fell into a pattern Mannoni generalizes in the following terms: "Any desire to awaken on the part of the child will be systematically stifled—so that, in the end, the child is convinced that 'he can't.' In any case, it is insofar as 'he can't' that he preoccupies the mother and is loved by her."[5]

Whatever glint of a fully formed body image Isabelle may have been acquiring at eighteen months, it was overwhelmed by the image of the fragmented body. She experienced her body in pieces. And each piece—her limbs, organs and orifices—remained "signifying marks" echoing or answering her mother's wounds and anxieties. The pieces of the body became "signifiers" in the unspoken dialogues of her "wordless relationship" with her mother. The pieces could not thereafter be integrated into the single image of a body Isabelle could recognize as her own, as herself.

Mannoni reports that at the beginning of the analysis, "in Isabelle's own words, the head and trunk were paralyzed; only the heart and legs were alive. The legs were either used to be naughty, or not used at all. The hands could not hold anything, and the eyes were frightened." Some parts of her body express her symbiotic tie to her mother. When she pictures (and experiences) useless hands, they are ciphers of what she must be to keep her mother's love. Analysis revealed that the "frightened eyes" echoed the frightened eyes of grownups who are alarmed when one doesn't eat and whose terror makes one's own neck ache with pain.

When the child does seek autonomy, she must do so through the body fragments themselves rather than a coordinated mastery of the body as a whole. Thus Isabelle's legs were the opposite of her useless hands. They permitted independence and motion by being "naughty"; when inactive, her legs were like the flowers she frequently drew to express her feelings: they "have a duty to remain fixed in the ground."

Her autonomy always carried a negative connotation, like "naughty." Or else it had to express itself in negations and refusals in the language of the fragmented body. Mannoni paraphrases Isabelle's explanation of a drawing she made of a mother and child:

> The mother's head is leaning to one side, as if she had a heartache or a headache. She has a little door on her belly. This little door, according to Isabelle, will become the door that Isabelle has in her ears, and that she will keep shut . . . , and she hears only what she wants to hear. The door is shut to grown-ups and, of course, at school.

Her fragmented body language makes even her protests against her symbiosis with her mother yet another manifestation of the symbiosis itself, removing her yet further from genuine autonomy: "As long as Isabelle was absorbed by her mother, her sole autonomy consisted in refusing food and in closing the door in her ear."

Isabelle's approach to language learning was blocked from the start. The door in her ear was shut to speech. Her own speaking was rife with dislocations and inversions. She was unable to locate an *I* in her discourse during the first several months of the analysis. She referred to herself as "one." She refused or inverted the agreed-upon meanings of words in her everyday communication and in what she heard at school. "She cried when given a present, and if she said yes, one was never sure whether she meant no. She was left-handed, and when she said, 'I'm going down,' she would go up."

She was similarly recalcitrant to the symbolic conventions of arithmetic. "It was obvious that what mattered for the child was that she not learn that 1 + 1 = 2—that is, be in agreement with the plus sign as understood by others. For Isabelle, plus had always been able to mean minus." Mannoni's interpretation stresses Isabelle's inability to place herself within the age hierarchy of her family, just as she could not place herself in space or locate herself in discourse as an *I*. "'Why am I the third of five, as you say? I say I'm just as much the fourth or ninth—anyway my name is Emilie, not Isabelle.'"

As therapist, Mannoni is looking to find how the child's learning difficulties are entangled in the intersubjective situation in which he or she lives:

> In these questions of dyslexic re-education, we often come up against prepsychotic structures, as in the case of the feebleminded. What is not right in speech, handwriting, and spelling takes on a meaning in the body image, and even in the history of the subject. Most of these children live in ignorance or misapprehension: they do not accept their sex, they deny the disturbing familial situation in which they find themselves, and so on. . . . The inversions are therefore to be found in life, in the relations of the child with others; they are then expressed—in addition, I would say—in the educational sphere.

The retarded child's "inability to use speech as a mediator"[6] in relations with others results not so much from a dearth of meaning in the child's world as from an excess of meaning. When the mother-child relation is saturated with unrecognized and distorted meanings derived from the mother's own history and desire, the child remains "unknown to himself [and] will become the support of something essential within her; hence a *fundamental misunderstanding* between mother and child."[7]

Such a fundamental misunderstanding undermines the second promise of autonomy, the promise offered by language of participating on a par with others in symbolically mediated interactions. Lacan likes to call the acquisition of language the "second entry into language." It has to be understood in light of an entry into language that happens before you learn to speak. A newborn is already endowed with a name, with a designated place in the nomenclature and symbolic network of family relations, with some set of gender-encoded "traits" by virtue of being a "boy" or "girl" and with meanings designating his or her place in the parents' personal histories or "family legend." These raw materials of the individual myth are also, therefore, part of the first entry into language.

More importantly, though, the preverbal interaction of parents and child is already structured by language through the dynamic of what Lacan calls the "request" [*la demande*]. The needs agitating and animating an infant provoke its "cry," which is heard by others, especially the mother, as a *request for love.* She answers in the form of the care and satisfactions she provides. In Lacan's terms, the request for love is a message that is constructed by its recipient (the mother) rather than the sender (the *in-fans:* the speechless one), who first encounters his or her message only as it comes back from the other. This discourse of the Other is at once unconscious, since thus subject is not a speaker but an *in-fans,* and intersubjective, since it is composed of all the effects of the requests made of others and by others.[8]

This dialectic of the request for love and the naming and symbolic situating of the newborn are the "first entry" into language. Our original extreme dependence is not only a dependence on the physical care others provide us but also on their language-mediated labor and desire. The second entry into language requires us, drawing signifiers from the discourse *of* others, to participate in discourse *with* others, forming messages, requests, expressions and so on. And to do so in our own name.

The fundamental misunderstanding Mannoni locates in the disturbed mother-child relation blocks this second entry into language. The meaning of the child's request for love now comes back to him or her as an obscure but compelling demand on the part of the mother. The child is being asked to answer the mother's desire and fantasy in the protolanguage of his or her symptoms, incapacity or illness. Language does not emerge for the child as a field of shared meanings available to self and other alike, but remains the monopoly of the other.

The child still seeks autonomy, but is deprived of the shared rules and agreed-upon meanings of language needed to do so. His or her self-assertion may then take the extreme form of a refusal to speak at all, negation being the discursive gesture of last resort. Or, as with Isabelle, the struggle for autonomy may take the form of inverting the agreed-upon meanings of a language that cannot break loose from the hold of the Other's desire.

How does a mother come to place herself in the position of the Other, monopolizing the domain of meanings and blocking the child's approach to language? How do her own unrecognized wishes come to be expressed in the child's debility and incapacity? How does the child's autonomy come to represent a threat to the mother's identity and security, to her sense of worth and expectations of fulfillment?

Mannoni shatters the psychoanalytic stereotype of the "pathogenic" mother, along with the picture of a quasi-natural, incestuous bond between mother and child in need of the cultivating intervention of paternal authority. *The Backward Child and His Mother* gives a very different picture, even as it descends into the pathogenic depths of these relationships. Because Mannoni's therapeutic method calls forth the mother's actual voice and history, she is able to grasp the real-life mother whose practices, fantasies and relationships have such impact on her child. Even as Mannoni concentrates her attention on pathogenic mothers, she begins to recover the occluded *5th term* of Oedipal theory.

The wounds that afflict the women whose children are suffering from neurosis or psychosis are a record of what those women have been denied at the level of socially recognized, meaningful activity. Becoming a mother is often a compulsory role they have approached on the demand of husband or family. Or it is a promised fulfillment to offset whatever they have suffered or been deprived of in their own families and in their adult aspirations.

When they then face, virtually alone, the responsibility of caring for a child, especially one who is "ill," "difficult" or "slow," their further sacrifices are typically socially recognized merely as duty but become meaningful and a source of self-recognition precisely to the extent that their child cannot get along without them. The betrayal of the child's promised autonomy has been prepared by the social and family betrayal of that same promise for the women themselves. Their recognition, worth and happiness have been staked so exclusively on "being a mother" or "having a child" because the other paths to what they want to be and to have have been foreclosed.

Isabelle's mother was "a highly gifted woman who had begun higher mathematics when very young. Her education had been interrupted by the death of her own mother, with whom she had had ambiguous relations. 'I was very spoiled by Mummy,' she told me. 'She was always beating me.'"

Her mother's death had forced her to abandon her studies in order to care for her fourteen-year-old sister. She also mourned her mother's death by preserving the image of their victim-victimizer relation. Her mother had not only beaten her but also favored the younger sister "who had not done well in school." The difficulties of her new predicament lent themselves to her sadomasochistic image of the mother-daughter relation. First the younger sister and then Isabelle became her victimizers, she the victim in a replay of the original dyad.

Her life-history followed a path from victimized daughter to victimized mother. She sought compensation for her interrupted education in love and marriage only to find herself alienated in the anonymity of the role:

> While quite young, she met a brilliant boy who was passionately interested in mathematics and research. For her, he was the eternal student, yet successful in his job and a good father to his children. He was the image of everything the young woman had wanted to do when she was twenty. It was the husband who achieved the emancipation from maternal tutelage that she herself would have liked to enjoy—while she became, like

> her own mother, a housewife who devoted herself to her children. She had each of these children against her will. The first died before he was a year old. Then came the twins. She had no respite, and had given up her dream of continuing her studies. No sooner had the older children reached school age than she found herself pregnant with Isabelle, and felt condemned by fate to her role as mother and housewife. . . . The subsequent births [there were two children born after Isabelle] were accepted without incident. For each of them she was the dispenser of food that kept her children healthy. For each of them—except Isabelle. For Isabelle she was more. Isabelle had to be saved from herself; she had to be forced to live.

As recounted earlier, being a mother became meaningful—as duty—only when Isabelle reached eighteen months. She refashioned her alienated role by deriving from it the gratifications she had previously found in mourning and bitter disappointment. "Isabelle helped the mother to abandon her dreams of becoming an independent young woman. It was Isabelle who was to impose tyranny on the family, the mother returning to the role of victim."

The wound in Isabelle's mother's history might be described as follows: she was forced into a situation in which "being a woman" meant "not being a mathematician." Every preordained step toward "being a woman"—caring for her sister, falling in love, getting married, being pregnant—was a *real loss* of "being a mathematician." Only with Isabelle did "being a mother" and "having a child" become the *symbolic compensation* for that loss. The mother-child symbiosis then caused this interplay of real loss and symbolic compensation to radiate back out into the child's own existence.

Among the overdetermined meanings of Isabelle's inability to learn arithmetic is this symbiosis with a mother for whom being a woman negates being a mathematician. So, too, Isabelle's own gender-identity is caught in a paradox that echoes her mother's history: if I am a girl, I can have no life independent of mother; therefore, I must be a boy; but if I am a boy, mother will die. Isabelle had already begun to forge a path, however tormented, toward autonomy in articulating this paradox:

> "In the end, the little boy does the things that he likes and not what his Mummy likes." The child was discovering that one must do what one likes doing oneself, and not what Mummy would like one to like. But to do that one must be a boy. "In fact," said Isabelle, "the Mummy says to

> herself, 'It's a good thing I've got my little girl. What would I do if all my boys left me?'" [N.B. In fact two of the other children were girls.]. . . .
>
> In the distinction drawn by Isabelle between boy and girl, there is, in a reflected form, the problem of the mother who can accept herself as a girl only as the victim of a sadistic mode of action. By separating herself from her mother, Isabelle becomes a boy-girl (that is, she can achieve autonomy only at the cost of internal contradiction).

Mannoni's therapeutic procedure tries to take stock of the fact that Isabelle's separation from her mother has to begin with the "internal contradiction" of being a boy-girl. The paradox-ridden encoding of gender that has presided over her existence is part of the discourse within which she must now learn to speak, and to speak for herself. The path toward autonomy does not permit a fresh start. *Where it was, there must I become.*

There is no already constituted *I* the analyst might then merely resituate in a properly communicated set of meanings: "the important thing for the analyst is not so much to verbalize what is wrong as to be receptive to the confusion of a fragmented body that can locate itself nowhere." The individual's "second entry" into language cannot proceed except via the "first entry," that is, via the background discourse of the Other with all its contingent encodings, associations and paradoxes: "By trying, in the course of the analysis, to distinguish between the child's fantasy and the mother's, I lead the subject to assume his own history instead of remaining alienated in that of his mother. Nevertheless, the child's history is one that spreads over several generations. The nexus of the drama already exists at the level of the grandparents."[9]

Mannoni's perspective forces a clarification of the relation of dependence and autonomy and of subjectivity and intersubjectivity. Dependence is the precondition as well as the opposite of autonomy. Nurturance, or the cultivation of persons, requires that a child be introduced from infancy into the discourse of others. By the same token, autonomy is not the opposite but the corollary of unconstrained, self-developing interactions with others. The promise of participation in such interactions is the principle of separation from the mother. It is the horizon of growth and the orientation toward norms that no one transcends.

The passage from heteronomy to autonomy is never traversed once and for all. Passing from the necessary heteronomy of having one's identity, desire and history formed in the discourse of others to the promised autonomy of active participation in discourse on a par with others is not a single event and never an absolute achievement. In the emphatic experience of Mannoni's patients, the promise of autonomy is blocked because the child's dependence on the mother has become, for the mother, her only meaningful, socially recognized activity. In the *activity of mothering* she finds herself standing for the community in which the child will eventually participate. But in rigidifying her *identity as a mother* she is driven to take the place of the community, of others in general, in order to salvage her self-recognition.

In these circumstances it is easy to see how the damaged subjectivity of the child is the corollary of a distorted intersubjectivity. Classical psychoanalytic theory misses this connection because it translates this whole array of interpersonal, social, even political relations into mere "intrapsychic" events. As can be seen in the case of Isabelle, however, the distorted intersubjectivity of the mother-child relation is itself but a moment in the larger pathology that has marked Isabelle's mother with the effects of sexual inequality and channeled her life activity into compensatory, pathogenic forms.

The goal that Mannoni sets for psychoanalytic therapy is the repair of the promise of autonomy which has been blocked by the mother-child relation. It is a question of the second promise of autonomy. She approaches the analyst-analysand relation itself as the site where the patient can come to participate on a par with others. The place of these "others"—of the Other—is now being held by the analyst. More precisely, it is the analyst's task *to hold open the place of the potential partners of such a dialogic interaction,* since once the child acquires the capacity of participation in this normative sense the analysis should end and the analyst disappear.

The actual dialogue between analysand and analyst has to become an alternative to the distorted discourse of the other that has formed the child's damaged subjectivity. It has to establish, for the child, the horizon of participation on a par with others. It can establish the horizon but not realize such an "ideal speech situation." The child is groping within the analytic dialogue to find him- or herself as an *I* in the discourse of others which has already shaped his or her as yet unnarrated history.

As the analyst, Mannoni has to play the role of an actual and potential interlocutor by constantly monitoring the child's hesitant, often contradictory commitments to discourse. She receives the child's negations as genuine acts of expression. Unlike the parents, she does give these negations the meaning of an absence or incapacity. Unlike the medical and educational experts, she does not approach them as objectifiable deficiencies to be overcome with rehabilitation. She responds to the negations as a mastering, however distorted, of the *3rd term* or symbolic mediation which alone can distinguish child from mother and give him or her access to the communicative process:

> In the world of the dyslexic, we find both an inverted, incomplete body image and a wordless relationship with the mother that is so rich in significations that the child, in order not to be lost in them, escapes by seeking a third term, namely negation. And it is in this negation, itself a certain form of language, that a meaning must be found that will enable the subject first to find a correct structure for himself in a world that he accepts, and then—and only then—to begin to learn, not as a duty imposed by an adult, but because he himself wishes to.

The analyst's task, as interlocutor, is to receive—and thus send back—these negations as the individual's commitment to discourse, as a tentative, still distorted step toward autonomy and the ordeal of separation.

Mannoni is also careful, however, to permit the child not to commit him- or herself to the discourse in which he or she is narrating experiences and relationships. These narratives originate intersubjectively and unconsciously. While they comprise the child's "own history," they can be so laden with the oppressive meanings that come from the Other that the child can become extremely anxious about accepting the truth of these narratives, for its own sake or its mother's. The narratives often have to be told "impersonally," as though about someone else; even then the child is beginning to hear something other than the mother's voice. Only gradually can the stories be told in the first person and thus openly acknowledged as stories about oneself.

By means of this technique, Mannoni encourages the discourse itself to begin to emerge as the *3rd term* possessed by neither self nor other and thus a potential terrain of self-other interactions. The child's drawings can be made the occasions for such storytelling. Isabelle persisted in referring to herself as "one" rather than "I" in these narratives:

> The "third term" introduced happened to be the language of fable. The child could speak in the Imaginary language used in psychotherapy

> because the things referred to did not concern her. In Real life, to speak is a commitment, and she could not consent to that. . . . For language to be accessible to Isabelle, it had to contain a disguise, a possible escape. It was necessary that there should be a certain distance between self and others. . . .
>
> She was able to find this language with me because I remained as long as she wished on the plane of what did not, and yet did, concern her. I played the game of never committing her until she was ready to commit herself by being the flower that pricked. Before that she was one.

In her fables of flowers Isabelle gradually could represent herself acting on her own behalf. "It was on the occasion of the flower that pricked that Isabelle discovered the *I*. Quite spontaneously, she said to me, 'I'm going to be the flower that pricks.'"

The whole direction of Isabelle's treatment throws into question Lacan's notion that the name-of-the-father, *law-giver* and *castrator,* is the agent of the child's separation from the mother and entry into the symbolic. The *3rd term* that gave Isabelle access to speech, to the ordeal of separation and to the promise of autonomy did not come from the Father but from the language of fables. The intervening *3rd term* that emerges as Mannoni nurtures the patient's various commitments and noncommitments to discourse is simply the appeal to participate in a communication, a communication not dictated by the desire of the Other.

The name-of-the-father does of course lay claim to the principle of separation and the power of the *3rd term.* Male dominance needs this claim as a strategy of legitimation. Ideologies and practices of the male-headed restricted family give the claim material force, and psychoanalytic theory offers justifications for it. The whole of Mannoni's work, on my reading, goes against the grain of these claims, legitimations, justifications. Though she herself often draws on the Lacanian name-of-the-father to explain mother-child symbiosis or the salutary role of her patients' husband-fathers, the case histories in fact give no empirical or theoretical reason to conclude that the symbolic *3rd term* comes of necessity from paternal authority.

Fathers do intervene with positive effects. In the relatively isolated, restricted family, he may simply be the most available third party who introduces interests, demands and desires that are not locked into the mother-child relation. The more severe the division of labor between husband and wife the more easily he will seem to fulfill this role. But this is also a misleading circumstance.

With Isabelle, for example, Mannoni did indeed observe that the father's involvement with the child and her acquisition of language coincided. Was it not the father, therefore, who brought the child into the symbolic and liberated her from the dyadic snare? On the contrary. It was not that the father brought the symbolic, but rather that the child's belated mastery of the symbolic finally awoke the father to her presence. Isabelle's father had not recognized her in her state of incapacity and deficiency:

> The father was interested only in the older children; only a child who could speak and express himself properly won his attention. It was not until Isabelle was cured that he took any notice of her. It may be worth mentioning incidentally that this father took so little notice of the child that when he had driven her to the hospital to have her tonsils out at the age of three years, she was unable to "recognize" him for three days.

What was missing from Isabelle's existence was not paternal authority or the mother's reference to paternal authority. What was missing was her father's recognition of her. She lived in a world that was inhabited by someone who did not acknowledge her presence and therefore himself remained an unnameable absence for her.

The patriarchal prejudices encrusted in Freudian and Lacanian theory keep insisting that the name-of-the-father is source of separation, autonomy and symbolic mastery. And Mannoni's work certainly shows how tragically pathogenic and autonomy-robbing mothering can actually be. Yet her therapeutic practice is itself the key to an alternative understanding of autonomy and of mothering. Isabelle had to be cured before her father noticed her. The dialogue in which Isabelle first discovered the promise of autonomy was conducted by a woman, that is, Mannoni herself, not a Father. It centered not on the pronouncement of a paternal law but on picture-stories about flowers.

Because Mannoni's own therapeutic practice serves to repair the promise of autonomy thwarted in distorted mother-child relations, it can likewise provide a theoretical model of the dialogical and autonomy-enhancing dimension of childrearing. It is in this sense that a psychoanalytic method devoted to pathologies can nonetheless recover the genuine normative benchmarks—without accepting the validity of the prevailing patriarchal norms.

Mannoni's approach to therapy sheds light on mothering. For women themselves play the double role of real and potential interlocutor with their children. They practice a dialogic receptivity to a child in the process of acquiring a stable body image and a capacity to speak. They recognize the ambiguities of a child's commitments and noncommitments to discourse. They balance play and reality. A therapeutic practice devoted to autonomy and participation is, therefore, a kind of inventory of the techniques of mothering. It shows nurturance in its capacity to induce and reward separation; it reveals practices of mothering that, far from being the "natural" bond of family life, are the source of culture, learning and sociality.

Even so, the most successful therapeutic practice can only establish the *promise* of autonomy for individuals. The social and institutional formations that produce and reproduce distorted intersubjectivities and damaged subjectivities continue to make their claims on patients. Freud assiduously avoided the role of social reformer. Though Mannoni's own proposals for reform and transformation are tentative rather than systematic, she introduces a needed perspective of social criticism and aspiration whenever she evaluates the failures and possibilities of her own clinical work, including its institutional setting.

The promise and limits of Isabelle's progress reveal an unfinished struggle. Isabelle's own initiatives were the measure of her progress:

> What struck me as remarkable about this case was the way the child was led quite spontaneously to elucidate her own problems—and how, by doing so, she was able to recover in turn her psychomotor stability, a sense of rhythm, a sense of direction, a taste for reading, and the idea of numbers. Moreover, her IQ became normal: 93.

The constraints of family and society continued, however, to make their claims on Isabelle. She asked to terminate therapy and attend boarding school. Mannoni acknowledges that she herself misconstrued how thoroughly intermingled this request was with the request of the Other: "Isabelle avoided a more extensive analytic investigation by asking for an intensive educational program. In fact, this demand concealed the wish of the parents: in making it her own, the child was reliving the difficulties of her childhood." Analysis is terminable or interminable in accord with how one's life-history continues its engagement with family, community and polis. In the case of Isabelle, the terminated analysis left her to be robbed of her autonomy yet again:

"After the interruption of psychotherapy, educational progress was negligible; in other words, the acquisition of reading and arithmetic that had been achieved during psychotherapy, without the help of specialized re-education, remained at an identical level despite the efforts of specialized re-educators.

"The re-education establishment discharged the child, who was then sent to an institution for the feebleminded, from which in turn she was discharged for behavioral problems."

Conclusion

12

Why a Cultural Critique of Psychoanalysis

"In the Wake of Home"

MANY WOMEN and men's anguished and insurgent feelings, desires and fears were gathered into articulate critique by Adrienne Rich's phrase, *compulsory heterosexuality.* But Rich has also evoked the hold that the image of the conjugal couple can have on our most recurrent wishes. Her poem "In the Wake of Home"—addressed perhaps to her reader, perhaps to her lover or her child or even herself—begins as follows:

> You sleep in a room with bluegreen curtains
> posters   a pile of animals on the bed
> A woman and a man who love you
> and each other   slip the door ajar
> you are almost asleep   they crouch in turn
> to stroke your hair   you never wake
>
> This happens every night for years.
> This never happened.[1]

What do the fabricated, idealizing images of the conjugal family have to do with the Oedipus complex? After all, Oedipal theory tells a son's story filled not with the bedtime rituals of Ozzie and Harriet but with bloody, lawless fantasies of incest and patricide. It is the stuff of ancient tragedies not fairy tales.

Yet it is Rich's insight that *home* is always created "in the wake of home." Like the Freudian *Nachträglichkeit,* home takes shape and becomes meaningful through the back-forming imagination. It marks a yearning to return to where you never were:

Home, home!
and the hole torn and patched over
will gape unseen again.

Even where love has run thin
the child's soul musters strength
calling on dust-motes   song on the radio
closet-floor of galoshes
stray cat   piles of autumn leaves
whatever comes along
—the rush of purpose to make a life
worth living past abandonment
building the layers up again
over the torn hole   filling in[2]

The meaning of home, the shape of home, the tie to home, are products of our imaginations and of the culture that furnishes binding images. The heterosexual couple is such an image, continually fabricated, endlessly idealized. It has become the cipher through which our society attempts to fill the unseen gaping hole of our backward-glancing longings. Psychoanalysis affirms this imaginary heterosexual couple by placing it at the heart of the Oedipus complex, at the origin of desire and law, sexuality and identity.

Psychoanalysis's complicity with compulsory heterosexuality has affected its intellectual habits, its conceptual style and its therapeutic strategies. Yet psychoanalysis does have a role to play in the cultural critique of compulsory heterosexuality, patriarchy and male dominance. But to enlist it in that role at the same time requires a cultural critique *of* psychoanalysis.

Several important critical starting-points lay scattered, half dormant, in Freud's work. He postulated that a little boy's incestuous impulses toward his mother and rivalrous hostility toward his father are often matched by a love for his father and rivalry toward his mother. He further postulated that the socially privileged outcome of the Oedipus complex—namely, the achievement of a strongly masculine identity and unambiguously heterosexual desires—was decidedly rare. The norm was not normal. The purely heterosexual Oedipus complex, the so-called "simple positive Oedipus complex," seldom occurred. Rarer still was its "dissolution" without traces of inner conflict.

Yet these insights never prompted a critique of compulsory heterosexuality. Freud never saw the cultural pathology in the Oedipal norm itself. He did not reassess the Oedipal norm of heterosexuality, even when he acknowledged the importance of "bisexuality." He interpreted bisexuality narrowly in terms of two Oedipal scenarios, the "positive" (heterosexual) and the "negative" (homosexual) Oedipus complex. He might have asked what gives this ideal its normative force, its compulsoriness, since hardly anyone has the "simple positive Oedipus complex." Stumped, Freud concluded that the relative strength of the "simple positive Oedipus complex" was purely a matter of an individual's innate sexual constitution. He satisfied himself with the spurious tautology that the weaker a boy's innate "bisexuality" the easier his adaptation to heterosexuality and masculinity.

Freud further eschewed any critique of specific institutions and practices by examining social life only through the undifferentiated idea that civilization exacts such a high price of repression on the instincts that neurosis has become the common modern fate. His hypothesis was one-dimensional: the more civilization advanced the more it inhibited instinctual life. He saw no need to discriminate between one set of social arrangements and another. He never examined how the institutions that repress sexuality also shape it. The effects of civilization seemed just as inevitable as the individual's innate disposition. Civilization and disposition were the two pincers of ineluctable fate. They became Freud's alibi for his lack of a *cultural* critique of the Oedipus complex.

Nevertheless, the more Freud dissociated Oedipal theory from cultural critique the more his concepts acquired an unacknowledged, uncritical cultural content. The "mother" and "father" of the Oedipus complex were symbolic constructs far removed from his patients' flesh-and-blood parents. This imaginary heterosexual couple were the *2nd* and *3rd terms* of the Oedipal triangle of I—mother—father. They were not, however, mere misguided stereotypes. Rather, they were the unacknowledged condensation of symbols, meanings and images crucial to the workings of patriarchy and compulsory heterosexuality.

Lacan and Ricoeur helped establish that the *3rd term* is really the cluster of symbols which have historically designated fatherhood in Western culture, even though they were quite unmotivated to advance a critique of either patriarchy or compulsory heterosexuality. How this patriarchal heritage and these names-of-the-father affect the conduct of real-life fathers is the question that psychoanalysis and cultural critique ought to share. Likewise, the *2nd term* of the Oedipus complex bore little resemblance to the real-life mothers of Freud's patients. The Oedipal mother, too, is a symbolic entity, fabricated, for example, in the masculine discourse on love. She inhabits male fantasy as an idolized *and* degraded model of women. How this symbolic construct affects real-life mothers and actual mother-child relationships is the question completely neglected in the clinical and theoretical narratives of Freud, Lacan and Ricoeur. Its absence is a measure of these theorists' androcentrism and further reflects the failure of psychoanalysis to see itself as a mode of cultural critique.

So What, in Sum, Is the Oedipus Complex?

Since the classical Oedipal triangle turns out to represent the *I*'s relation to a symbolic mother and a symbolic father, these symbolic *2nd* and *3rd terms* have to be reinterpreted in relation to their real-life counterparts. The real-life father is, as Lacan recognized, a *4th term* of the Oedipus complex; the real-life mother, who is simply blotted out in psychoanalytic theory, is the *5th term*. Heuristically and for the purposes of critique, the Oedipus complex becomes, therefore, a five-term structure. But what does it ultimately mean to say that the symbolic mother is not identical to the real-life mother? the symbolic father not identical to the real-life father?

It is first of all to stress that when women and men take up their roles in the modern family they are faced with deeply contradictory imperatives and conflicting expectations. Maud Mannoni's case of Isabelle reveals how Isabelle's mother approached becoming a wife and a mother as a loss of identity, a sinking into anonymity, because marriage and pregnancy abruptly ended her potential career as a mathematician. At the same time, the symbolic meaning of motherhood which she had derived from her childhood relationship with her own mother had expressed itself in victim-victimizer scenarios. The unplanned birth of her new, apparently retarded child occasioned a new synthesis: she replenished her depleted identity by becoming a mother-victim forced to care for a burdensome child. Meanwhile, Isabelle's own individual myth was being fatefully spun from this web of symbolic and real motherhood.

The distinction between symbolic and real can also easily be misread. Consider how rigidly Lacan separates the *3rd* and the *4th term*. The symbolic father then looks like an inevitable, nearly unchanging feature of "culture" as such, while the real-life father is relegated to a transitory, changing "society." Such a conception contributes to the anti-modern strain of Lacan's thought. Real-life fathers are pitied their burdensome task of having to uphold the very pillars of culture and law while a thoroughly individualistic, bureaucratized society is reducing them to powerless cogs. Lacan's hypostatization of the split between the symbolic and the real-life father obscures how it is precisely the real-life father's actual power *within* the household and in his social relations with women at large that lets him become the support of the symbolic names-of-the-father which in turn serve, among other things, to legitimate his power over his wife and to create the domestic scene of his often abusive authority. The "symbolic" and the "real," the *3rd term* and the *4th,* are knitted together as well as split apart.

The heuristic idea of a five-term structure reveals how the Oedipus complex maps not only the child's family relations but also the various social and political relations which are reflected and refracted in the specific family relations themselves. The Oedipus complex is an individual drama woven from the meshing of family and community, family and polis, family and economy. The individual's drama is never altogether unique. Nor is it simply universal. It shares in some common history. The Oedipal drama refuses to reduce to the triangle of an *I* loving and hating Mother and Father, because it is the scene of the parents' and child's entanglement in that larger shared history.

When Hamlet sees his anticipated accession to kingship preempted, usurped, by his mother Gertrude's marriage to Claudius, he "regresses" to a debilitating preoccupation with her marital vows, her desires and her sexuality. When he is called upon to prove himself worthy of his father's mantle by avenging his murder and exposing Claudius, he finds himself mirroring not his murdered father but his murderous uncle—"a satyr" who is "no more like my father / Than I to Hercules."[3] The schism between the symbolic father (King Hamlet) and the real-life father (Claudius) divides Hamlet, prince and son, against himself.

When Freud's dreams herald his father's heroism while veiling his supposed or actual cowardice, Freud the dreamer is probing the gap between the symbolic and the real-life father in search of the meaning of his own professional and civic choices and his own identity as a citizen and a Jew.

When Kafka in a single gesture credits the stability of his parents' marriage and household solely to his father's willfulness, repudiates his mother's efforts to reconcile father and son *and* denounces the father's brutal treatment of his employees, he shows himself to be hopelessly caught in a dilemma from which he cannot extricate himself. He cannot fully recover his sense of justice, because his rejection of capitalist power relations is being fed by the same emotional wellsprings as his envy of his father's acts of male dominance.

When the Rat Man is most in the grip of his Oedipal crisis—mourning his father's death, avoiding progress in his studies, postponing decisions about the woman he loves—the sources of his predicament have nothing to do with any primal "Oedipal" attachment, past or present, to his mother. They lie instead in his identification with his father's two courtships, one for love and one for money. This identification bifurcates his own desires into a sexually stifled idealization of his fiancée and a series of sexual episodes in which working-class women and his sisters become the objects of his attempted seductions, voyeurism and sexual assaults. He keeps trying to prove his sexual capacity with them by exerting the social superiority or power he holds by virtue of his class and gender.

All these Oedipal dramas map the son's relation to his parents across the social and political relations that come into play in his immediate experience and in the parental, marital and family histories he encounters. Contrary to Freud, the political and social relations are not "outside" the family. Nor, on the other hand, are the child's active experiences and abiding perceptions within the family simply the offshoot of these social and political processes. Contrary to the functionalism favored by many Marxists, from Engels to Althusser and Chodorow, the dynamics of sexuality and gender in family life are not fully meshed into the gears of a total social and political order. Nor, contrary to Ricoeur, do the conflicts and contradictions within the modern restricted male-headed family ultimately resolve themselves in a synthesis with capitalism and the modern state.

Less ironclad, less finished concepts and metaphors are needed to account for the Oedipus complex. Family life is much more ragged, tentative and fluctuating than the Freudian "psychic mechanism," the structuralist "system," "capitalist patriarchy," Marxist "totality" or Hegelian "ascending dialectic" admits. Modern families and family relationships are indeed caught up in the social relations (market, community, gender) and political relations (citizenship, patriarchy, power) which organize the society at large, but there is no singular "logic" which determines what those many-layered relations actually are.

Even though the Lacanian individual myth gives a glimpse onto the social world in which the real-life father lives, it ultimately stays within the orbit of Freud's intrapsychic paradigm. The Oedipus complex remains a purely mental representation. Psychoanalytic theory has been weak when it comes to explaining how this mental representation is supposed to take up residence in the psyche. Freud went the biological route: the Oedipus complex is the psychic inheritance by which the species provides the individual with guiding representations of sexual reproduction and death. Lacan went the structuralist route: the Oedipus complex comes from the indelible rules of kinship which "from the dawn of history" have represented law, culture and language through the figure of the Father. Biologism and structuralism hardly differ in this instance. The rules of reproduction or of kinship are assumed to directly imprint the individual psyche, giving it a blueprint of identity and desire.

The origins of the Oedipus complex are thus cast outside all of society's historically changing features. Freud certainly considered the Oedipus complex a modern predicament, but he kept explaining it as the inevitable outcome of human sexuality. Lacan set out to ground the pathologies of the Oedipus complex in the modern era, but ended up merely trumpeting the agelessness of patriarchy. If the Oedipus complex is given no "site" other than the individual psyche, its actual formation within the psyche inevitably gets attributed to some suprahistorical source—whether biology, heredity, structure or "culture." The theoretical import of Freud and Lacan there reaches its limit. The "site" of the Oedipus complex has to be rethought.

Structure of Feeling

An alternative emerges when exemplary Oedipal narratives, including autobiographies and novels as well as psychoanalytic case studies, are approached historically. The Oedipus complex then looks at once less privatized *and* less universal. It is a *structure of feeling,* in the sense that it is the "matrix of perceptions, appreciations, and actions" which boys typically draw upon in shaping their identity and their desire under the specific pressure of their society's prevailing values and its typical crises. I am pushing the meaning of Raymond Williams' concept of structure of feeling more in the direction of what Pierre Bourdieu calls *disposition* and *habitus*.[4]

Let us therefore rephrase the response to the question *What is the Oedipus complex?* As a structure of feeling, the Oedipus complex is a repertoire of representations and responses which men begin to acquire in early childhood to establish, interpret, orient their identity and their desire. This repertoire itself is forged from the process through which the modern market and polis displace the traditional sociality of community and religion, transforming the family, creating new sources of the self, solidifying new forms of the sexual division of labor. This formative process is strongly stamped with the institutions of modern patriarchy and compulsory heterosexuality.[5]

Freud's own life and thought matured in the midst of just such a set of crisis-ridden changes. Like the obsessional Rat Man and the modernist Kafka, Freud drew upon the Oedipal repertoire in responding to the major personal and professional events of his life. Freud's theory of mind, the Rat Man's neurosis and Kafka's practice of writing belong to the same structure of feeling. These very disparate phenomena are not, to be sure, identical, nor are they mere "expressions" of the same mentality. But the lives of the psychoanalyst, the neurotic and the writer elaborate upon the same fund of dispositions. The Oedipal matrix enables *and* limits the representations and responses through which they actively relate to their social and sexual world.

The general context in which these three offspring of the Habsburg Empire acquired the Oedipal structure of feeling is readily identifiable. Their families were bourgeois, liberal, urban secular Jews who were just one generation past the rural and religious life of the *stetl*. Even more to the point, these sons were raised to expect that they could—and must—find fulfillment in a synthesis of career, citizenship and marriage. But the seams that joined these roles one to another were also fault-lines, traversing and threatening every attempt at synthesis.

Freud's practice of his profession derived its meaning and motivation from a crisis of citizenship. When he discovered as a young man that anti-Semitism would continually jeopardize full citizenship and participation even in enlightened Vienna, he abandoned his dream of politics as vocation and turned to science and eventually psychiatry. He came to invest his psychoanalytic theory with covert, compensatory political fantasies.

When Kafka at once repudiated career and coveted marriage, he found himself torn asunder by the masculine ideal that united the figure of the businessman and that of the husband. In his individual mythology, the one could not exist without the other. He filled his emotional life with three all-absorbing, lengthy betrothals each of which he broke off at the eleventh hour. His diaries and letters reveal how completely his writing—the hours of composing as well as the forms of the composing—was an ingenious gambit in the Oedipal game. Writing was first of all a refusal of profession, since it did not amount to a career and yet freed him to invest nothing of himself in the bureaucratic-legal career at which he actually earned his living. And, at the same time, writing was a refusal of marriage. His need to write always justified his postponement of the wedding, and invariably he eventually broke the engagements in order to keep the writing going.

When the Rat Man discovered that the marriage plans his mother was cooking up for him simply awaited the start of his legal career, he ceased making progress in his studies. He anticipated the role of husband with a combination of ambivalence (connected to his father's marital history), guilt (connected to his own inclinations to sexual violence) and loathing (connected to his bifurcated vision of women as virgins and whores). His identity floundered on the joint between profession and marriage, dividing him against himself and further debilitating his desire. The sort of crisis which Freud parried by theorizing and Kafka by writing incapacitated the Rat Man altogether.

It is indeed my view that Freud's fashioning of Oedipal theory was itself a strategic response to the many-sided *and* largely unsolvable problems of his own social, political, sexual world. Distilled to a triangular, familial, ultimately intrapsychic conflict, these problems were made to appear curable. Through his self-analysis and his treatment of the Rat Man he concluded that the crises to which the Rat Man's life and his own were susceptible originated in primal fantasies of incest and patricide. To reach this conclusion he carried out the threefold revisionism that fixed father, mother and self in their rightful positions in the Oedipal triangle.

To adduce the *Oedipal father,* Freud refashioned the crisis of Austro-Hungarian liberalism into the personal drama of a son's conflict with his father. He distilled a fixed, ever-recurring conflict between fathers and sons from the open-ended, still unresolved historical process that was urbanizing and secularizing Jewish communities while at the same time betraying the concomitant promise of citizenship and national identity.[6]

To adduce the *Oedipal mother,* he transfigured the first object of his own erotic attachment—the working-class Czech nanny, a devout Catholic and petty thief, who stimulated his first sexual experiences—by neutralizing her significance and transferring it instead onto his mother, whom he remembered as young, beautiful and cultivated.[7]

And to adduce the *Oedipal self,* Freud radically shifted his therapeutic and theoretical perspective. In precipitously abandoning his "seduction" theory of hysteria in the midst of clinical failures and intellectual crisis, he first of all replaced the fathers' faults and misdeeds with the child's erotic wishes and fantasies. The individual's desire rather than the moral dramas of family and society became the focus of the Oedipal scenario. However, since his clinical experience in fact never did definitively refute his women patients' traumatic memories, he also gradually completely remodeled the incestuous fantasies on the experiences of little boys rather than girls or young women. Only at that point did the Oedipus complex firmly rest on a desiring male *I.*[8]

These three maneuvers yielded the Father, Mother and Son of the Oedipal triangle and substantially resolved Freud's personal, professional and intellectual impasses. As regarded his self-analysis, Oedipal theory effaced the father's real or imagined fault and authenticated the son's symbolic guilt. As regarded his practice, it shifted his therapeutic efforts onto a terrain where he might succeed. The prospect of cure had returned.

The intricate stratagem of displacements and reductions that produced the "discovery" of the Oedipus complex was not, however, simply error. Intellect was following the contour of movements within society itself. Freud's thought mimicked a social process in which the relations among household, market, community and polis were being completely restructured.

When, for example, he adduced the Oedipal father, he was shadowing a central project of modern patriarchy, namely, the separation of household and polis on an axis of private and public spheres. The mythically eternal parents took precedence over mutable politics in defining the sources of moral relationships and personal identity. As a privatized space at once imaginary and real, the household provided a scene of individual male authority distinct from, yet complicit with, the political scene of potential or supposed male equality.

In adducing the Oedipal mother, Freud was responding to other important institutional and ideological mechanisms. The actual interpenetration of the capitalist economy and the household—specifically, the upstairs-downstairs of class relations within the bourgeois household itself—was veiled by fabricating a pure, internalized family: *I—Mother—Father*. Freud removed real women from (the representation of) the primal scene by effacing the presence of their childrearing and housekeeping labors. The mother could then reappear in pristine, purely symbolic form, ready for adulation or degradation as the occasion required.

So many rudiments of psychoanalytic theory were developed in the course of Freud's self-analysis that it should not be surprising that his thought was a complex response to the specific social and political circumstances of his own life-history. There is a vibrant reflexivity in psychoanalysis, even where Freud himself fails to take stock of the connections between theory and lifeworld.

How far does this reflexivity go?

The Oedipal structure of feeling was not simply the "object" of psychoanalytic reflection, it also motivated and shaped that reflection. Conversely, Freud's theoretical moves oftentimes symptomatically reveal the ideological and institutional processes at work within the Oedipus complex itself. I want to suggest something more as well. Freud's theoretical reduction of the Oedipal structure of feeling to an intrapsychic structure corresponds to a dynamic *within* that structure of feeling itself. The imaginary heterosexual couple are the culturally produced fantasy to which the individual has recourse when in need of a home, a place of origin that might compensate for the dislocations, losses, injuries, deprivations that have happened "in the wake of home." Conflicts that arise from class relations or the transformations of community or the inequalities between men and women are folded back into the civic privatism of the modern male-dominated family. That, too, is part of the Oedipal structure of feeling.

Freud did not of course fully grasp the reflexivity between theory and lifeworld. He failed to the exact extent that he separated the psychoanalytic enterprise from cultural critique. His evocations of the underworld notwithstanding, Freud wanted the *science* of psychoanalysis to stand on more Olympian terrain. He did not admit that it remains eyeball deep in the social lifeworld from which it emerges. What is tellingly absent from his work is a critical reflection on the institutional-symbolic matrix that most significantly shapes the Oedipal structure of feeling: namely, *compulsory heterosexuality* and *modern patriarchy*.

Compulsory Heterosexuality

Compulsory heterosexuality is more than a taboo on homosexuality. It also organizes the social subordination of women. An array of institutions, practices and values pressures women to remain dependent on men and blocks their avenues to independence. Poverty, ostracization and isolation have been the cost of deviating from the heterosexual path in search of economic, sexual or emotional freedom from men. To the extent that marriage is a haven in a heartless world *for women,* it is because male dominance destroys or impoverishes all other shelters.

Many of the motifs of the Oedipus complex are simply the effects of this cultural pathology as it rebounds in the psychosexual development of boys. Growing up is at once a boy's schooling in male power and his continual encounter with its corrosive effects. The Oedipus complex not only takes its shape from the imperatives of compulsory heterosexuality, but it is also simultaneously shaped, that is, misshaped, by the moral dissonance that female subordination and homophobia create.

Men cannot impose dependence on women without suffering a distortion of their own sense of independence. Like the Hegelian master, men find their self-esteem perpetually challenged by the fact that the independence they so much prize is itself dependent on the other's labor and on her unfreedom. The ideal of self-sufficiency that men are prone to adopt as a measure of their autonomy is the imaginary counterpart, the inverted image, of the dependence they impose on women. It is a denial of interdependence. Men look for the proof of their own strength and autonomy in women's subordination.

The masculinized promise of autonomy is not only articulated in the many cultural images of self-sufficient heroes, it is also reinforced in the most elementary practices and values of capitalist society, from entrepreneurship to corporate or bureaucratic careerism. The experience of equality that boys are supposed to acquire in their rivalries and reconciliations with their father is itself continually compromised. The meaning of being an equal is dogged by the inequalities that disturb the very roles in which equality is to be realized: In the market, the father is visibly a part of the inequalities of command and obedience, profit and exploitation, status and failure, whether as an employer (like Kafka's father) or an employee (like the Rat Man's). In the household, the son sees his father in his role as a husband wielding a more or less tyrannical, more or less patronizing, authority over his wife.

The social relations between men and women thus also become an unacknowledged core of inequality around which revolves the son's search for equality with his father. He cannot see himself in his father without embracing some new share in male dominance. The promise of autonomy is corrupted as it is masculinized. The meaning of masculinity is inflected with dominance, subordination and inequality within the very framework of experiences of equality.

The norm of heterosexuality is simultaneously imposed on the male child's horizon of expected growth, identity and desire. The Oedipal moment so dogmatically foregrounded in psychoanalytic theory—namely, the moment the little boy assumes an erotic attachment to his mother, mediated by his rivalry and identification with his father—is not at all a passage into the true biological or cultural meaning of sexuality. It is more often a catastrophic revision of the child's complex attachments to his mother, a contradictory set of identifications with his father and a constraining projection of his future desires. Compulsory heterosexuality forges an imaginary equivalence between becoming-a-man and desiring-a-woman, and a fantasmal, nearly psychotic perception of "woman" as the "mother/whore."

How dogmatic this norm actually is among psychoanalytic theorists can be seen in the tenacious hold it has on even the most insightful revisionists of Freudian theory. André Green, for example, explores a rich variety of tragic relationships in ancient and modern drama and yet tacitly reverts to the terms of compulsory heterosexuality when it comes to generalizing the stakes of his interpretation:

> Every man is born of a person of the same sex and of a person of the opposite sex. He establishes difference by including himself in the couple that constitutes him and excludes him. He himself excludes the similar and mates with the Other.[9]

Green metaphysicalizes heterosexuality by equating becoming-a-man with desiring-a-woman. Gender identity and sexual desire are assumed to completely overlap. The boy or young man in this scenario wants to have sex with his mother because of her difference (that is, sexual difference); he simultaneously discovers his identity (that is, his selfsameness) in his likeness to his father. Killing the father is a dream of coming into his own identity.

What creates the "ineluctibility," as Green likes to say, of this unity of identity and desire, gender and sexuality? Green is left to locate the sources of Oedipus in the circumstances of human sexual reproduction. The cultural route opened by Lacan comes back around to the biological route favored by Freud. The male and female roles in reproduction are unambiguously assimilated to the social roles of father and mother. The male's path to forming his masculine identity and cultivating his heterosexual desire seems necessary because sanctioned by biology. By failing to grasp how heterosexuality is a *socially* compulsory institution, the theorist gives it the aura of a natural necessity.

As psychoanalysts metaphysicalize heterosexuality, they pathologize every deviation from the "simple positive Oedipus complex." Because they fail to take account of the moral disturbances and the pathologies that arise from within the heterosexual scenario, they view every alternative scenario as somehow exceptional. Yet the "simple positive Oedipus complex" is itself elusive, rare, perhaps even a theoretical fiction. It would therefore seem that the child's individual myths are more likely formed from the alternative scenarios themselves, the unexplored non-simple and non-positive complexes.

Psychoanalysis has not asked how our desires and identities resist the regime of compulsory heterosexuality. It has always offered the falsely generalized theme of the conflict between instinct and civilization in place of an in-depth exploration of what makes heterosexuality compulsory in our society. It has generally abdicated its social responsibility, especially to gays and lesbians. It has failed to explore the dysfunctions, sufferings, injustices, the damage, which the regime of compulsory heterosexuality imposes on the very formation of sexual identities, gay and straight. Neither the injustices which continually haunt homosexual experience nor the moral and psychological distortions which inhabit heterosexual experience get put within the purview of psychoanalysis.

Green himself begins by arguing for the cultural, theoretical and clinical significance of all those tragedies that do not follow the patterns of Sophocles' Oedipus. They are the dramas of the non-simple, non-positive Oedipus complex. But Green ends up reading each one simply as an instance where "the positive Oedipus complex breaks down." The resulting scenarios are described in a cascade of misogynist and homophobic pseudo-concepts. The *Orestia,* Green argues, shows "the nodal [point] of primary masochism linked to the symbolic relation to the mother"; *Othello* that "of psychotic homosexuality degraded into masochism"; *Iphigenia* that "of moral masochism and the suicidal feminine"![10] In the midst of so many feminine and homosexual pathologies, Oedipus' tragic actions seem downright wholesome. Unsullied masculinity and heterosexuality retain their aura of normality.

The ballast of prejudice that weighs upon psychoanalytic theory's paradigms and fundamental concepts casts doubt on all its claims about sexuality. Psychoanalysis is overdue for viewing itself with a more critical, skeptical eye. Thanks to gay and lesbian writers and the new historians of sexuality, it is becoming increasingly clear how completely social prejudice and ignorance have dominated our scientific, historical and psychological knowledges of sexuality. A fruitful agnosticism is dislodging the deep-seated, unwarranted certitudes. John Boswell has put it quite succinctly: "Whether human beings are 'homosexual' or 'heterosexual' or 'bisexual' by birth, by training, by choice, or at all is still an open question."[11]

Modern Patriarchy

Every effort at making flat assertions about sexuality and sexual identity should, therefore, be met with considerable skepticism. From what standpoint can positive descriptions or reliable facts be advanced? Skepticism is all the more appropriate when it comes to determining the historical provenance of the Oedipus complex.

Does the Oedipus complex belong to the dawn of civilization, fully in evidence with Sophocles' *Oedipus Rex?* Is it a phenomenon limited to the Victorian mind, an obsession at first unconscious and then theoretical? Does it accompany capitalism? or the *haute bourgeoisie?* or the middle-class? or Western modernity?

These questions will not receive answers that are precise enough theoretically or dense enough empirically except through multiple, interdisciplinary efforts. I do, however, believe that the most plausible hypothesis to emerge from the critique of psychoanalytic theory—and the one most likely to give fruitful direction to further, more empirical work—postulates that the Oedipus complex is a structure of feeling that took shape with modernity, more precisely, Western modernity.

Carole Pateman has persuasively shown that Freud's whole theoretical project was a meditation on *modern* patriarchy. When Freud speculated on what he considered the earliest origins of paternal authority and the rule of law among men, he gave the "primal horde" a decidedly modern cast. The forms of equality he attributed to the sons who made a civilized order by killing (and idolizing) the primal father were in fact the modern forms of equality linked to civic and economic individualism: the equality of citizens and equality in the marketplace. Freud was contributing to the theory of the social contract.

The features of modern patriarchy have been outlined by Pateman and, in a less critical vein, by Paul Ricoeur.[12] First, modern patriarchy establishes the meanings of citizenship and equality in a masculine form. In modern Western societies, becoming the equal of other men as a citizen in the public sphere of the polis has been firmly linked to becoming the unrivaled ruler over a woman and children in the private sphere of the household. Second, even as the modern conceptions and institutions of civil society overcame "patriarchalism," the new patriarchal order drew on the rich fund of symbols of fatherhood which reach back to ancient, even prehistoric times. These designations of fatherhood became available to interpret and legitimate the new forms of male power that were now organizing along the axis of public and private. The father as law-giver or provider or castrator became, as it were, privatized.

I think it is a mistake to interpret the joining of civil equality and masculinity as an organic connection. Such an interpretation is common to Pateman's critique and Ricoeur's celebration of modern patriarchy. The articulation of civil equality and masculinity is conjunctural rather than intrinsic. Historically it happened that equality was joined to masculinity thanks to the separation and complementarity of private and public spheres. And it is certainly the case that the effects of this linkage have continued to ramify through our experiences of both equality and masculinity. Nevertheless, the linkage is also recurrently disturbed and challenged from within.

On the one hand, the fusion of the roles of citizen and husband is never altogether stable and is further unsettled by the vicissitudes of a man's related role in the economy (employer, employee, bureaucrat, professional, entrepreneur). Ricoeur believes that the organizing principles of polis, family and market are synthesized in masculinity or, more precisely, in the form of maturity embodied in masculinity and heterosexuality. But the apparent norm is itself pathogenic. Consider men's common tendency to threateningly assert their authority at home, making shows of force, demanding shows of obedience, in response to the uncertainties or disappointments of their civic or economic endeavors. The modern patriarchal synthesis which effectively defines masculinity in our society is rife with conflicts that continually unhinge the maturation and moral development of men. How a boy responds to his father's domestic acting out bears heavily on his own eventual relationships and character.

And, on the other hand, the synthesis of civil equality and masculinity is disturbed by women's claims to rights and equalities. Reproductive rights challenge modern patriarchy's rule over the private sphere. The participation of women in the polis continually alters the meanings and institutions of the public and private spheres. In policy and in everyday life, women have exposed the private domain of inequality on which the public domain of masculine equality has rested. Whenever a wife and mother asserts her rights to dignity or autonomy, she is appealing to norms and rules that are not subordinate to the "name-of-the-father." Women may appeal to their rights as citizens or as persons or as women—such is the complexity of "rights talk" in modern societies—but they definitely appeal to modern norms of equality that run counter to patriarchy. They displace the conjunction of equality and masculinity.

These sorts of displacements become part of the politics of the family. Children are not only witness to marital conflict, they are also avid interpreters of it. They are eager to know who is right and what is right; they are also of course often desperate for harmony. They sometimes take sides, sometimes withdraw, sometimes test out visions of right that transcend him-against-her. In these real dramas of moral development, children encounter the conflicting norms which regulate the social and political relations between men and women. The name-of-the-father is not the supreme or ultimate norm because paternal authority is continually challenged and exceeded not merely by rebellious impulses but by alternative moral norms. Psychoanalysis has in general ignored this whole dimension where, once again, the formation of the Oedipus complex is inseparable from the social and political world in which parents and children live.

What Is Missing

What is missing from psychoanalytic theory is the moral-political dimension of the Oedipal structure of feeling. What is missing from psychoanalytic therapy is the moral-political dimension of individual myths and pathologies.

Psychoanalysis has had many reasons, some of them quite compelling, for steering clear of these troubled waters. On balance, however, they do not hold up very well. The theoretical justifications for bracketing an intellectual engagement with questions of justice or social reform and eschewing a therapeutic engagement with the tangled moral relations of everyday life is wearing thin.

Consider once more the "seduction" theory. Freud's repudiation of it is celebrated by psychoanalysts as the origin of psychoanalysis proper. It was, however, an escape as well as a discovery. The pragmatic, almost desperate prestidigitation which turned an utter theoretical and therapeutic crisis into a triumphant starting-point fooled its author as well as his followers.

Years after he supposedly overcame the seduction theory, Freud reported interviewing a potential patient who he quickly surmised had suffered some sexual trauma. When he suggested as much, the guilty father, who was standing behind her in Freud's consulting room, broke down and cried. Neither the father nor the daughter ever came to see him again. This tableau reveals the unacknowledged problem in a nutshell. The seduction theory threatened to leave Freud with no *practice,* that is, no therapeutic method and no professional livelihood. The ethical and practical complexities to be resolved were probably insurmountable. How could he cure daughters without exposing their abusive fathers? The crude fact was that fathers would not pay to be exposed as child-abusers. Moreover, Freud did not have the institutional, legal or community context from which to intervene more decisively in his patients' family lives. His theoretical revision did not unravel any of these problems. It simply side-stepped them. The evasiveness sticks in the craw of his triumphant Oedipal theory.

When Freud had to assess why his patients were not cured when they became conscious of their traumas, he did not question the therapeutic powers of introspection but concluded that the young women's memories of seduction must be false. He did not ask what it might take, beyond remembering, for women who had been seduced by a father, uncle or brother to repair, or even just disintricate themselves from, what was really an ongoing moral morass, a violation of trust and a family lie, that could continue long after the perpetrator had died.

This question, like the institutional and ethical questions, became moot as soon as Freud made the overt substitution of Oedipal fantasy for sexual trauma and the covert substitution of little boys' experience for young women's. Oedipal theory thus salvaged the self-reflective, introspective method of treatment Freud had so arduously worked out in his "self-analysis" and with his first patients. He could resume building a practice on the voluntary, confidential dialogue between analyst and analysand.

Freud's method was retrospective as well as introspective. The Oedipus complex's temporality was just the opposite of a trauma's. A trauma leaves the patient no place to stand, no place from which to speak, because the fundamental trust on which a family's moral relations depend has been broken. The Oedipus complex, however, belongs to the remote past. It is infantile and archaic. To "remember" this past, through psychoanalytic constructions and interpretations, never requires you to reenter a moral scene which could still cry out for resolution, including resolutions that might be unachievable. Rather, Oedipal rememoration places you in a narrative where your desire and identity seem to have originated in a kind of moral *prehistory*.

Freud in this way put psychoanalytic therapy "beyond" the uncertainties that come with any moral-political domain. The costs of his advance were considerable. He in effect had to turn his back on his first significant group of patients. He was driven to assume that sexual coercion was not traumatic, that it was not in itself of psychological consequence; he could then, for example, simply exclude the Rat Man's whole history of sexual assaults from his case history. Buried in the foundations of psychoanalysis was a failure to recognize the moral origins of neurosis, and the failure to recognize the institutional and professional constraints on psychoanalytic therapy itself. These blindspots became part and parcel of the intellectual heritage of psychoanalysis.

To secure the space of introspection, psychoanalytic therapy approaches the family not as a living set of ongoing relationships but as an intrapsychic representation. Moral relations become irrelevant. Psychoanalysis may compel you to "take responsibility" for the desires formed in the remote past of the Oedipus complex. But there is actually nothing to hold anyone, yourself or others, responsible for.

According to Shoshana Felman, Lacan's reflections on language and the psychoanalytic dialogue amount to just such an internalization and neutralization of responsibility: "The analytic speech act by which the subject recognizes, and performatively names, his desire and his history (insofar as the misapprehension of the one has structured the other) has to be completed, consummated, by an ultimate analytic act of speech that Lacan calls the *assumption* of one's history, that is, the ultimate acceptance and endorsement of one's destiny, the acknowledgment of responsibility for the discourse of the Other in oneself, as well as the forgiving of this discourse."[13]

The appeal of such a process is undeniable. It seemingly enables individuals to pursue a process of self-reflection and healing that does not require anyone else's cooperation. It is an expression of one's freedom. It promises to enrich our highly developed, highly valued capacity for elaborating on our inner reality. Psychoanalysis gives individuals access to the endless unique folds of meaning which ultimately connect our idiosyncratic individual histories to the larger culture into which we are born: "the discourse of the Other in oneself."

But Lacan, like Freud, supposes that this dialectic occurs in a place abstracted from historical time and space. The psychoanalytic dialogue connects a subhistorical domain (drives, imagos, signifying chains) to a suprahistorical domain (culture, kinship, the law of the Father). The Oedipus complex or individual myth is reduced to the representation that mediates between the two. Lacan eventually dropped the reference to society and history originally evoked in the *4th term*. The increasingly abstracted "subject" of Lacanian theory is constituted in the reduced field of dual (*I—Mother*) and triadic (*I—Mother—Father*) relations.

The Future of Psychoanalysis

The imperatives of modern patriarchy got the better of Lacanian psychoanalysis. Lacan reduces the whole problem of the moral-political relations that shape the individual's life to the subject's relation to the name-of-the-father. He assumes, dogmatically, that the paternal metaphor subsumes all of social life's norms, rules, regulative ideals, projected values. He can therefore equate the paternal metaphor with the Law. Contrasted to this suprahistorical domain is the subhistorical domain of the unconscious, which Lacan then identifies with "primal repression"—that is, those yearnings and desires which were never conscious in the first place, because they were formed in advance of the inarticulate subject's capacity to recognize them. The subject's relation to a primal law stems from this primal repression itself, since, according to Lacan's axioms, a law is the barrier to (the recognition of) a desire.

As John Rajchman shows, Lacan believes that our conscience forms only as this primal repression and primal law fall under the aegis of the paternal metaphor. Moral experience can accordingly be reduced to the dyads and triads of modern patriarchy:

> The sublime inner demand of the moral law is not with us from the start. It finds its place inside us only through the internalizing mechanisms that comprise the Oedipus complex. Lacan has a "structural" account of this complex. It is not that we *happen* to internalize paternal interdictions or paternal figures of interdiction. It is rather through such figures and interdictions that we come to represent in and to ourselves the "primal" or "structural" fact that we are constituted through repression of our desire. "Structurally" speaking, the Mother is this object from which the Law separates us, and the Father is the agency or "word" of this separation. The internalization of the parental figures is only the way each fills out the fundamental structure. The law thus *consists* in primal repression; internalization is the only way an Imaginary identity can be built up from it.[14]

Lacan stacks the theoretical deck by obliterating all reference to the many-layered sources of the child's moral experience which do not refer back to the name-of-the-father: expressive play with peers; the rules that the mother or other primary caretakers tacitly evoke in their interactions with the child; the mother's own struggle for recognition and autonomy vis-à-vis the father or society at large; economic and civic practices that generate ideas of fairness and equality.

To get at these experiences, Lacan would have to break out of the orbit of intrapsychic representation and the closed circuits of "structure." His return to the three-term structure signals his abandonment of the dense weave of historical institutions and practices that are bound up with the formation of the Oedipus complex as a structure of feeling. The "structural" Mother and Father are after all merely the symbolic *2nd* and *3rd* terms. It is in the divergence between the real-life and the symbolic father (the *4th* and *3rd terms*) and between the real-life and the symbolic mother (the *5th* and *2nd terms*) that children encounter the puzzles and conflicts of wealth, power and sociality.

Citizenship, class, ownership, wealth and debt, gender, community, the social relations between men and women, ethnicity and race, forms of power and so on—all these features of the social world are found *in* the Oedipus complex. I suspect that Lacan reduced the moral universe to unconscious desire and paternal Law to avoid the consequences, theoretical and therapeutic, of having to make psychoanalysis address this disparate, volatile field of relationships.

By foregrounding primal repression and paternal Law, Lacan tried to give the cultural project of psychoanalysis a skeptical, libertarian turn. Since, as Rajchman puts it, "no form of society can rule out the singularity of our desires," since "there can be no social arrangements in which we should all be content to fit," we had best engage in "a sort of constant cultural resistance to the tyranny of the very idea of an objectively good human arrangement."[15]

These slogans verge on what Jürgen Habermas has provocatively called "young conservatism" to designate the anti-modern strain in postmodernism.[16] What indeed does it mean to call for "freedom" in the form of a resistance to organized social change? Lacan insists on disconnecting the therapeutic effort from questions of justice, the common good or moral rightness. Such a gesture can seem essential to the therapist's neutrality and a guarantee of the patient's freedom. But it at the same time obscures the injustices, the social wrongs and the moral harm which are a direct or indirect part of every individual's formative experiences. Surely attention to this moral-political dimension would severely complicate the therapeutic project. It would also lead therapist and patient into the fallible process of knowing a wrong from a loss, a disappointment from a betrayal, a flaw from a misdeed. But ignoring the moral uncertainties and politics of everyday life has eroded psychoanalysis's contribution to society and narrowed its therapeutic scope.

The ethic of introspection which has grown up around the culture of psychoanalysis and around the therapy culture more generally is a valuable part of contemporary society. But its value and validity are now in need of reexamination by practitioners and clients alike. The Woody Allen scandal sent a self-critical shiver through the New York psychoanalytic community. In the words of *Husbands and Wives,* "Why do I have the feeling $50,000 of psychotherapy is dialing 911?" The charges of sexual abuse horrified those for whom Woody Allen symbolizes what it means to be "in analysis"; the thought that the charges may have been trumped up redoubled the horror. Whatever the truth, the feeling of the fracture of a family's moral universe was palpable.

Psychoanalysts have traditionally liked to keep their distance from social work. Their motivation has come to seem related more to a desire for prestige than a devotion to "science." But can they any longer justify how remote their own theoretical paradigms, therapeutic methods and professional identity are from urgent questions of community welfare and social reform? Sexual abuse is but one arena where psychoanalysis falls short. It is an especially telling shortcoming because of the history of psychoanalysis. Nearly a century after Freud's famous paradigm shift, sexual violence is psychoanalytic theory's own return of the repressed. It is time for the paradigm more generally to be rethought all over again. Psychoanalysis needs to reinvent its cultural project, both as a therapeutics and an ethics. Interrupted or isolated attempts have been made by important, exceptional psychoanalysts, including the "anti-psychiatrists" R. D. Laing and David Cooper, "radical" therapists like Joel Kovel and, on what unfortunately became the margins of the Lacanian movement, Maud Mannoni. A larger project looms. For it is time for psychoanalysis to figure out how its powers to heal can join with the cultural critique of male dominance, compulsory heterosexuality and modern patriarchy.

NOTES

Introduction

1. Sigmund Freud, "Female Sexuality" (1931), *The Standard Edition of the Complete Psychological Works,* ed. and trans. James Strachey (London: Hogarth Press, 1961), 21:228–229.
2. Ibid., p. 226.
3. Ibid., p. 228.
4. Michel Foucault, *The History of Sexuality, Volume I: An Introduction,* trans. Robert Hurley (New York: Vintage Books, 1980), p. 49.
5. Ibid., p. 46.
6. Ibid., p. 38.
7. Jonathan Goldberg, "Sodometries," in *English Inside and Out: The Places of Literary Criticism,* ed. Susan Gubar and Jonathan Kamholtz (New York: Routledge, 1993), pp. 68–86.
8. Sandra Lee Bartky, "Foucault, Femininity, and the Modernization of Patriarchal Power," in *Feminism and Foucault: Reflections on Resistance,* ed. Irene Diamond and Lee Quimby (Boston: Northeastern University Press, 1988), p. 63. Several essays in this collection make a case for Foucault's significance for feminist theory.
9. Adrienne Rich, "Compulsory Heterosexuality and Lesbian Existence," in *Powers of Desire: The Politics of Sexuality,* ed. Ann Snitow, Christine Stansell and Sharon Thompson (New York: Monthly Review Press, 1983), p. 183.
10. Ibid., p. 191.
11. Ibid., p. 201.

Chapter 1

1. Sigmund Freud, "The Dissolution of the Oedipus Complex," (1924) *The Standard*

Edition of the Complete Psychological Works, ed. and trans. James Strachey (London: Hogarth Press, 1961), 19:173 (hereafter cited as *S.E.*).

2. Freud, *The Ego and the Id* (1923), *S.E.* 19:31–32. "Anaclitic" refers to an erotic instinct that borrows or "leans" on the bodily functions exercised in the satisfaction of some basic need.
3. Freud, *Introductory Lectures on Psycho-Analysis* (Part III) (1917), *S.E.* 16:337.
4. Cf. Freud, "Some Psychical Consequences of the Anatomical Distinction between the Sexes" (1925), *S.E.* 19:248–258; "Female Sexuality" (1931), *S.E.* 21:225–243; *New Introductory Lectures on Psycho-Analysis* (1933), Lecture XXXIII: "Femininity," *S.E.* 22:112–135; *An Outline of Psycho-Analysis* (1940 [1938]), Chapter VII: "An Example of Psycho-Analytic Work," *S.E.* 23:183–194.
5. Freud, "A Special Type of Choice of Object Made by Men" (1910), *S.E.* 9:168–169.
6. Ibid., p. 169.
7. Ibid.
8. Ibid., p. 172.
9. Ibid.
10. Ibid., p. 173.
11. Ibid., p. 171.
12. Freud's English translators usually render *Nachträglichkeit* as "deferred action." Freud often used the term to refer to traumas that have no significant impact on a person's feelings or behavior until long after the original event. His earliest remarks on the temporality of traumas and symptoms go back to 1895: cf. *The Project for a Scientific Psychology, S.E.* 1:356–359. Freud discusses the problem extensively in his efforts to explain the "primal scene" he constructed in his analysis of the Wolf Man:

> At the age of one and a half the child receives an impression to which he is unable to react adequately; he is only able to be moved by it when the impression is revived in him at the age of four; and only twenty years later, during the analysis, is he able to grasp with his conscious mental processes what was then going on in him. The patient justifiably disregards the three periods of time, and puts his present ego into the situation which is so long past. And in this we follow him, since with correct self-observation and interpretation the effect must be the same as though the distance between the second and third periods of time could be neglected. Moreover, we have no other way of explaining the events of the second period. (*From the History of an Infantile Neurosis, S.E.* 17:45n.)

Several commentators radicalized the concept of *Nachträglichkeit* in the direction of what I am calling *retrodetermination.* Jacques Derrida argued that if a perception or experience is at first deferred, then there is no original perception or experience in the first place. He believes this paradox applies to all perception and experience. Because human experience is embedded in language, which according to the Saussurean model produces meaning through the structured "differences" among linguistic elements, the "reconstitution of meaning after the fact [*après coup*]" is the only way meaning ever attaches to specific perceptions and experiences. Cf. "Freud et la scène de l'écriture," in *L'écriture et la différence* (Paris: Editions du Seuil, 1967), p. 317. Jacques Lacan pursued a similar line of argument. Unconscious signifiers are in themselves meaningless but produce meaning when strung together and punctuated, just as phonemes are combined and segmented to make words, words to make sentences, sentences to make discourses. Meaning awaits the punctuations; it requires "the retroaction of the signifier." Lacan associates this "retroaction" with the discontinuous temporality that "restructures" the subject and thus "resubjectifies" past experience. Freud, according to Lacan's commentary on the Wolf Man, "accepts all the resubjectifications of the event which seem necessary to explain its effects at every turn where the subject is restructured, that is, for however many restructurations of the event are at work, as he says, *nachträglich,* after the fact [*après coup*]." Cf. "Fonction et champ de la parole et du langage en psychanalyse," in *Ecrits* (Paris: Editions du Seuil, 1966), p. 256. Gilles Deleuze, from whom I have adapted the notion of an infantile and adult "series," realized that Freud's whole model of psychic causality had to be revised in light of the *Nachträglichkeit.* The so-called "primal object" of the Oedipus complex could not be the "cause" of a later object; rather, the maternal object of the infantile series and the object of the adult series find their meaning and their connection to one another in relation to a "virtual object." "Our mother simply occupies, in the constitutive series of our present, a certain place with respect to the virtual object, which is necessarily filled by another figure in the series which constitutes another subjectivity, taking account always of the displacements of this [virtual] object = *x*." Gilles Deleuze, *Répétition et différence* (Editions de Minuit, 1966), p. 139. Deleuze's account is unsatisfactory simply to the extent that he disregards the cultural and social content of this "virtual object." The intermediary construct needed to effect, after the fact, a connection between the infantile and adult objects is itself an amalgam of cultural meanings and social relationships yet to be fully identified. It is not an empty signifier or *x*.

13. Freud, *Group Psychology and the Analysis of the Ego* (1921), *S.E.* 18:129.
14. Freud, *An Autobiographical Study* (1925), *S.E.* 20:37.
15. Freud, *Three Essays on the Theory of Sexuality* (1905/1915), *S.E.* 7:197.
16. Freud, "Family Romances" (1909), *S.E.* 9:239.
17. I am alluding here to Lacan's terminology in which desire is conceived as a *manque* manifested either in the form of a *manque-à-avoir* (wanting-to-have) or a *manque-à-être* (failing-to-be). As the varying resonances of the term *manque,* and its English equivalents, indicate, Lacan's concept is more a site of ambiguities than theoretical clarification. Rather than endowing the *manque-à-avoir/manque-à-être* polarity with the status of an abstract, all-embracing categorization of the forms of desire, I think it is more fruitful to define, as here, the social relations and cultural meanings that coalesce in a particular specification of the form of desire.
18. Freud, *Group Psychology and the Analysis of the Ego* (1921), *S.E.* 18:105.
19. René Girard, *Violence and the Sacred,* trans. Patrick Gregory (Baltimore: The Johns Hopkins University Press, 1977), p. 170.
20. Ibid., p. 182.
21. Ibid., p. 180.
22. Freud, *Notes upon a Case of Obsessional Neurosis* (1909), *S.E.* 10:206n.
23. Freud, "Two Encyclopaedia Articles" (1923), *S.E.* 18:246.
24. William Shakespeare, *Hamlet Prince of Denmark,* ed. Willard Farnham (Baltimore: Penguin, 1970), I.v.188–189.

25. See my *Culture and Domination* (Ithaca: Cornell University Press, 1987), pp. 3–56 for a discussion of the antagonism between traditional and critical theory generally, and pp. 184–199 for a discussion of the specifically psychoanalytic version of this antagonism.

Chapter 2

1. Paul Ricoeur, *Freud and Philosophy: An Essay on Interpretation,* trans. Denis Savage (New Haven: Yale University Press, 1970), especially, pp. 188–213 on the Oedipus complex, and pp. 494–551 on the general problem of linking the Freudian economy of desire to the interpretation of cultural symbols.
2. Paul Ricoeur, "Fatherhood: From Phantasm to Symbol," trans. Robert Sweeney, in *The Conflict of Interpretations* (Evanston: Northwestern University Press, 1974), pp. 468–497.
3. Ibid., p. 478.
4. Ibid., pp. 471–472.
5. Ibid., p. 475.
6. Ibid., p. 474.
7. Ibid.
8. Ibid., p. 476.
9. G. W. F. Hegel, *Phenomenology of Spirit,* trans. A. V. Miller (New York: Oxford University Press, 1977), p. 118.
10. Ricoeur, "Fatherhood: From Phantasm to Symbol," p. 477.
11. Ibid.
12. Ibid., p. 478.
13. For Freud's view, see "The Dissolution of the Oedipus Complex" (1924), *S.E.* 19:173–182.
14. Ricoeur, "Fatherhood: From Phantasm to Symbol," pp. 479–480.
15. Ibid., p. 480.
16. G. W. F. Hegel, *Philosophy of Right,* trans. T. M. Knox (New York: Oxford University Press, 1967), para. 163 note.
17. Ricoeur, "Fatherhood: From Phantasm to Symbol," p. 480.
18. Ibid., p. 481.
19. Ibid., p. 482.
20. Ibid., p. 483.
21. Ibid., p. 484.
22. Ibid., p. 480.
23. Ibid., p. 486.
24. Ibid.
25. Ibid., p. 490.

26. Ibid., p. 491.
27. Ibid., pp. 492–493.
28. Ibid., p. 478.
29. C. B. Macpherson, "Democratic Theory: Ontology and Technology," *Democratic Theory: Essays in Retrieval* (Oxford: Oxford University Press, 1973), p. 33.
30. Macpherson, "Market Concepts in Political Theory," ibid., p. 194.
31. Ricoeur, "Fatherhood: From Phantasm to Symbol," p. 493.
32. Ricoeur, *Freud and Philosophy,* p. 549.
33. Ricoeur, "The Demythization of Accusation," *The Conflict of Interpretations,* p. 350. This important essay complements "Fatherhood: From Phantasm to Symbol."
34. Ibid.
35. Immanuel Kant, *Religion within the Limits of Reason Alone,* trans. Theodore M. Greene and Hoyt H. Hudson (New York: Harper Torchbooks, 1960), p. 36.
36. Ricoeur, "Guilt, Ethics, and Religion," *The Conflict of Interpretations,* p. 435.
37. Ricoeur, "The Demythization of Accusation," p. 350.

Chapter 3

1. Jacques Lacan, "De nos antécédents," *Ecrits* (Paris: Editions du Seuil, 1966), p. 71. See also p. 72n.
2. Jacques Lacan, "The Neurotic's Individual Myth," *The Psychoanalytic Quarterly* 48:3 (1979), p. 416. According to Jacques-Alain Miller's prefatory notes, the original lecture was presented under the auspices of Jean Wahl at the Sorbonne in 1953.
3. Ibid., p. 423.

Chapter 4

1. Freud, *Notes upon a Case of Obsessional Neurosis* (1909), *S.E.* 10:182.
2. Claude Lévi-Strauss, "The Structural Study of Myth," *Structural Anthropology,* trans. Claire Jacobson and Brooke Grundfest Schoepf (Garden City, NY: Anchor Books, 1967), pp. 202–228.
3. Freud, *Notes upon a Case of Obsessional Neurosis,* p. 210.
4. Ibid., p. 171.
5. Ibid., p. 211.
6. Ibid., p. 199.
7. Ibid., p. 200.
8. Ibid., pp. 205–206.
9. Ibid., p. 218.
10. Ibid., p. 238.

11. Ibid., p. 240.
12. Shakespeare, *Hamlet Prince of Denmark,* II.ii.116–119.
13. Ibid., p. 241.
14. Ibid., pp. 243–244.
15. Ibid., p. 244.
16. Ibid., p. 246.
17. Jacques Lacan, "The Neurotic's Individual Myth," *The Psychoanalytic Quarterly* 48:3 (1979), p. 415.
18. Freud, *Notes upon a Case of Obsessional Neurosis,* p. 211.
19. Ibid.
20. Ibid., p. 177.
21. Ibid., p. 267.
22. For a commentary that follows the classical assumptions, see Patrick J. Mahony, *Freud and the Rat Man* (New Haven: Yale University Press, 1986), pp. 52–55.
23. Lacan, "The Neurotic's Individual Myth," p. 424.
24. Ibid., p. 423.
25. Jacques Lacan, "Fonction et champ de la parole et du langage en psychanalyse," *Ecrits* (Paris: Editions du Seuil, 1966), p. 302. My translation. *Ecrits: A Selection,* trans. Alan Sheridan (New York: W. W. Norton, 1977), p. 88.
26. Freud, *Notes upon a Case of Obsessional Neurosis,* p. 204.
27. Lacan, "The Neurotic's Individual Myth," p. 417.

Chapter 5

1. Freud, *Three Essays on the Theory of Sexuality* (1905), *S.E.* 7:228.
2. Jeffrey Moussaieff Masson, *The Assault on Truth: Freud's Suppression of the Seduction Theory* (New York: Farrar, Straus and Giroux, 1984), p. 113.
3. Sigmund Freud, *The Origins of Psycho-Analysis,* ed. Marie Bonaparte, Anna Freud and Ernst Kris and trans. Eric Mosbacher and James Strachey (New York: Basic Books, 1954). The revised translation can be found in *S.E.* 1:175–397. See also Masson, pp. xv–xxiii.
4. Freud's letter was included in Max Schur, *Freud Living and Dying* (New York: International Universities Press, 1972), p. 104. Cited in Masson, p. 9.
5. Masson, p. 10.
6. Freud, Letter 69, *S.E.* 1:259.
7. Ibid., p. 261n.
8. Freud, *An Autobiographical Study* (1925), *S.E.* 20:34.
9. Ibid., pp. 34–35.
10. Masson, pp. 14–54.
11. Ibid., pp. 123–128.

12. Marie Balmary, *Psychoanalyzing Psychoanalysis: Freud and the Hidden Fault of the Father,* trans. Ned Lukacher (Baltimore: The Johns Hopkins University Press, 1982), pp. 103, 108.
13. Freud, *S.E.* 1:259.
14. Balmary, p. 38.
15. Freud, *S.E.* 1:263, 265.
16. Balmary, p. 94.
17. Ibid., p. 128.
18. See Masson, pp. 119–134.
19. Maya Angelou, *I Know Why the Caged Bird Sings* (New York: Bantam, 1971), p. 65.
20. Ibid., p. 61.
21. Ibid., p. 63.
22. Ibid, pp. 70–71.
23. Ibid., p. 72.
24. Ibid., p. 71.
25. Christine Froula, "The Daughter's Seduction: Sexual Violence and Literary History," *Signs* 11:4 (Summer 1986), pp. 621–644.
26. Freud, *Fragment of an Analysis of a Case of Hysteria* (1905), *S.E.* 7:26.
27. Steven Marcus, "Freud and Dora: Story, History, Case History," in Charles Bernheimer and Claire Kahane (eds.), *In Dora's Case: Freud—Hysteria—Feminism* (New York: Columbia University Press, 1985), p. 61. The essay is also included in Steven Marcus, *Freud and the Culture of Psychoanalysis: Studies in the Transition from Victorian Humanism to Modernity* (New York: W. W. Norton, 1984), pp. 42–86.
28. Maria Ramas, "Freud's Dora, Dora's Hysteria," in Bernheimer and Kahane, pp. 151, 163–164.
29. Madelon Sprengnether, "Enforcing Oedipus: Freud and Dora," in Bernheimer and Kahane, p. 256.
30. Freud, *Notes upon a Case of Obsessional Neurosis* (1909), *S.E.* 10:234.
31. Ibid., p. 235. See also pp. 205–206.
32. Ibid., p. 300.
33. Ibid., p. 261.
34. Ibid., p. 262.
35. Ibid., p. 263.
36. Ibid., p. 278.
37. Ibid., pp. 278–279.
38. Ibid., p. 314.
39. Ibid., pp. 273, 292.
40. Ibid, p. 279.

Chapter 6

1. Carl E. Schorske, "Politics and Patricide in Freud's *Interpretation of Dreams,*" *Fin-de-Siècle Vienna: Politics and Culture* (New York: Vintage Books, 1981), pp. 181–207.
2. Alvin W. Gouldner, *The Future of Intellectuals and the Rise of the New Class* (New York: Continuum, 1979), pp. 62–67.
3. Schorske, "Politics and Patricide," p. 191.
4. Freud, *The Interpretation of Dreams* (1900), *S.E.* 4:196.
5. Ibid., p. 217n.
6. Schorske, pp. 197, 203.
7. Carole Pateman, "The Fraternal Social Contract," *The Disorder of Women: Democracy, Feminism and Political Theory* (Stanford: Stanford University Press, 1989), p. 43.
8. Ibid. p. 39.
9. Ibid., p. 43.
10. Freud, *Civilization and Its Discontents* (1930), *S.E.* 21:101.
11. Ibid.
12. Eve Kosofsky Sedgwick, *Between Men: English Literature and Male Homosocial Desire* (New York: Columbia University Press, 1985).
13. Freud, *Civilization and Its Discontents,* p. 104.
14. Franz Kafka, *The Sons* (New York: Schocken Books, 1989), pp. 113–167. The passage quoted is on p. 148.
15. Ibid., p. 135.
16. Ibid., pp. 136–137.
17. Ibid., p. 137.
18. Ibid., p. 154.
19. Ibid., p. 156.
20. Ibid., p. 162.
21. Ibid., p. 163.
22. Ibid., p. 132.
23. Freud, "Dostoevsky and Parricide" (1928), *S.E.* 21:184.
24. Adrienne Rich, "Compulsory Heterosexuality and Lesbian Existence," in *Powers of Desire: The Politics of Sexuality,* ed. Ann Snitow, Christine Stansell and Sharon Thompson (New York: Monthly Review Press, 1983), pp. 177–205.
25. Freud, "Dostoevsky and Parricide," p. 184.
26. Freud, *The Ego and the Id* (1923), *S.E.* 19:32.
27. Ibid., p. 33.
28. Freud, "The Paths to Symptom-Formation," *Introductory Lectures on Psycho-Analysis, S.E.* 16:368–369.
29. The case history of the Wolf Man provides the most detailed discussion of Freud's con-

struction of a primal scene memory. Cf. Freud, *From the History of an Infantile Neurosis* (1918 [1914]), *S.E.* 17:29–47, 89–103.

30. Carole Pateman, "Genesis, Fathers and the Political Sons of Liberty," *The Sexual Contract* (Stanford: Stanford University Press, 1988), p. 106.

31. Ibid., p. 107. Cf. Gregory Zilboorg, "Masculine and Feminine: Some Biological and Cultural Aspects," *Psychiatry* 7 (1944), pp. 257–296.

32. Pateman, "The Fraternal Social Contract," p. 51.

Chapter 7

1. Carole Pateman, *The Disorder of Women: Democracy, Feminism and Political Theory* (Stanford: Stanford University Press, 1989), p. 34.

2. Partha Chatterjee, "A Response to Taylor's Invocation of Civil Society," *Working Papers and Proceedings of the Center for Psychosocial Studies* 39 (Chicago: Center for Psychosocial Studies, 1990), p. 9. Chatterjee's response is to Charles Taylor, "Invoking Civil Society," *Working Papers and Proceedings of the Center for Psychosocial Studies* 31 (Chicago: Center for Psychosocial Studies, 1990).

3. Ibid., p. 8.

4. Ibid.

5. Chatterjee's reflection on the nation and community and on nationalism and the politics of postcolonial societies shares a number of themes with the very important work of Benedict Anderson, *Imagined Communities: Reflections on the Origin and Spread of Nationalism,* Revised Edition (New York: Verso, 1991 [1983]).

6. G. W. F. Hegel, *Philosophy of Right,* trans. T. M. Knox (New York: Oxford University Press, 1967), pp. 261–262.

7. Chatterjee, p. 7.

8. Carl E. Schorske, "The Ringstrasse, its Critics, and the Birth of Urban Modernism," *Fin-de-Siècle Vienna: Politics and Culture* (New York: Vintage Books, 1981), pp. 24–115.

9. Schorske, "Politics and Patricide in Freud's *Interpretation of Dreams,*" ibid., p. 203.

10. Freud, *Extracts from the Fliess Papers, S.E.* 1:261.

11. Ibid., p. 263.

12. Schorske, pp. 192–193.

13. Ibid., pp. 205n–206n.

14. Freud, *S.E.* 1:262.

15. Freud, *The Psychopathology of Everyday Life* (1901), *S.E.* 6:49–52.

16. Peter Stallybrass and Allon White, *The Politics and Poetics of Transgression* (Ithaca: Cornell University Press, 1986), pp. 159–160. For Freud's published account, see *The Psychopathology of Everyday Life* (1901), *S.E.* 6:49–52. See also Jim Swan, "Mater and Nannie: Freud's Two Mothers and the Discovery of the Oedipus Complex," *American Imago* 31:1 (1974), pp. 1–64.

17. See Schorske, pp. 191–193.

18. Quoted in Peter Gay, *Freud, Jews and Other Germans: Masters and Victims in Modernist Culture* (New York: Oxford University Press, 1978), p. 90.
19. Freud, *Notes upon a Case of Obsessional Neurosis* (1909), *S.E.* 10:293.
20. Ibid., p. 290.
21. Ibid., p. 286.
22. Ibid., pp. 297–298.
23. Ibid., pp. 301–302.
24. Ibid., p. 298.
25. Kafka, *The Sons,* p. 146.

Chapter 8

1. Jacques Lacan, "L'agressivité en psychanalyse," *Ecrits* (Paris: Editions du Seuil, 1966), pp. 121–122; "Aggressivity in Psychoanalysis," *Ecrits: A Selection,* trans. Alan Sheridan (New York: W. W. Norton, 1977), p. 26.
2. Ibid., p. 122; trans., p. 27.
3. *Kant's Political Writings,* ed. Hans Reiss and trans. H. B. Nisbet (Cambridge: Cambridge University Press, 1970), p. 54.
4. Jacques Lacan, "The Neurotic's Individual Myth," *The Psychoanalytic Quarterly* 48:3 (1979), p. 424. The phrase "a kind of original experience of death" comes from a passage of the original lecture not included in this version edited by Jacques-Alain Miller. Cf. Jacques Lacan, "Le mythe individuel du névrosé, ou 'Poésie et vérité' dans la névrose" (Paris: Centre de Documentation Universitaire, 1956), p. 27.
5. Jacques Lacan, "Le stade du miroir comme formateur de la fonction du Je," *Ecrits,* p. 99; "The Mirror Stage as Formative of the Function of the I," *Ecrits: A Selection,* p. 7.
6. Lacan, "The Neurotic's Individual Myth," p. 425.
7. Stuart Schneiderman, "Lacan's Early Contributions to Psychoanalysis," in *Returning to Freud: Clinical Psychoanalysis in the School of Lacan,* ed. and trans. Stuart Schneiderman (New Haven: Yale University Press, 1980), p. 6.
8. Ellie Ragland-Sullivan, *Jacques Lacan and the Philosophy of Psychoanalysis* (Urbana and Chicago: University of Illinois Press, 1986), p. 55. For her fuller discussion of the mirror stage, which she eventually assimilates to the mother-child relation, see pp. 16–30.
9. For an excellent account of the events that split the Lacanian movement just before Lacan's death and the intellectual currents that shaped what has become a self-proclaimed orthodoxy preserving the true word of Lacan, see Monique David-Menard, "Lacanians Against Lacan," trans. Brian Massumi, *Social Text* 6 (Fall 1982), pp. 86–111.
10. Louis Althusser, "Ideology and Ideological State Apparatuses (Notes towards an Investigation)," *Lenin and Philosophy,* trans. Ben Brewster (New York: Monthly Review Press, 1971), p. 162. See also the essay "Freud and Lacan," pp. 189–219. An extremely important variation and extension of Althusser's appropriation of Lacan is Fredric Jameson, "Imaginary and Symbolic in Lacan: Marxism, Psychoanalytic Criticism, and the Problem of the Subject," *Yale French Studies* 55/56 (1977), pp. 338–395.

11. It would be more accurate to say that this is a representation of *an* intersection of the household and the market, since they also intersect through the real-life mother's practices and role. The changing history of the household as a unit of consumption rather than production as well as the sexual division of labor shape all these relationships. On the problems Habermas encounters in trying to distinguish the family and the market as, respectively, an institution of the "lifeworld" and an institution of the economic "system," see Nancy Fraser, "What's Critical about Critical Theory? The Case of Habermas and Gender," *New German Critique* 35 (Spring/Summer 1985), pp. 97–131.
12. Lacan, "Le stade du miroir," p. 99; trans., p. 7.

Chapter 9

1. Stuart Schneiderman, *Rat Man* (New York: New York University Press, 1986), p. 11.
2. Patrick J. Mahony, *Freud and the Rat Man* (New Haven: Yale University Press, 1986), p. 36.
3. Schneiderman, *Rat Man,* p. 10.
4. Freud, "On the Universal Tendency to Debasement in the Sphere of Love" (1912), *S.E.* 11:179.
5. Ibid., p. 180.
6. Ibid., p. 181.
7. Ibid., pp. 181–182.
8. Ibid., p. 183.
9. Ibid.
10. Ibid., p. 185.
11. Ibid., p. 183.
12. Ibid., p. 182.
13. Ibid., pp. 184–185.
14. Ibid., p. 185.
15. Ibid., p. 190.
16. Silvia Bovenschen, "The Contemporary Witch, the Historical Witch and the Witch Myth: The Witch, Subject of the Appropriation of Nature and Object of the Domination of Nature," trans. Jeannine Blackwell, Johanna Moore and Beth Weckmueller, *New German Critique* 15 (Fall 1978), p. 100.
17. Ibid., pp. 102–103.
18. Ibid., p. 95.
19. Ibid., pp. 107–108.
20. Nancy Chodorow, *The Reproduction of Mothering: Psychoanalysis and the Sociology of Gender* (Berkeley: University of California Press, 1978), pp. 166–167.
21. Carol Gilligan, *In Different Voices: Psychological Theory and Women's Development* (Cambridge: Harvard University Press, 1982).

22. The following statement exemplifies both the hypothesis regarding social reproduction and the psychic determinism of Chodorow's position: "women's and men's personality traits and orientations mesh with the sexual and familial division of labor and unequal ideology of gender and shape the asymmetric location in a structure of production and reproduction in which women are in the first instance mothers and wives and men are workers. This structure of production and reproduction requires and presupposes those specific relational modes, between husband and wife, and mother and children, which form the center of the family in contemporary society. An examination of the way that gender personality is expressed in adulthood reveals how women and men create, and are often committed to creating, the interpersonal relationships which underlie and reproduce the family structure that produced them." Ibid., p. 190. Iris Marion Young has shown how this sort of statement lends itself sometimes to a weak thesis, sometimes to a strong thesis in Chodorow's work. In the strong form, *male domination,* in the sense of a whole complex of social institutions that distribute power, opportunities, wealth and so on unequally to men and women, is not distinguished from *gender differentiation,* in the sense of the "cultural categorization" that shapes "individual psychology and experience." "The failure to distinguish male domination from gender differentiation" ultimately leads Chodorow, in Young's view, to explain male dominance with reference to psychology rather than structures of power, distribution and wealth: "To regard male domination as identical with or derivable from gender differentiation, however, is to overpsychologize the social phenomena of male domination." Iris Marion Young, "Is Male Gender Identity the Cause of Male Domination?" in *Mothering: Essays in Feminist Theory,* ed. Joyce Trebilcot (Totowa, NJ: Rowman and Allanheld, 1984), pp. 129–146.
23. Jessica Benjamin, *The Bonds of Love: Psychoanalysis, Feminism, and the Problem of Domination* (New York: Pantheon, 1988), p. 135.
24. Ibid., p. 162.
25. Ibid., p. 151.
26. Ibid., p. 174.
27. Ibid., p. 152.
28. Ibid., p. 162.
29. Ibid., p. 163.
30. Ibid., pp. 96–114.
31. Ibid., p. 165.
32. Ibid.
33. Ibid., p. 181.

Chapter 10

1. Shakespeare, *Hamlet Prince of Denmark,* III.iii.51-56.
2. Shakespeare, III.iii.57-60.
3. Jacques Lacan, "Fonction et champ de la parole et du langage en psychanalyse," *Ecrits* (Paris: Editions du Seuil, 1966), p. 278. All translations are my own. English version: "The Function and Field of Speech and Language in Psychoanalysis," *Ecrits: A Selection,*

trans. Alan Sheridan (New York: W. W. Norton, 1977), p. 67.

4. Ibid.; trans., ibid.

5. Ibid.; trans., ibid. My italics.

6. Cf. Max Weber, "Domination and Legitimacy," *Economy and Society,* ed. Guenther Roth and Claus Wittich (Berkeley: University of California Press, 1968), 2:945–955. In Weber's usage "domination" means "the situation in which the manifested will (*command*) of the *ruler* or rulers is meant to influence the conduct of one or more others (*the ruled*) and actually does influence it in such a way that their conduct to a socially relevant degree occurs as if the ruled had made the content of the command the maxim of their conduct for its own sake. Looked at from the other end, this situation will be called *obedience*" (p. 946). Legitimation concerns the process of justifying the exercise of domination; according to Weber, there are three different principles of legitimation. The "'validity' of a power of command" can (1) be expressed "in a system of consciously made *rational* rules (which may either be agreed upon or imposed from above) which meet with obedience as generally binding norms whenever such obedience is claimed by him whom the rule designates"; (2) rest on "personal authority" which is "founded upon the sacredness of *tradition*"; or, (3) "personal authority" that has "its source in the very opposite, viz., the surrender to the extraordinary, the belief in *charisma,* i.e., actual revelation or grace resting in such a person as a savior, a prophet, or a hero" (p. 954). While these principles of legitimation—rational rules, tradition and charisma—define the "'pure' types," the forms of legitimation and the corresponding forms of domination "occurring in historical reality constitute combinations, mixtures, adaptations, or modifications of these 'pure' types" (ibid.).

7. Lacan, "D'une question préliminaire à tout traitement possible de la psychose," *Ecrits,* p. 556; "On a Question Preliminary to any Possible Treatment of Psychosis," *Ecrits: A Selection,* p. 199.

8. Ibid.; trans., ibid. See also Guy Rosolato, "Du Père," *Essais sur le symbolique* (Paris: Editions Gallimard, 1969), pp. 36–58.

9. Claude Lévi-Strauss, *The Elementary Structures of Kinship,* trans. Bell, Sturmer and Needham (Boston: Beacon Press, 1969).

10. Gayle Rubin, "The Traffic in Women: Notes on the 'Political Economy' of Sex," in Reyna Reiter (ed.), *Toward an Anthropology of Women* (New York: Monthly Review Press, 1975), pp. 157–210.

11. Jürgen Habermas, *Legitimation Crisis,* trans. Thomas McCarthy (Boston: Beacon Press, 1975), p. 18. My italics.

12. Lacan, "Fonction et champ de la parole," p. 277; trans., p. 66.

13. Lacan, "D'une question préliminaire," p. 583; trans., p. 221.

14. Lacan, "Fonction et champ de la parole," p. 285; trans., p. 73.

15. Lacan, "D'une question préliminaire," p. 579; trans., p. 218.

16. Lacan, "Subversion du sujet et dialectique du désir dans l'inconscient freudien," *Ecrits,* p. 813; "The Subversion of the Subject and the Dialectic of Desire in the Freudian Unconscious," p. 311.

17. Jacques Lacan, "The Neurotic's Individual Myth," *The Psychoanalytic Quarterly* 48:3 (1979), pp. 422–423.

18. Jessica Benjamin, "Authority and the Family Revisited, or, A World Without Fathers?" *New German Critique* 13 (Winter 1978), p. 51. See also her "The End of Internalization: Adorno's Social Psychology," *Telos* 32 (Summer 1977), pp. 42–64. For a discussion of Horkheimer and Adorno's adaptation of psychoanalytic theory to critical social theory, see Mark Poster, *Critical Theory of the Family* (New York: Seabury, 1980), pp. 53–62.
19. For a full, uncritical account of this aspect of Lacanian orthodoxy, see Ellie Ragland-Sullivan, *Jacques Lacan and the Philosophy of Psychoanalysis* (Urbana and Chicago: University of Illinois Press, 1986), pp. 54–56, pp. 300–304.
20. Here I rejoin the crucial core of Chodorow's problematic.

Chapter 11

1. Maud Mannoni, *The Backward Child and His Mother: A Psychoanalytic Study,* trans. A. M. Sheridan Smith (New York: Pantheon, 1972), pp. 61–62.
2. Ibid., p. 182. All references to the case of Isabelle occur between pp. 177-207. Quotations from other passages in the book will be cited separately.
3. Ibid., p. 55.
4. Ibid., p. 60. Mannoni finishes the sentence with the gloss "—what we analysts call the 'castration experience.'" This very Lacanian formulation presupposes that the archetype of all experiences of separation is castration since it is the symbolic father who is considered the agent of separation. I have of course already challenged this bit of psychoanalytic reasoning, and will return to Mannoni's occasional affirmation of Lacan's understanding of the name-of-the-father.
5. Ibid., p. 63.
6. Ibid., p. 67.
7. Ibid., p. 62.
8. Lacan, "La direction de la cure et les principes de son pouvoir," *Ecrits* (Paris: Editions du Seuil, 1966), esp. pp. 624–633; "The Direction of the Treatment and the Principles of its Power," pp. 260–269. Also, "Pour une logique du fantasme," *Scilicet* 2/3 (1970), pp. 223–273.
9. Mannoni, p. 61.

Chapter 12

1. Adrienne Rich, *Your Native Land, Your Life* (New York: Norton, 1986), p. 56.
2. Ibid., p.58.
3. Shakespeare, *Hamlet Prince of Denmark,* I.ii.140, 152–153.
4. Raymond Williams developed the concept of structure of feeling in several contexts, without ever providing a systematic or synthetic discussion. See, principally, *The Long Revolution* (New York: Columbia University Press, 1961), pp. 72–100; *Marxism and Literature* (New York: Oxford University Press, 1977), pp. 128–135; "The Bloomsbury Faction," *Problems in Materialism and Culture* (London: Verso, 1982), pp. 148–169. See

also Pierre Bourdieu, *Outline of a Theory of Practice,* trans. Richard Nice (Cambridge: Cambridge University Press, 1977), pp. 72–95, 159–197. The phrase "a matrix of perceptions, and actions" occurs on p. 82.

5. The Oedipal structure of feeling is, as Bourdieu might say, at once a "structuring structure" (since the individual male actively draws upon it to represent his relationships in and to his social world) and a "structured structure" (since the whole repertoire of representations and responses he can draw upon is itself a collectively evolved and limited set of symbolizations, valuations, skills, scenarios, social perceptions). Psychoanalytic theory thinks of the Oedipus complex as a kind of synthesis or mediator between a subhistorical "intrapsychic" domain (the erotic drives, parental imagos) and a suprahistorical domain (incest prohibition, rules of kinship, law of the Father). With the concept of an Oedipal structure of feeling, I am using Bourdieu's notion of the *embodiment* of dispositions to place both the Oedipal repertoire and its individual embodiments on the historical plane where social institutions are formed and change. I have been guided by Bourdieu's suggestive argument that it would be wrong

   > to reduce to their strictly sexual dimension the countless acts of diffuse inculcation through which the body and the world tend to be set in order, by means of a symbolic manipulation of the relation to the body and to the world aiming to impose what has to be called, in Melanie Klein's term, a "body geography," a particular case of geography, or better, cosmology. The child's initial relation to its father or mother, or in other terms, to the paternal and maternal body, which offers the most dramatic opportunity to experience all the fundamental oppositions of mythopoeic practice, cannot be found as the basis of the acquisition of the principles of the structuring of the ego and the world, and in particular of every homosexual and heterosexual relationship, except insofar as that initial relation is set up with objects whose sex is defined symbolically and not biologically. The child constructs its *sexual identity,* the major elements in its social identity, at the same time that it constructs its image of the division of work between the sexes, out of the same socially defined set of inseparably biological and social indices. In other words, the awakening of consciousness of sexual identity and the incorporation of the dispositions associated with a determinate social definition of the social functions incumbent on men and women come hand in hand with the adoption of a socially defined vision of the sexual division of labour.

   Bourdieu, *Outline of a Theory of Practice,* pp. 92–93.

6. See pp. 110–112 above; and Carl E. Schorske, "Politics and Patricide in Freud's *Interpretation of Dreams,*" *Fin-de-Siècle Vienna: Politics and Culture* (New York: Vintage Books, 1981), pp. 181–207.

7. See pp. 136–139 above; and Peter Stallybrass and Allon White, *The Politics and Poetics of Transgression* (Ithaca: Cornell University Press, 1986), pp. 149–170.

8. See pp. 87–108 above; Marie Balmary, *Psychoanalyzing Psychoanalysis: Freud and the Hidden Fault of the Father,* trans. Ned Lukacher (Baltimore: The Johns Hopkins University Press, 1982); and Jeffrey Moussaieff Masson, *The Assault on Truth: Freud's Suppression of the Seduction Theory* (New York: Farrar, Straus and Giroux, 1984).

9. André Green, *The Tragic Effect: The Oedipus Complex in Tragedy,* trans. Alan Sheridan (Cambridge: Cambridge University Press, 1979), p. 217.

10. Ibid., p. 187.

11. John Boswell, "Revolutions, Universals, and Sexual Categories," in *Hidden from History: Reclaiming the Gay and Lesbian Past,* ed. Martin Duberman, Martha Vicinus and George Chauncey, Jr. (New York: Meridian, 1990), p. 23.

12. Carole Pateman, "Genesis, Fathers and the Political Sons of Liberty," *The Sexual Contract* (Stanford: Stanford University Press, 1988), pp. 77–115; and *The Disorder of Women* (Stanford: Stanford University Press, 1989). Paul Ricoeur, "Fatherhood: From Phantasm to Symbol," trans. Robert Sweeney, *The Conflict of Interpretations* (Evanston: Northwestern University Press, 1974), pp. 468–497.

13. Shoshana Felman, "Beyond Oedipus: The Specimen Story of Psychoanalysis," in *Jacques Lacan and the Adventure of Insight: Psychoanalysis in Contemporary Culture* (Cambridge: Harvard University Press, 1987), p. 131.

14. John Rajchman, "Lacan and the Ethics of Modernity," *Representations* 15 (Summer 1986), p. 52.

15. Ibid., pp. 52–53, 55.

16. "The 'young conservatives' recapitulate the basic experience of aesthetic modernity. They claim as their own the revelations of a decentered subjectivity, emancipated from the imperatives of work and usefulness, and with this experience they step outside the modern world. On the basis of modernistic attitudes they justify an irreconcilable antimodernism. They remove into the sphere of the far-away and the archaic the spontaneous powers of imagination, self-experience and emotion." Jürgen Habermas, "Modernity—An In Complete Project," in *The Anti-Aesthetic: Essays on Postmodern Culture,* ed. Hal Foster (Port Townsend, WA: Bay Press, 1983), p. 14.

Index

ch. 4, Rat Man (F. & Lacan) in relat to Ant.
- Ant's ident ctr'd on mirror-relat to bifurc'd fr.
- C. cd. be both ½'s, real & symbolic, or rather activate both ½'s
  - symbolic fr: stoic masculin as cult'l ideal
  - real fr.: transp'n of that ideal - powerhungry rival
    - C. talks as tho he only wants Ant to reform & ret. to triumvir
    - C. acts as tho he really wants Ant to screw up & allow C. to defeat him.

- Cleo. resembles Brenkman's def'n of mo/whore/Oed. mo as symbolic construct "fabric'd in the androcentric field of m. intersubjectiv." (85)
- Chargcarg. re Cleo: Sh. destabil's source-view of Cleo as foreign threat/seductress thru interpol'n of mo-motif. See Adelman again.
  - Role of mo. is admitted but only obliquely & in denig'd form (or contain'd) by being estranged in Cleo. as exotic

ch. 9, "Mo-Whore": if cult'l codes/repr's → "mo." in Oed complex, then I ought to look at those in EM per. to see how maternal images in A&C func. (165)

Woodward Gardens
nr Dubose & Mission